I0225091

Educational Visions: Lessons from 40 years of innovation

Editors:
Rebecca Ferguson,
Ann Jones,
Eileen Scanlon

]u[

ubiquity press
London

Published by
Ubiquity Press Ltd.
Unit 322-323
Whitechapel Technology Centre
75 Whitechapel Road
London E1 1DU
www.ubiquitypress.com

Text © the authors 2019

First published 2019

Cover design by Amber MacKay. This cover has been designed using open resources from Freepik.com, Pexels and Pixabay. Front cover images by @ tuiphotoengineer and Pixabay; back cover image by Stocksnap.

Print and digital versions typeset by Siliconchips Services Ltd.

ISBN (Paperback): 978-1-911529-80-4
ISBN (PDF): 978-1-911529-81-1
ISBN (EPUB): 978-1-911529-82-8
ISBN (Kindle): 978-1-911529-83-5

DOI: https://doi.org/10.5334/bcg

This work is licensed under the Creative Commons Attribution 4.0 International License (unless stated otherwise within the content of the work). To view a copy of this license, visit http://creativecommons.org/licenses/by/4.0/ or send a letter to Creative Commons, 444 Castro Street, Suite 900, Mountain View, California, 94041, USA. This license allows for copying any part of the work for personal and commercial use, providing author attribution is clearly stated.

The full text of this book has been peer-reviewed to ensure high academic standards. For full review policies, see http://www.ubiquitypress.com/

Suggested citation:
Ferguson, R., Jones, A. and Scanlon, E. (eds). 2019. *Educational Visions: Lessons from 40 years of innovation*. London: Ubiquity Press. DOI: https://doi.org/10.5334/bcg. License: CC-BY 4.0

To read the free, open access version of this book online, visit https://doi.org/10.5334/bcg or scan this QR code with your mobile device:

Contents

Figures

Tables

Authors' Biographies

Dr Ann Jones
For publication list, see http://oro.open.ac.uk/view/person/acj4.html
ORCID: https://orcid.org/0000-0003-0853-8545
I am interested in mobile learning and social and affective uses and aspects of technologies, and also in how informal learning can be supported by technology, especially mobile devices. My most recent OU teaching contribution was to 'The critical researcher: educational technology in practice', a module in our then MA in Open and Distance Education (MAODE).

I have been a member of the Computers and Learning research group (CALRG) since its inception, and have been convenor and also deputy convenor for considerable periods of time as well as being a part time PhD student within the group in the early years, and have also supervised a number of CALRG PhD students. I am now part of the organising committee.

My current research interests include mobile learning and social and affective uses and also how informal learning can be supported by technology, especially mobile devices and how this can support language learning.

Finally, I co-edit the Journal of Interactive Media in Education, a peer-reviewed open access online journal in educational technology.

Professor Bart Rienties
For publication list, see http://oro.open.ac.uk/view/person/bcr58.html
ORCID: https://orcid.org/0000-0003-3749-9629

I am Professor of Learning Analytics and Associate Dean of Academic Professional Development at the Institute of Educational Technology at The Open University UK. As Associate Dean, I lead a group of academics who provide university-wide professional development and innovation courses and conduct evidence-based research of how professionals learn. As an educational psychologist, I conduct multi-disciplinary research on work-based and collaborative learning environments and focus on the role of social interaction in learning, which is published in leading academic journals and books. My primary research interests are focussed on learning analytics, professional development, and the role of motivation in learning. Furthermore, I am interested in broader internationalisation aspects of higher education. I have successfully led a range of institutional/national/European projects and received a range of awards for my educational innovation projects.

Dr Canan Blake

For publication list, see https://iris.ucl.ac.uk/iris/browse/profile?upi=CTBLA57 and http://oro.open.ac.uk/view/person/ct6.html
ORCID: https://orcid.org/0000-0003-1311-0092
My research has mainly focused on evaluation of technology-enhanced learning in different environments, including computer-supported collaborative learning, mobile learning and interactions in massive open online courses. This research has led to development of frameworks for the interactions of learners in several technology-enhanced learning environments and evaluation methodologies. I have convened the CALRG, organised its annual conferences and contributed to supervision for postgraduate research students carrying out research in main CALRG themes. My most recent role involves mentoring EdTech start-ups to acquire research-informed evidence for their products and services, and working with Masters students in educational technology.

Chris Edwards

For publication list, see: http://oro.open.ac.uk/view/person/che2.html
ORCID: https://orcid.org/0000-0002-0585-2697
I am a lecturer in the Institute of Educational Technology with over twenty years' experience of teaching at the OU. I joined to produce teaching materials in the collaborative Supported Learning in Physics Project (SLIPP), that introduced OU methods to teaching A-Level Physics in context and researched their effectiveness. I now chair the Masters module, Openness and innovation in eLearning and am Staff Tutor for the Online and Distance Learning qualifications. I support the University's Quality Enhancement activities with a focus on understanding, using new data methods and structures, the student experience of study pathways in a range of subjects and in the Open degree programme of study. I was a researcher on the recently completed TeSLA project developing and researching embedded e-authentication tools for online assessment.

Dr Christothea Herodotou

For publication list see http://oro.open.ac.uk/view/person/ci746.html
ORCID: https://orcid.org/0000-0003-0980-1632
I am a Senior Lecturer in the Institute of Educational Technology (IET), interested in the design and evaluation of technologies for learning (i.e., online platforms, mobile applications, digital games). I hold funding from the National Science Foundation, Wellcome, and ESRC for researching learning in online citizen science communities with the aim of making science more accessible and productive for young people (https://education.ucdavis.edu/ccs-learn-cit-sci). I lead the process of launching citizen science projects on nQuire (www. nquire.org.uk); a learning platform that aims to educate the public in scientific thinking, and which was designed in collaboration with the BBC. Also, I am the evaluation lead of a university-wide initiative that uses predictive analytics to support student performance and retention (https://analyse.kmi.open.ac.uk). I am the lead author of the edited book 'Citizen Inquiry: Synthesising Science and Inquiry Learning'. In the past, I held funding from the British Academy and BERA to capture the impact of mobile applications on young children's science learning and development as well as internal funding (eSTEeM) to improve how virtual microscopy is embedded in online courses. I also chaired the Masters course 'Technology enhanced learning: practices and debates'.

Professor Denise Whitelock

For publication list, see http://oro.open.ac.uk/view/person/dmw8.html
I am the Interim Director of the Institute of Educational Technology at The Open University, UK. I am a Professor of Technology Enhanced Assessment and Learning and have over 30 years' experience in Artificial Intelligence for designing, researching and evaluating online and computer-based learning in Higher Education. I have a long history of working with the CALRG and developed many research projects with its members.

I recently led the UK's contribution to the Adaptive Trust e-Assessment System for Learning (TeSLA) http://tesla-project.eu/ project. The overall objective of the TeSLA project was to define and develop an e-assessment system, which ensures learners' authentication and authorship in online and blended learning environments while avoiding the time and physical space limitations imposed by face-to-face examination.

I am currently the Editor of Open Learning: The Journal of Open, Distance & e-Learning.

My work has received international recognition as I hold visiting chairs at the Autonoma University, Barcelona and the Open University of Catalonia.

Professor Eileen Scanlon

For publication list, see http://oro.open.ac.uk/view/person/es5.html.
ORCID: https://orcid.org/0000-0003-1180-682X

I am the Regius Professor of Open Education and Associate Director of Research and Innovation in the Institute of Educational Technology at The Open University, UK. As Associate Director, I have institutional responsibility for developing research strategy in educational technology. My teaching and research experience has been gained across OU roles including course manager, postgraduate research student, module team member and chair, CALRG research group director and research centre director, principal investigator on research council grants including large cross-institutional and inter-institutional externally and internally funded research projects. I am particularly interested in learning science and in journeys between formal and informal learning, and I am one of the organisers of the FutureLearn academic network. https://iet.open.ac.uk/people/eileen.scanlon

Professor Jane Seale
For publication list, see http://oro.open.ac.uk/view/person/jks282.html
ORCID: https://orcid.org/0000-0002-4279-7463
My teaching and research interests lie at the intersections between disability, technology and inclusion. My work focuses in particular on the factors that influence or sustain the digital exclusion of disabled learners. Prior to joining the OU, I broke new ground with my 2006 book 'E-learning and Disability and Higher Education', by developing a theoretical framework for understanding and analysing successful and unsuccessful accessibility practices in higher education. This led to fruitful teaching and research collaborations with members of CALRG at the OU. I worked with members of CALRG to embed the 2006 book into a new module on accessibility for the Masters in Online and Distance Education. I also collaborated with Martyn Cooper to review the range of accessibility tools available to teachers and evaluate how successful they have been in helping teachers in higher education and further education develop accessible e-learning materials and activities for disabled learners. In 2016, I joined the OU and I have continued my contribution to CALRG activities through the Ed-ICT International Network in which, alongside Tim Coughlan and Chetz Colwell, I have worked with international researchers in Canada, US, Germany and Israel to identify solutions to the disadvantages that disabled students experience through lack of access to technologies and associated inclusive practices.

Kate Lister
For publication list, see http://oro.open.ac.uk/view/person/kml322.html
I manage accessibility and inclusive practice at The Open University, UK, and am an associate for Advance HE. My role involves driving and coordinating inclusive practice in The Open University, supporting staff to be accessible and inclusive by design, and championing disabled student needs at different echelons of the University. My background is in educational technology, language learning, and accessible and inclusive pedagogies in international contexts; I worked in Germany, Spain and China before moving to the UK to take up my

current role. My core research interests are accessibility and inclusive practice in pedagogy, student mental health and wellbeing in the curriculum, and technology that can support and empower disabled students.

Professor Martin Weller

For publication list, see http://oro.open.ac.uk/view/person/mjw5.html
ORCID: https://orcid.org/0000-0002-8339-146X
I'm a Professor of Educational Technology and my interest has always been in the application of new technology to academic practice. I lead the OER Hub research team, running a portfolio of projects examining the impact of open educational practices.

I joined the OU in 1995, as a Lecturer in Artificial Intelligence. I chaired the OU's first major elearning course, T171, in 1999 with nearly 15,000 students. This involved a number of strategic shifts in the OU to make it an online provider. I was the first director of the virtual learning environment, recommending the adoption of Moodle. I am currently academic director for the Learning Design project and also Director of the OER Hub.

My research area is in open education and digital scholarship – I blog about this, and have authored two books, The Digital Scholar and The Battle for Open (both available under open licence).

I'm a regular and reasonably well known blogger at Edtechie.net

Professor Mike Sharples

For publication list, see http://oro.open.ac.uk/view/person/ms8679.html
ORCID: https://orcid.org/0000-0001-7081-3320
I am Emeritus Professor of Educational Technology at the Institute of Educational Technology, The Open University, and Honorary Visiting Professor at the Centre for Innovation in Higher Education, Anglia Ruskin University. My research involves human-centred design of new technologies and environments for learning. I inaugurated the mLearn conference series and was Founding President of the International Association for Mobile Learning. As Academic Lead for the FutureLearn company (www.futurelearn.com), I informed the design of its social learning approach. I am currently Academic Lead for the nQuire project with the BBC to develop a platform for inquiry-led learning at scale (www.nquire.org.uk). I established the 'Innovating Pedagogy' series of annual reports and was lead editor of the series from 2012 to 2016 (www.open.ac.uk/innovating). I am co-editor of the 'Routledge Advances in the Learning Sciences' book series and author of over 300 papers in the areas of educational technology, learning sciences, science education, human-centred design of personal technologies, artificial intelligence and cognitive science.

Professor Patrick McAndrew

For publication list, see http://oro.open.ac.uk/view/person/pm526.html
ORCID: https://orcid.org/0000-0002-9016-154X

I am Emeritus Professor of Open Education at The Open University and led the Institute of Educational Technology (IET) from 2013 to 2019. In my research, I took a leading part in the development of approaches to open and free learning. Recent projects in this area include OpenLearn, OLnet, Bridge to Success and the OER Research Hub. These projects combine practice and research on the impact of openness. I have had an active role in over 40 funded projects across other areas of technology-enhanced learning such as accessibility, evaluation and learning design.

Dr Rebecca Ferguson

For publication list, see http://oro.open.ac.uk/view/person/rf2656.html
ORCID: http://orcid.org/0000-0002-8566-8231
I am a Senior Lecturer at The Open University, focusing on educational futures, learning analytics, MOOCs, innovating pedagogy and online social learning. I have been a pedagogic adviser to the FutureLearn MOOC platform since its foundation, supporting its development of conversational learning and its recent move towards microcredentials. I am also one of the coordinators of the FutureLearn Academic Network (FLAN), linking academics from over 140 partner institutions around the world and helping to develop a focused research agenda. As lead author on the 'Innovating Pedagogy' reports published each year by IET, I work with colleagues to explore new forms of teaching, learning and assessment in order to guide educators and policymakers. I am also an executive member of the Society for Learning Analytics Research (SoLAR) and was Program Chair for its international conferences in 2018 and 2019.

Dr Tim Coughlan

For publication list, see http://oro.open.ac.uk/view/person/tc6295.html
ORCID: https://orcid.org/0000-0002-0891-5438
I am a Lecturer in the Institute of Educational Technology at The Open University. My research interests cross the areas of Education and Human-Computer Interaction, and focus on the design and evaluation of systems that support inclusion, creativity, and openness in learning. I first joined CALRG in 2010 as a researcher on the 'Out There and In Here' project, which explored how a range of technologies could be applied to create inclusive collaborative fieldwork activities. Supporting access to learning through the appropriate design of technology has been a consistent theme in my work. This has included applying participatory research and design methods with students, analysing feedback at scale from students with declared disabilities, understanding how open courses can be developed collaboratively to widen participation in education, and creating new means for students to talk about their support needs and represent the successes and challenges they have experienced.

Professor Sir Timothy O'Shea
I am Honorary Professor of Innovation in Learning & Teaching at IET Open University and Emeritus Professor of Digital Education & Machine Learning at the University of Edinburgh. I am a former Vice-Chancellor and Principal of the University of Edinburgh. I have worked as a researcher in the Computer Science Department of the University of Texas at Austin, the Bionics Research Lab at the University of Edinburgh the Systems Concepts Lab, Xerox PARC, California and at the Institute of Educational Technology. In 1978, I founded the Computers and Learning research group at The Open University and was promoted to a personal chair in Information Technology and Education at the University in 1986. I was appointed Pro-Vice-Chancellor of The Open University in 1993 before moving to Birkbeck College as Master in 1997 and then to the University of Edinburgh as Vice Chancellor in 2002.

Foreword

Timothy O'Shea

This book was produced to mark the Computers and Learning research group's fortieth year. The CALRG, as it is known, has a special place in the history of The Open University. When it was established back in 1978, The Open University was still young, and only in its eighth year of the innovative teaching of students at a distance.

From the outset there was a recognition of the potential of the computer to assist and enrich our students' experience of being distance learners. In1975 we offered remedial tutorial Computer Assisted Learning (with feedback) via terminals in study centres, simulations at science summer schools and day schools and a specially designed programming language to help psychology students construct cognitive models.

The folk who came together in 1978 to form this very interdisciplinary research group understood that we had to make effective use of these newly developing technologies and we were very ambitious. We wanted to develop a research group that would cross faculty boundaries and be world leading. The Open University is the twentieth century's greatest educational experiment. As such the group saw it could be considered as a test bed with which to explore all the possible ways that the quality of student learning could be impacted by the judicious and imaginative use of computers in our courses. This proved to be a very wise endeavour!

The group is based in the Institute of Educational Technology with founder members including academics from Psychology, and the Education, Mathematics and Science Faculties, the then Student Computing Services and the staff based in regional offices. The original vision of a group with a strong international reputation for research excellence and with a mission to help deliver better learning experiences for students, has persisted and flourished.

The group understood that a large cohort of PhD students would be vital for the development of a research community so I offer a special acknowledgment both to current PhD students and to all the past PhD students who are the lifeblood of the group.

Thanks to the PhD programme and the work of various research staff over the years, the group has had an enviable record of external funding for research, well cited publications and well documented contributions to the success of The Open University in the various UK research assessment exercises.

As the chapters of this book demonstrate, the group is a key influencer in the research and development of educational technology worldwide. The members of the group have contributed to theory development, been technological innovators and conducted very large scale teaching experiments. The group's unique position comes from supporting and being embedded in a University whose raison d'etre derives from the application of educational technology in distance education.

CHAPTER I

Introduction

Ann Jones, Eileen Scanlon and Rebecca Ferguson

This chapter forms the introduction to the book, "Educational Visions" and describes the nature of the book. It presents the four principles or visions which inform the work of the Computers and Learning research group (CALRG) and are reflected in this book, and then provides the context with a discussion of the innovative nature of the early Open University. The CALRG is then described briefly before the introduction of a further framework used in the book to analyse the factors that make educational innovations successful, the Beyond Prototypes model. The last section describes the organisation and contents of the rest of the book.

Introduction

This book, "Educational Visions", informs future developments in educational technology, by reviewing the history of computers and education, covering themes including learning analytics and design, inquiry learning, accessibility and learning at scale. The lessons from these developments, which evolve, recur and adapt over time give an indication of the future in the field. The book informs readers about what is already known and demonstrates how they can use this work themselves.

"Educational Visions" is based on the research of the Computers and Learning research group (CALRG). Based at The Open Unversity, CALRG is the

How to cite this book chapter:
Jones, A., Scanlon, E. and Ferguson, R. 2019. Introduction. In: Ferguson, R., Jones, A. and Scanlon, E. (eds). *Educational Visions: Lessons from 40 years of innovation*. Pp. 1–12. London: Ubiquity Press. DOI: https://doi.org/10.5334/bcg.a
License: CC-BY 4.0

longest-running UK research group in the field of educational technologyy. The Open University celebrated its 50th birthday in 2019, whilst the research group recently celebrated its 40th anniversary. The production of the book drew on the CALRG's 40th-birthday celebrations and conference to extract themes and generate content of interest to a broad audience.

The core principles of the approach to educational technology reflected in this book are:

1 Teams can successfully teach any number of students at a distance
2 Learning is accessible for everyone
3 Teaching is adapted to meet learners' needs
4 Learners engage enthusiastically with STEM learning.

These four principles give the research a practical emphasis linked to the application of educational technology to the benefit of learners. The principles also form the visions that are discussed and considered in the book. "Educational Visions" traces 40 years of research in this area, showing how these four visions are being achieved, identifying challenges that have been overcome; those that still remain, and extracting general themes in educational technology.

The structure of the book aligns with these four visions. In each case, the lead author on one chapter is a researcher with a global reputation, who examines the foundations of work towards this vision and how that work has developed over 40 years. A second chapter related to the vision is authored by researchers currently active in this field, describing current work and future directions. This approach allows for a balance between historical analysis and current thematic application.

The structure of each chapter is also related to a framework (Beyond Prototypes) which explains why educational technology initiatives worldwide succeed and why they often fail. This framework highlights that initiatives only succeed if they are guided by a vision and if they take account of the whole complex system of interacting factors that impact on educational technology (pedagogy, technical aspects, ecology of practices, technical context, student community, teacher community, technical communities, pedagogic research community, revenue generation, environment, policy context and funding). A fuller description of this framework and a graphical representation are provided further on in this introductory chapter and chapter authors use this framework as a recurring theme. The aim is not only to introduce successful educational technology projects but also to make it clear why they are successful when so many others are not.

Each chapter includes examples and/or case studies of significant work, the effect this work has had and its implications for the future. These examples include FutureLearn (a MOOC platform with more than ten million learners), the Conversational Framework (widely used to structure and understand online teaching and learning), iSpot (used internationally by citizen scientists) and learning analytics tools. The remainder of this chapter briefly introduces The Open University, its mission, the CAL research group and the Beyond Prototypes Framework before offering some comments on the chapters that follow.

The Open University

The Open University was established in the UK in 1969 – and celebrated its 50th anniversary in 2019. Its mission was and still is to be open to people, places, methods and ideas. During the 1960s, only a small percentage of the UK population attended university. In 1970, a year after the OU started, but before courses were available, the figure was 8.4%. A primary aim for The Open University was to extend access to higher education to a much wider population.While he was leader of the British Labour Party, Harold Wilson wrote an outline for the 'university of the air' and the Labour Party's 1966 manifesto included a commitment to establish such a university – building on the idea that the then relatively new technologies: radio, film and television, could bring university education within reach of a much larger audience. Once he was Prime Minister, Wilson appointed Jennie Lee as Arts Minister and to take charge of the project.

The Open University (OU) Charter was signed in April 1969 and by 1972 the university had 36,000 students, increasing to 72,000 by 1979 when 130 under-graduate courses were offered. The OU's core vision and mission, to be open to people and places, methods and ideas, has not changed significantly during its 50 years.

Open to people and places

OU courses originally consisted of written course materials, sent out by post to students who studied part time. In addition, through a partnership set up with the OU, BBC (British Broadcasting Corporation) programmes were also made and broadcast in non-peak broadcasting times. Today, the BBC no longer produces broadcast programmes for OU courses, but the two organisations still work in partnership, co-producing programmes for all BBC tv, radio, digital and online channels/platforms. Printed course materials still play a role, but much is online.

Students were allocated to regional centres and to tutors who worked in the geographical areas associated with these centres. The tutors supported the students' work, marked their assignments and held tutorials at local centres during the evenings or on Saturdays. No qualifications were needed in order to start a course with The Open University: a radical idea at the time.

Generally, students were able to study wherever they lived in the UK and even when working abroad. Since then there has been a growth in students working from non-UK locations although it is not always possible to take courses from anywhere in the world.

Open to methods

The university pioneered new approaches to teaching, especially in STEM (Science, Technology, Engineering and Maths) areas where students did not have a traditional laboratory to hand. The idea of the Home Experiment Kit was developed. This involved posting out home chemistry sets, fruit-flies and, more recently, home computers. The very first science Home Experiment Kit included a small, compact microscope. Further examples are described in Chapter 8.

Residential schools run at traditional university campuses were set up where students could use laboratories, have face-to-face lectures, and work collaboratively on projects. However, the first Chancellor of the OU also foresaw the importance of computers:

> *I predict that before long actual broadcasting will form only a small part of the University's output. The world is caught in a communications revolution, the effects of which will go beyond those of the Industrial Revolution of two centuries ago. .... As the steam engine was to the first revolution, so the computer is to the second."* (Crowther, 1969)

Extract from Speech by Lord Crowther, first Chancellor of The Open University at the presentation of the Charter, 23rd July 1969.

Open to ideas

Probably the earliest 'big' idea was that of 'course teams' that would develop and produce courses for the students. In addition to content specialists, these included editors, administrators and educational technologists. Course materials underwent several drafts, which were commented on in course team meetings. Another significant example of the OU being open to ideas was its decision to develop a partnership with the BBC in 1971. This early collaboration meant that the programmes used in OU courses were made by BBC producers, in conjunction with academics, and so were able to benefit from the high production values of the BBC as well as including ingenious ways of helping students to visualise complex phenomena.

Modern technologies were used from very early days as the University developed ways of teaching science at a distance. A media mix that was heavily text based also included broadcast TV, audio and, from the mid 1970s, the use of computers. From the very beginning, the need for advising the University on the role of educational technology was acknowledged. A paper by the first Vice Chancellor, Lord Walter Perry, to the Planning Committee in July 1969 emphasised that Open University staff should include those with skills in "all the modern methods of educational technology" (Perry, 1969). By March 1970, the Institute of Educational Technology (IET) had been established. One of the

IET's roles was to "provide the Course Teams with continuous diagnostic feedback as a basis for remedial guidance, revision and recycling".

The CAL research group

The Computers and Learning research group (CALRG) was set up in 1979: housed in IET with founding members located in IET, Psychology and Computing. The first objective of the CAL research group was "to carry out a coordinated programme of research into ways computers can be used to improve the quality of education" (Jones and Scanlon, 1981). In their later edited book, Jones, Scanlon and O'Shea, (1987) explained that all the work described within the book "had a distance education (or training) setting in mind" (Preface, p.x), hence there was not only a strong commitment to researching teaching, but also a desire to understand how technology could improve teaching and learning within the distance learning context of the OU.

From the beginning, a significant part of the CAL research group's work was carried out by PhD students: both full time and part time. Members of the group were drawn from across the OU and were involved in the University's teaching in various ways: as authors, critical commentators, and evaluators, who shared "a strong commitment to improving education in general and distance education in particular by the application of new information technologies" (Jones, Scanlon and O'Shea, 1987, p.1). Thus, the part-time students chose areas of investigation that could be applied in their professional lives and to issues related to teaching.

Models of Learning: a cognitive science approach to understanding the learner

During the late 1970s and the 1980s, the CALRG was influenced by the rise of cognitive science, which embraces a number of different disciplines: (see, e.g. https://plato.stanford.edu/entries/cognitive-science/), and, in particular, the application of artificial intelligence (AI) research. Such research was often located in the United States (e.g. Carnegie Mellon, MIT, Stanford) and in the UK in Edinburgh, Sussex, and the MRC Applied Psychology Unit in Cambridge. One founding member of the CALRG developed a "self-improving" quadratic tutor, (O'Shea, 1979), and another researcher (Eisenstadt, 1982) wrote a unit on AI for a cognitive psychology course.

Following AI-influenced approaches, some CALRG researchers were interested in developing production systems – computer programs consisting of a set of rules; ways of deciding different rules, and an interpreter to run the system – for psychological modelling, building theories about how people learn. To do this they collected student protocol data – where protocols are concerned with the process of carrying out a cognitive task (Ericsson and

Simon (1980). This data could be used to construct production rule models which could then be used to predict the kinds of error that students were likely to make. Such models are valuable for examining learning but can also be embedded within tutoring systems (see for example O'Shea's "self improving" tutor, O'Shea, op. cit.).

Perhaps predictably, the fields and specific areas where such work was applied were those with sufficiently well-defined problems to benefit from such an approach. These included maths, physics problem solving, programming and graph interpretation skills. Many of the new approaches to teaching pioneered by The Open University related to STEM subjects and so there was a particular need to conduct research into teaching in these areas. This emphasis on STEM areas has persisted, and is reflected in Vision 4: Learners engage enthusiastically with STEM learning, although there has also been research in many non-STEM areas, including language learning, which is discussed briefly below. Overall, there has always been a strong interest in supporting student learning through designing instruction to help improve student performance, so the relationship with teaching is strong. Early goals also included theory development, e.g. understanding how physics problem-solving skills were developed.

Some developed models of learning that were used within courses. For example, O'Shea developed a computer game, modelled on the fraction buggy (Brown and Burton, 1978), which was embedded into teaching on an influential educational course for teachers: "Developing Mathematical Thinking". Indeed, cognitive science research had a significant impact on mathematics education more generally, see Siegler (2003).

CALRG research and evaluation have also fed into course design, sometimes directly and at other times more indirectly through studying students closely and developing an understanding of how the design of course materials influences students' understanding and learning. Good learning design is particularly important where students are learning at a distance. The production of Open University courses included a cycle of draft material which was commented on by the course team, which typically included both designers and media experts. In addition to the internal comments and suggestions, external readers would also read and comment on the materials. Some courses were developmentally tested – involving a more complete 'run-through', often by students.

As noted by Jones, Kirkup and Kirkwood (1992): *"... it is particularly important to test out any element of practical work, whether it is a laboratory-style home experiment or the use of a computer, as students will be on their own if and when any problems occur"* (p105). Their work on the Microcomputers for Schools project in the 1980s described how materials developed for teaching teachers were designed. They drew attention to the practical work texts, which were laid out in a three-column format, *"where the first column gave the keypress required, the second gave a photograph of the screen display that appeared as a result of that action, and the third column provided a commentary"* (p106).

The Beyond Prototypes Framework

So far we have discussed how some of the educational technology research at the OU, conducted by members of CALRG, has fed back into and influenced the design of OU teaching material, its courses. However, there is also the larger question of how educational technology research, sometimes referred to as technology-enhanced learning (TEL) can be applied in education more generally and, when the research is focusing on development, how it can lead to useful and usable products.

A recognition that successful TEL innovations needed to be interdisciplinary led to the establishment of the ESRC (Economic and Social Research Council) TEL programme, which ran from 2008 to 2013. This programme awarded funding to eight TEL projects. Reflecting on these, Richard Noss, who directed the programme, wrote: "*So the issue is this one: in general, despite the fact that all projects successfully designed and built effective prototypes of systems: the question is how to move from prototype to product.*" (Scanlon et al., 2013, p. 4). He continued: "*So this report is concerned with how to move from academic research and innovative prototypes to effective and sustainable products and practices.*" (Scanlon et al, op. cit. p.5).

In order to do this, an interdisciplinary team of educational technologists analysed and evaluated TEL research and selected key examples to study in further detail. Drawing on these they developed a framework: "Beyond Prototypes", which is used to frame and consider both the historical and the contemporary research discussed in the book. The framework is based on four Key Insights from the research (see Scanlon et al, op. cit. pp. 5–8).

1 TEL involves a complex system of technologies and practices. In order to embed significant TEL innovation successfully, it is necessary to look beyond product development and pay close attention to the entire process of implementation.
2 Significant innovations are developed and embedded over periods of years rather than months. Sustainable change is not a simple matter of product development, testing and roll-out. Persistent intent is needed.
3 TEL innovation is a process of bricolage. This process includes informed and directed exploration of the technologies and practices required to achieve an educational goal. It involves experimentation to generate fresh insights, and creative use of available resources. It also requires engagement with a range of communities and practices.
4 Successful implementation of TEL innovation requires evidence that the projected educational goal has been achieved. Reliable evaluations must be carried out; their findings disseminated and acted on. Methods of evaluation are required that can be applied to processes of innovation and to institutional change, as well as those that can be applied to shifts in technology usage.

At the heart of the Beyond Prototypes model is Key Insight 1 – the 'TEL complex'. The framework is represented in figure 1 which is reproduced below:

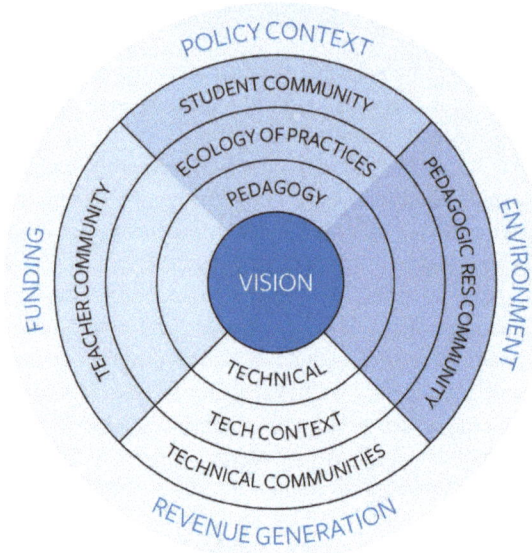

Figure 1.1: The Beyond Prototypes Model of the TEL Complex. Adapted from Figure 1 in Scanlon et. al. (2013) with thanks to the TLRP/TEL programme for permission to use this figure.

In order for TEL innovation to be successful, key elements must be considered. These are:

- pedagogy: "an extremely complex and distinctive process which involves both student and teacher engagement, delivering a set of educational services by means of specific channels." (Scanlon et. al., 2013 p.28);
- technical components that support the pedagogy in order to achieve the aim of enhancing learning in a specific way;
- the ecology of practices and technical context. These are important because any TEL will be implemented in a specific context. For example, internet coverage may be sporadic or unavailable (see, e.g. Gaved and Peasgood, 2017);
- the communities involved in the TEL complex, including students, teachers, researchers and technical developers or supporters.

Whilst it would be beyond the scope of this book to apply the complete framework for the research discussed, each chapter illustrates how aspects of the TEL complex work in practice. So, in Chapter 7 Rienties and Jones describe how the learning analytics research currently being undertaken involves a number of different communities in the University and how 'data wrangling' (a process which provides learning analytics information about University courses) involves a series of discussions with the academics involved in developing those courses.

Continuing work with the nQuire tool illustrates how persistent intent works (Key Insight 2). The nQuire tool was originally developed during a three-year project funded by the ESRC/TEL programme (2007–2010); Sharples et al (2015).

At the end of the successful project, a prototype tool was available. This required considerable further development, and was taken forward in a number of projects, (see e.g. Sharples, Aristeidou, Herodotou, Mcleod and Scanlon, 2019) as described by Scanlon and Herodotou in Chapter 9. In 2019 the nQuire tool was used by over 200,000 people as part of a citizen science project, Gardenwatch, to fill in a gap in information about the nature of UK gardens as habitats for wildlife.

Much of the emphasis of CALRG research has been on STEM subjects. However, the group has also been involved in research outside STEM and it continues this trajectory. Notable examples of research into how educational technology can support learning in other areas and contexts includes, for example, the use of mobile technologies to support language learning especially in informal contexts. This research has also been applied to support migrants' language learning, see, e.g. Kukulska-Hulme (2019) as noted in chapter 10. Another example is the work carried out by Charitonos on how microblogging (particularly the use of Twitter) can help to support and connect learning across museums and classrooms (see, for example Charitonos, 2019). A final example is Jones's work on affective issues in learning technologies, including using computer-mediated role play for investigating and supporting children's socio-emotive development and expression (Jones, 2010).

Even when research has originated in STEM contexts, it is often applied and further developed in numerous other non-STEM contexts, or in contexts where the types of scientific inquiries are very varied. One good example of this is the nQuire project, discussed by Sharples in the concluding chapter. The first nQuire project developed and evaluated an inquiry tool that could be used on mobile devices or on a computer to support school children's personalised scientific inquiries. Such inquiries included investigating whether an Urban Heat Island existed in the new city where one school was located. Other inquiries investigated healthy eating, bird feeding behaviour and how cheese rots. Parts of the investigations took part in the field, other parts at home and in the classroom.

This line of research is a good example of persistent intent. It has continued over a very long period, developing a platform that can support inquiries at a large scale, with a very broad definition of science.

The work on learning design, and our understanding of the learning process, which began in the 1970s (see chapter 6) is also applied to a very wide range of topics. In chapter 7, Rienties discusses its application to OU course or module design, whilst Ferguson (chapter 3) and Sharples (chapter 10) focus on different aspects of how research into the pedagogic process and learning design has fed into the development of MOOC platforms.

The remainder of this book is organised as follows: (this chapter is included in the list for completeness).

Chapter 1: Introduction
Ann Jones, Eileen Scanlon and Rebecca Ferguson
Introducing CALRG and giving the background to the group; setting out the visions, and placing them in context; introducing the framework and its importance for educational technology.

Chapter 2: Teaching and Learning at Scale: Foundations
Patrick McAndrew
Studies of how distance learning can be supported by TEL and how these methods can scale. This chapter relates to Vision 1: Teams can successfully teach any number of students at a distance.

Chapter 3: Teaching and Learning at Scale: Futures
Rebecca Ferguson
Recent developments in this area, particularly massive open online courses (MOOCs.) This is the second chapter relating to Vision 1: Teams can successfully teach any number of students at a distance.

Chapter 4: Accessible Inclusive Learning: Foundations
Tim Coughlan, Kate Lister, Jane Seale, Eileen Scanlon and Martin Weller
The development of open learning, and work on accessibility. This chapter relates to Vision 2: Learning is accessible for everyone.

Chapter 5: Accessible Inclusive Learning: Futures
Tim Coughlan, Kate Lister, Jane Seale, Eileen Scanlon and Martin Weller
Current work on open learning and accessibility and future directions. This is the second chapter relating to Vision 2: Learning is accessible for everyone.

Chapter 6: Evidence-Based Learning: Foundations
Ann Jones, Bart Rienties and Canan Blake
Developing a coordinated programme of research into ways computers can be used to improve the quality of education. This chapter relates to Vision 3: Teaching is adapted to meet learners' needs.

Chapter 7: Evidence-Based Learning: Futures
Bart Rienties and Ann Jones

How this research programme has developed, with a focus on the relationship of learning design and learning analytics. This is the second chapter relating to Vision 3: Teaching is adapted to meet learners' needs.

Chapter 8: STEM Learning: Foundations
Eileen Scanlon, Christothea Herodotou, Denise Whitelock and Chris Edwards
Origins of work on learning and teaching STEM subjects at a distance. This chapter relates to Vision 4: Learners engage enthusiastically with STEM learning.

Chapter 9: STEM Learning: Futures
Christothea Herodotou, Eileen Scanlon and Denise Whitelock
Current and future work on areas including citizen science, inquiry learning and virtual field trips. This is the second chapter relating to Vision 4: Learners engage enthusiastically with STEM learning.

Chapter 10: Visions for the Future of Educational Technology
Mike Sharples
Drawing the themes together.

References

Brown, J. S. and Burton, R. R. (1978). Diagnostic models for procedural bugs, Cognitive Science Volume 2, Issue 2, April–June 1978. Pages 155–192.

Charitonos, K. (2019). Crossing over settings, practices and experiences: connecting learning in museums and classrooms. In: Looi, Chee-Kit; Wong, Lung-Hsiang; Glahn, Christian and Cai, Su eds. *Seamless Learning: Perspectives, Challenges and Opportunities.* Springer, pp. 111–137.

Crowther, Lord. (1969). Speech by Lord Crowther, first Chancellor of The Open University at the Presentation of the Charter, 23rd July 1969. Retrieved from: https://www.open.ac.uk/library/digital-archive/pdf/script/script:5747089b4a53f

Eisenstadt, M. (1982). Design features of a Friendly Software Environment for Novice Programmers, in (Eds. Marc Eisenstadt, Mark T Keane and Tim Rajan), Novice Programming Environments: Explorations in Human-Computer Interaction and Artificial Intelligence, Routledge, UK.

Ericsson, K. A., & Simon, H. A. (1980). Verbal reports as data. *Psychological Review, 87*(3), 215–251.

Gaved, Mark and Peasgood, Alice (2017). Fitting in Versus Learning: A Challenge for Migrants Learning Languages Using Smartphones. *Journal of Interactive Media in Education*, 2017(1), article no. 1.

Jones, A. and Scanlon, E. (1981). A review of research in the CAL group: A report of the first annual conference, November, CALRG Technical Report No. 27, Open University, Milton Keynes.

Jones, Ann; Scanlon, Eileen and O'Shea, Tim eds. (1987). *The Computer Revolution: New Technologies for Distance Teaching*. Brighton: Harvester Press.

Jones, A., Kirkup, G. and Kirkwood (1992). Personal computers for distance learning (London, Paul Chapman).

Jones, Ann (2010). Affective issues in learning technologies: emotional responses to technology and technology's role in supporting socio-emotional skills. *Journal of Interactive Media in Education*.

Kukulska-Hulme, A. (2019). Mobile Language Learning Innovation Inspired by Migrants. *Journal of Learning for Development – JL4D*, 6(2) pp. 116–129.

O'Shea, T (1979). International Journal of Man-Machine Studies Volume 11, Issue 1, January 1979, Pages 97–124.

Perry, W. (1969). *Establishment of an Applied Educational Science Unit*, Council Paper C/II/3. Milton Keynes: Open University.

Scanlon, Eileen; Sharples, Mike; Fenton-O'Creevy, Mark; Fleck, James; Cooban, Caroline; Ferguson, Rebecca; Cross, Simon and Waterhouse, Peter (2013). Beyond prototypes: Enabling innovation in technology-enhanced learning. Open University, Milton Keynes.

Sharples, Mike; Scanlon, Eileen; Ainsworth, Shaaron; Anastopoulou, Stamatina; Collins, Trevor; Crook, Charles; Jones, Ann; Kerawalla, Lucinda; Littleton, Karen; Mulholland, Paul and O'Malley, Claire (2015). Personal inquiry: orchestrating science investigations within and beyond the classroom. *Journal of the Learning Sciences*, 24(2) pp. 308–341.

Sharples, Mike; Aristeidou, Maria; Herodotou, Christothea; McLeod, Kevin and Scanlon, Eileen (2019). Inquiry learning at scale: pedagogy-informed design of a platform for citizen inquiry. In: *Proceedings of the Sixth (2019) ACM Conference on Learning @ Scale – L@S '19*, ACM Press, New York, NY, USA, article no. 29.

Siegler, R. S. (2003). Implications of cognitive science research for mathematics education. In Kilpatrick, J., Martin, W. B., & Schifter, D. E. (Eds.), A research companion to principles and standards for school mathematics (pp. 219–233). Reston, VA: National Council of Teachers of Mathematics.

CHAPTER 2

Teaching and Learning at Scale: Foundations

Patrick McAndrew

The Open University (OU) offered a radical change in how higher education was considered in the UK from the 1960s. A fundamental change was to allow access to those who wanted to learn, without their needing to show prior success in qualifications. Alongside this expansion in offering access there also needed to be a rethink in how learning could operate at scale. Higher education has a tradition of individual responsibility that was not suited to the complexity of the task, rather the OU needed to take a team approach to designing, building and operating the learning experience.

Addressing such complexity is one part of the model in Beyond Prototypes (introduced briefly in Chapter 1), recognising the complexity that occurs when applying Technology Enhanced Learning (TEL). Each part of the model can be seen to act in the development of the OU: persistence in achieving the aims of the OU to meet the needs of a new body of students; bricolage in being prepared to experiment with new ideas and new technologies; and, an underlying dependence on evidence to help understand and address the problems that are faced at scale.

How to cite this book chapter:
McAndrew, P. 2019. Teaching and Learning at Scale: Foundations. In: Ferguson, R., Jones, A. and Scanlon, E. (eds). *Educational Visions: Lessons from 40 years of innovation.* Pp. 13–32. London: Ubiquity Press. DOI: https://doi.org/10.5334/bcg.b. License: CC-BY 4.0

Beyond Prototypes

The Beyond Prototypes model sets out four different aspects of innovations that are summarised in the report (Scanlon et. al., 2013):

1. The TEL complex
"TEL involves a complex system of technologies and practices. In order to embed significant TEL innovation successfully, it is necessary to look beyond product development and pay close attention to the entire process of implementation."
2. Persistent intent
"Significant innovations are developed and embedded over periods of years rather than months. Sustainable change is not a simple matter of product development, testing and roll-out."
3. Bricolage
"TEL innovation is a process of bricolage. This process includes informed and directed exploration of the technologies and practices required to achieve an educational goal. It involves experimentation to generate fresh insights, and a creative use of available resources. It also requires engagement with a range of communities and practices."
4. Evidence
"Successful implementation of TEL innovation requires evidence that the projected educational goal has been achieved. Reliable evaluations must be carried out; their findings must be disseminated and acted on. Methods of evaluation are required that can be applied to processes of innovation and to institutional change, as well as those that can be applied to shifts in technology usage." (Scanlon et al, 2013, p6–7]

Considering the OU through the Beyond Prototypes framework

In this chapter those four aspects of the Beyond Prototypes model emerge from the work of the OU, including the Computers and Learning research group (CALRG) as part of the Institute of Educational Technology (IET).

The challenge of forming the first modern open university was undeniably complex, and the solutions proposed recognised both the complexity in the situation and also space for further development. The first section of this chapter considers how complexity was addressed by those working to bring the university together as they thought through how teamwork, and the role that educational technology needs to play, could work in practice.

In the second section the persistence of the work is considered. In particular considering how the university addressed the challenge of being open to learners. One of the fundamentals of the approach to distance education taken by The Open University is its open entry system. Open entry allows anyone to choose to study any subject that is offered. There are no prerequisites; at one stage this also meant that students could choose to study at different levels (though the fee system now in place makes that choice much more limited). This does not mean though that all choices will lead to equal success or that success can be measured on the same basis for all learners. Over time systemic threats to operation have occurred driven from funding models that have impacted unfairly on the part-time sector. These pressures have meant the OU has needed to show persistence in remaining true to its mission and yet avoid the complacency inherent in being a market-leader.

The third element is experimentation; "bricolage". The OU arose through a process of experimentation and willingness to try alternative approaches to support students to learn at a distance. The Open University came into operation at a time when new tools and new ways of thinking were available to reconsider the way correspondence education worked, and so provide a fuller experience of distance education that would be accepted as comparable to that from more conventional higher education providers. Being prepared to try new approaches has been very successful, however there are also risks in then settling into an accepted approach and providing a legacy position. The difficulty of being an innovator from a dominant position is recognised (Rogers, 1995) and can lead to susceptibility to losing position to other more disruptive innovators. At several points in the OU's history such disruption has threatened, as technology offered alternative ways for other providers to operate without the investment at scale of the OU. Nonetheless, the OU remains the leading distance and part-time provider of higher education in the UK. This is in part due to a willingness to itself disrupt its own models for working.

The fourth component of the Beyond Prototypes model is evidence. The OU established an evidence-based approach from the beginning, driven by the need to prove the quality of its approach and show value. Through research mainly carried out in the Institute of Educational Technology, the OU has always surveyed its students at scale and monitored the performance and satisfaction of its students. The role of evidence has been refreshed in more recent years through the availability and use of analytic measures.

Meeting complexity through teams at the OU

The establishment of The Open University arose out of a mix of political and practical ambitions in the 1960s that made its existence at first uncertain for reasons that included "demand was not proven, many students would leave early and degree-level work could not be taught in such a way" (Weinbren, 2015, p11). On the other hand, there had been considerable thought and planning into the idea of the OU, with the ideas captured in the original Planning

Report (HMSO, 1969). That report set out the different components of OU teaching and also how the OU might be structured in order to address those elements.

A key starting point was that the aim was not just to produce a correspondence approach to higher education. Instead the full range of components that made up a university were considered. That meant as a consequence that a more complex framework was required in designing The Open University than had been applied in established correspondence education. In keeping with the original concept of a "University of the Air" the Planning Report highlighted a role for broadcast as a replacement for the lecture of more conventional higher education. The report noted the "logistical advantages" of the lecture with broadcast providing scope to improve on quality and economies of scale so that they were "likely to achieve results at least as good as and often better than those secured by the normal live lecture". Six educational aims were assigned to the use of broadcast. Three being of benefit to a general audience:

a) Allow presentation of topics with high impact.
b) Share cultural value to a wider audience.
c) Promote awareness of the possibilities of higher education.

Together with three being of benefit to those who became students:
d) Support preparation so that there would be lower "fall-out" rate of those who do then sign-up.
e) Avoid the need for students to travel to attend events.
f) Help students to feel part of the university and in contact with its staff.

The use of broadcast was only seen as one element in the OU approach to teaching, albeit one that attracted attention in establishing the OU. Those who founded the OU were clear that it was "neither practically possible nor pedagogically sound to rely on broadcasting as the principal or exclusive means of instruction in an operation designed to provide disciplined courses of university level" (HMSO, 1969, p6). Instead it was proposed that a staff body be established that could support the mix of broadcast with printed materials and also offer the students the support that was needed. Some guidance for the aims of the OU came from work in the US, and several early appointments and visiting consultancies drew on experiences in independent and correspondence study there. While it is hard to give single credit for such work it is worth noting one contribution as described by Moore (1990) of the previous experience by Charles Wedemeyer in attempting to establish an Articulated Instructional Media project (AIM) at the University of Wisconsin to offer degree level education at a distance. Quoting Wedemeyer, Moore states that AIM "was an experimental prototype with three fatal flaws: it had no control over its faculty, and hence its curriculum; it lacked control over its funds; and it had no control over academic rewards (credits, degrees) for its students. The implications were clear: a large-scale, non-experimental institution of the AIM type would have to start with complete autonomy and control" [quoted in Moore, 1990, p. 292.]. Whether drawn directly on this experience or not, these three points do appear to have been considered in the formation of the OU as an autonomous entity structured to have academic faculty, independent finance, and awarding powers.

The structure was also planned in greater detail with the Planning Report proposing six different substructures, four areas that were considered essential, with two further areas seen as desirable.

The four core areas can be summarised as:

1. Central administrative office – to take control of the finances and to recruit and administer the students.
2. Academic departments – faculty on academic contracts that would be responsible for the content as a whole.
3. Specialised academic related staff to support the methods of teaching and media required, including broadcast through the BBC.
4. Administration of the part-time tutors and student counselling services, this was seen as being distributed across regions and nations.
   The further two areas outlined in the Report were:
5. An operational research unit to be "established as an early priority" to undertake studies in support of new methods of teaching.
6. To set up its own publications department.

The division of labour in the structure that was planned was very much reflected in the eventual setup of the university, with integration of each area around the structuring of a "course team" approach to ensure that responsibility for the student experience, and the materials and media that supported it, would be a shared one. The ambitious aim for the OU was to establish four foundational courses for study across key disciplines, to support those with different media, including broadcast, and to offer those courses to 25,000 learners within two years of being established. The "course team" emerged as a concept that has since become a core element of the university's success and provided resilience to several challenges. That the concept was not fully formed was acknowledged by those who worked on it at the time as "an enormous bit of improvisation" and the contributions needed had to rapidly evolve, "nobody for example realised that you actually had to have professional editors" (Mike Pentz, Dean of Science, speaking in 1979) (Open University, 1979). The lessons of that early stage were that not only did content have to be produced, it also needed to be integrated into a learning experience and the students supported to achieve the right outcomes. The role of research and evidence was important and from an early stage data on student performance was included, through surveys of students at scale and targeted projects to understand student needs.

Formation of IET, the Institute of Educational Technology

In forming The Open University as a complex organisation there was recognition that there was a need to invest not only in the discipline-based materials needed by the students, but also in the way that learning would operate for the students. The Planning Report had noted the need for research into educational technology: "We propose, therefore, that an operational research unit of the University be established as an early priority in order to undertake the necessary studies. Indeed the continuation, as an integral feature of the University, of experimental work particularly in relation to the learning process may eventually prove to be one of the University's distinctive contributions to education generally." (HMSO, 1969, p16). (Experimentation certainly did continue; the current and next planned phase for such work is discussed in the next chapter.)

The OU was established in 1969, gaining its charter in April 1969, and during its first year a decision was made to establish a unit to bring together staff development and research. A paper provided to the Council of the University (Perry, 1969) stated that the "role of The Open University as a major innovator in education" required "not only academic personnel distinguished in their respective disciplines, but also staff with special skills in all the modern methods of educational technology." The paper therefore "recommended the immediate establishment of an Applied Educational Sciences Unit" with responsibilities that included "service for course teams and contributing towards a professional development programme for University staff." Research was flagged as likely to increase as "academic staff become more conversant with the techniques of educational technology, and the workload with course teams decreases". These actions are also reflected in a later book considering the early days of the OU authored by the first Vice Chancellor, Walter Perry, saying "The Planning Committee had recommended most strongly an ongoing programme of research into the operation of the University. ... I therefore proposed that the Department of Applied Educational Sciences should be combined with the group of Research Officers into a single Institute. ... My suggestion was accepted ... and the Institute of Educational Technology was born." (Perry, 1977, p81). The role of the Institute of Educational Technology was summarised in a further paper to Senate in 1970 in terms of the impact needed on OU instructional materials:

"(1) They will all have been extensively tested and validated on representative samples of students and volunteers.

(2) They will make provision for individual differences, by permitting some choice of route and rate towards the course objectives.

(3) They will utilise the various media and supporting services to best advantage.

(4) They will demand participation from the student and will provide him with frequent assessments of his progress.

(5) They will provide the Course Teams with continuous diagnostic feedback as a basis for remedial guidance, revision and recycling." (Open University, 1970, p1).

The formation of IET provided one indication that the OU considered that the way in which it taught needed to both be different to conventional approaches and to evolve and change over time. The aim was to be innovative and to embrace the use of technology where it was appropriate to do so.

Persistent approach in developing distance education

The Open University has operated for 50 years on the basis that students can be enabled to learn at a distance. The very existence of the university is a testament to its persistence in ensuring the approach works. Having started by recruiting to its then maximum capacity of 25,000 students in 1971, it is the UK's largest university in terms of numbers of students taught, both expressed as a total number and as full time equivalent. Over its 50 years more than 2 million people have become its students, and nearly 500,000 have received qualifications. In 2018 it had over 170,000 students studying (though that is below the peak of over 250,000 in 2011/12). In addition, it offers free learning to over 7 million learners through its open educational resources (described further in forthcoming chapters) and a further 2 million supported by FutureLearn (Chapter 6). This is all in the context of a university that was created in uncertainty and amid questions as to whether it was offering education to an appropriate group of people.

Fundamentals for learning at scale

From its start The Open University adopted an open approach to higher education that may still be seen as going against accepted practice that access to such education is to be earned through achievement in earlier assessed education. The university system that developed in the western world and dominates in the world today is based on a model of scarcity. That model sees access to recognised education as less available as the levels increase. In particular post-secondary education is positioned as being for a privileged few. In relatively recent times that was reflected in a very clear way in the design and operation of the education system in the UK, with growth in the last 50 years to give access for more of the population into tertiary education. In 1960 approximate 5% of the population would attend university between the ages of 17–30, by 1970 this had risen to nearly 15% where it remained throughout the 70s and 80s. Then in the 1990s there was new policy and ambition with a push to attain 50% that led to increases in the numbers entering tertiary education, with 49% being claimed in 2017 (Guardian, 2017).

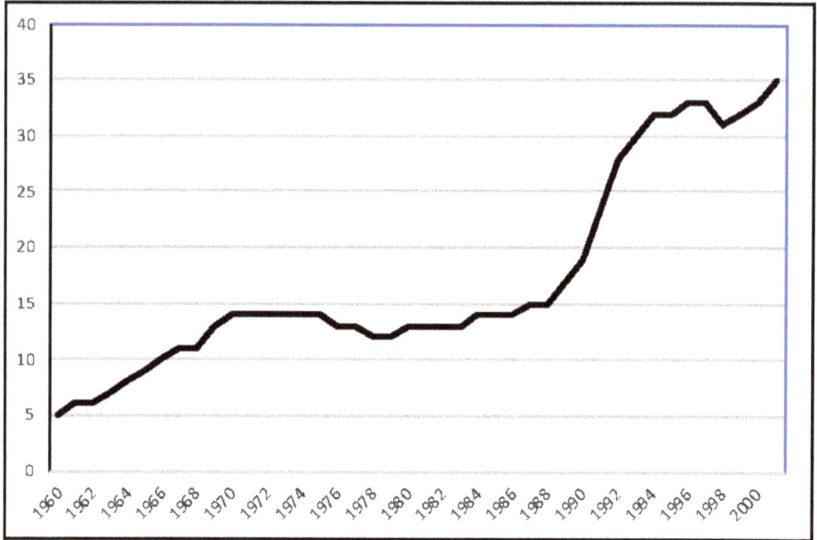

Figure 2.1: Age Participation Index of 17–30 year olds in university (%) 1960–2001: Adapted from Chowdry et al (2010).

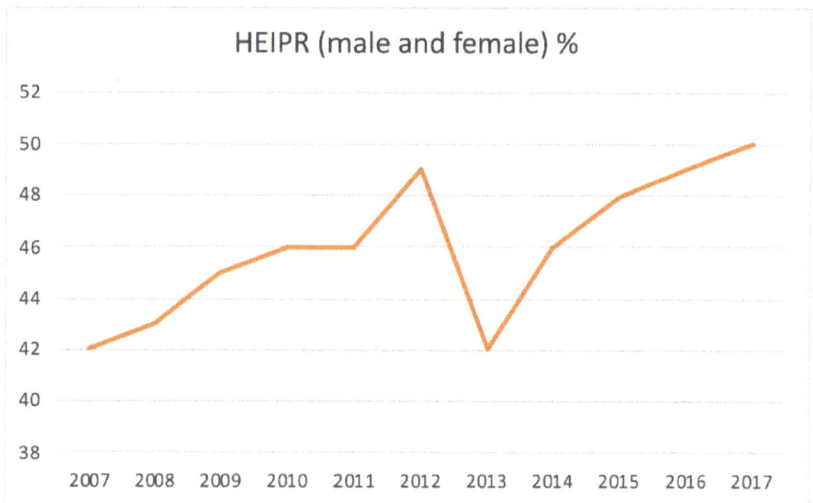

Figure 2.2: Higher Education Initial Participation Rate for England. Data from the Higher Education Statistics Agency (HESA) 2018.

The earlier trend towards greater entry to university in England is shown in Figure 2.1 above (adapted from Chowdry et al. (2010), using data from Finegold (2006)) and more recent data from HESA(2108) in Figure 2.2. Even with increasing attendance there was a need to diversify provision (Finegold, 2006). With 50% provision there remain both "the other half" and those that had left education before it expanded. Yet the dominant model remains one in which university study is undertaken during a period away from home and within a separate process from that of 'work'. Privilege remains built into the system with access gained on prior attainment, by seeking to filter out those who are not suitable at the start of the process. Prior qualifications are required with a requirement for "2 A-levels" an underlying assumption for eligibility for study.

The OU represents a persistent approach to push back at this existing model, through understanding both some of the truth in assumptions, and in looking at how to address them. A clear example of persistence is support for entry into study. An open entry approach to study inevitably means that on some measures The Open University will not look as successful as other universities. Past success is a good indicator of future success and at the point of entry that is most efficiently judged through grades achieved in previous formal examinations, with a correlation between those and future results identifiable, though weak (Birch and Rienties, 2014). While accepting such a link provides an overall picture, it is not the case at an individual level that learners with low or no previous qualifications will not succeed. Indeed the idea that there is a "limited pool of ability" has been rejected in previous reviews of higher education (Dearing, 1997).

Do qualifications matter?

Being open entry and operating at scale means that it is possible to see the different performance of those from different backgrounds. Four lessons have been learned here:

1. Anyone may succeed. So using data such as prior study and economic background to determine whether someone should be allowed to try to study means that some of those who would have succeeded will have been excluded.
2. Prior qualifications are an indicator for initial success. Perhaps not surprisingly those who have already shown success in earlier study are more likely to succeed, however for all abilities of student there are similar points where they struggle and determination is needed.
3. Once success in OU study has been achieved then previous study history is almost irrelevant. This means that it is vital to support students to achieve that initial success and to set them on the path to success.
4. The measure of success is not necessarily the same for the student and the institute. The focus institutionally and culturally is often on a qualification.

This is reflected back if students are asked to state their aims. Overwhelmingly (nearly 90% of) OU students will indicate that their aim is to achieve a degree. However, in practice students may gain advancement or satisfaction without meeting the degree. In the past this was built into the highly modular study structure of the OU. Current structures risk labelling those who leave prior to the degree as failures at system level (so that in league tables or funder progress models these are not successes), and at institutional level (with metrics set on final outcomes rather than progress). Unless success is identified at the student level this risks individuals seeing themselves as failing, despite possibly having achieved academically more than they had ever done before.

Modelling performance

One revealing indicator for the way in which different factors impact on the success of students is the analysis of the cohorts of students used to help judge whether a module at The Open University is performing as expected. Such analysis allows comparison with historic measures of performance for student completion and attainment, adjusted to allow for the impacted of the student body that is recruited. While demographics for an individual are not a sufficient reason to infer their success or failure, at scale such demographics can help us understand whether a group as a whole is likely to perform better or worse. An historic factor analysis has been used for the last 10 years to take into account all measures available. Some of the factors considered are shown in Table 1.

Table 1: Factors in predicting student performance in Open University modules (information provided by Vicky Marsh and Jim Peard of The Open University).

Student motivation factors (demographics)	Module factors (choice of study)	Previous student experience
Occupation Gender Age Credit transfer	Discipline area Level Credits from the module Number of assessments in the module Credits gained in same discipline area Credits gained at same level of study	Previous OU study Previous study success Previous educational qualifications

The details of the modelling are interesting, though not important in the context of this chapter. Here the importance is that the 10 years of data show a high level of consistency for the factors that emerge and in differences between initial study and continued study. For initial study one of the top factors is highest previous educational qualification gained before study, for continuing students this does not appear as a top 10 factor in the analysis of statistically significant factors in determining student success. For new students three of the other top 10 factors are also related to their background while for continuing students there is only one remaining demographic factor, relating to the market segment that they come from rather than their personal background. In simple terms this implies that from OU data it is only at the start of study that likely success can be judged from personal background or achievements in earlier education. Once study has got underway then previous successful study within the OU is the strongest predictor. This indicates the short-sightedness of building a system of higher education that first filters out people based on already achieved qualifications, rather than giving them a chance to develop and prove themselves.

Commencing study

The difference in achievement in early study that does depend on previous preparation has also been addressed in the OU approach with initial study seen as part of learning to learn rather than as a way to filter out. The OU has

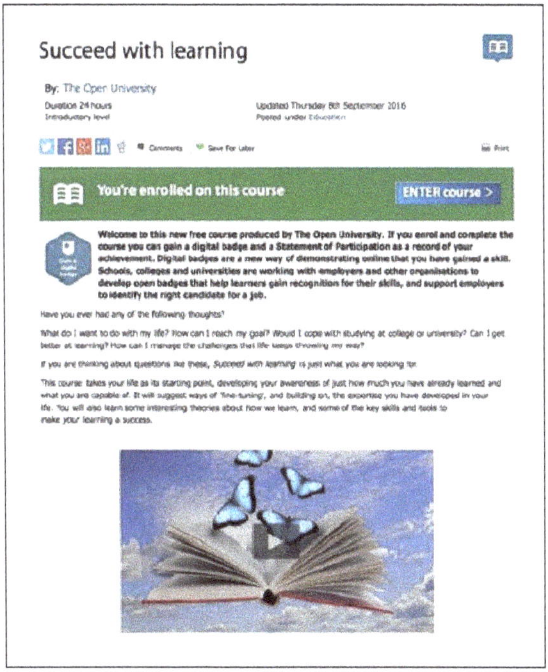

Figure 2.3: Available Badged Open Course: Succeed with Learning.

persistently looked to provide routes to support early study. Initially this was through gateway study with partner organisations, notably the National Extension College, and through foundation stages in the OU degrees. More recently it has supported those returning to education through programmes of *Openings* courses and, currently, through a range of *Access* provisions. Some of those changes reflect development over time, others the response of the OU to external factors. The value of the *Openings* approach was also demonstrated when it was used to support students facing difficulty in their study in US Community Colleges. In the Bridge to Success project (Law et al., 2012), material that was part of two *Openings* courses was reworked into open educational resources to support *Learning to Learn* and *Succeed with Math*. These resources were then used flexibly across a range of contexts by US Community Colleges, universities and other organisations such as charities. The success of these alternative bridging models both to inspire educators (Coughlan et al., 2013) and provide support for students (Pitt et al., 2013) showed that this is often an under-supported area where approaches in place in the OU can transfer successfully into other contexts. Updated versions of both of these courses remain freely available as *Succeed with Learning* and *Succeed with Maths* with badged recognition (Badged Open Courses) on the OpenLearn site (Law, 2016), Figure 2.3.

The current range of *Access* modules were designed to fit with the need for students in some parts of the UK to be eligible for loans to pay for study. This meant that the modules needed to become larger and eligible for accreditation as pre-university study. The reworking also allowed other changes so that the modules contain additional online study and revised assessment (Hills et al., 2018), both of which prepare the students more fully for further study (Butcher et al., 2018). While it might be tempting to see such *Access* modules as the poor relation in contrast to the main stream modules, in practice they are among the most highly rated modules for student satisfaction and have shown their value in improved performance, especially for those otherwise at risk, such as those with low previous educational qualifications. This shows action by the OU to give students, who would otherwise be in categories that might struggle with initial study, a route that can lead them to build up success with the OU and so improve their chances of further success.

Bricolage: Experimental approach to the learning experience

The OU supports learning at a distance for higher education in a changing environment both in terms of what students want and in how the technology can support it. By necessity the OU has needed to operate an experimental approach; initially in taking new steps into how to provide the scale that is needed, then to retain an innovative approach that evolves to make use of technology for educators and for students. Major changes have included adoption of online virtual learning environments, use of online conferencing and remote connections, and changes in how we assess students. These though have not come in isolation as one-off decisions, rather in each case there is a history of experimentation at a range of scales and of learning from external experiences.

Materials, cascaded support and feedback

The concept of materials as the basis for learning may initially feel wrong. That we can package up learning seems to draw us back to the Nurnberg funnel concept that we can simply provide the content and pour it in. The materials may have moved on from written texts to also include the use of other media such as broadcast, video and audio however if it is all there and can be sent in a big cardboard box then the student will be able to spend the time and come back having "learnt" it all. This, of course, is not the case and the idea of materials-based learning is not that the materials are everything, rather that they can provide an alternative to the high-contact approach and synchronous presentations seen in more traditional lectures. Furthermore the design of the experience around the materials can build in the tasks, activities, support and assessment that make learning more likely and do this in a way that can be scaled.

The design process for OU courses contained two innovations in particular. The first innovation is that the teaching component should be available within the content: while content is not necessarily king it is a vital component. The second innovation is that content would be closely supported by feedback to the learner.

Feedback has for some time been an unacknowledged element in education and learning. In Hattie's analysis (Hattie, 2008) of effects of educational innovations, feedback is ranked as one of the areas having highest likely impact, and yet this is a factor that often is either ill-defined or side-lined. The National Student Survey includes a rating for feedback. Assessment and feedback is the area in which the OU has consistently ranked highly in comparison with other UK universities. In 2019, it came first out of all higher education institutions with 85% compared to an average of 73% (OfS, 2019). For feedback to be so strong in the case of an institution where feedback has to be given at a distance is perhaps at first surprising. However this has been achieved through integration of feedback into the learning design and assessment of materials, to ensure feedback is provided at a scale that allows sufficient time and attention to be given to the individual.

Feedback at the OU operates both through its role in the design of the learning experience and in how support is provided. Materials are designed to be interactive and involve the learner in line with the materials-based approach. The materials need to talk to the learner, and ask them to be active. This can be achieved in print-based content by a combination of the language used and the addition of accompanying motivating activities, such as through watching broadcast programmes or through experimental kits. With availability of online content, interactivity is also through online activities, discussions and simulations, as part of the designed overall approach so that the structure of the module is made an active experience.

The second aspect of how feedback operates at the OU is through the cascaded model of support. An Associate Lecturer will typically support a group of approximately 20 people who are studying a module together. They will have started at a common point and while there will be flexibility in terms of day to day pacing of study there will be key synchronisation points where students need to supply material for assessment. Such assessment is designed to help the students gain understanding and receive feedback through the marking of the work. Typically the work will also be marked and form part of the assessed outcome of the module, however by design it is acting in a formative way – to help the student learn. The tension between marked work and feedback is well recognised in the literature with studies showing that feedback is the more important component for learning, while marks provide the higher motivation to complete, in line with other work where optional components for learning inevitably have a lower priority.

Distance learning works

Working in education or training it is very common to come across the attitude that there is nothing as good as face-to-face teaching and that anything that differs from getting people in the same place to learn is a compromise. This belief has been challenged over the years with correspondence education developing from the 18th century with the University of London, being the first higher education teaching establishment to provide correspondence education at scale. With the formation of The Open University in 1969, as described earlier, there was appreciation that the range of tools available could move on from correspondence models to alternative ways to connect with students. Overall it represented a rethinking of the approach to learning, considering the "Educational Technology" of how people learn.

The method that emerges from this work is one that values all the components in student activity. These include designing shared events, such as broadcasts, that motivate student engagement; providing content direct to the student, as written texts and other media (including physical experimental kits) that incorporated all that was needed to cover the required syllabus; and building in support through contact with tutors either face-to-face or through technology, such as via telephone. Bringing the whole method together was an approach to assessment that built in staged feedback from tutors that is tailored to the individual student and advises them how to improve, whilst ensuring a rigour that could be compared directly to other approaches to higher education.

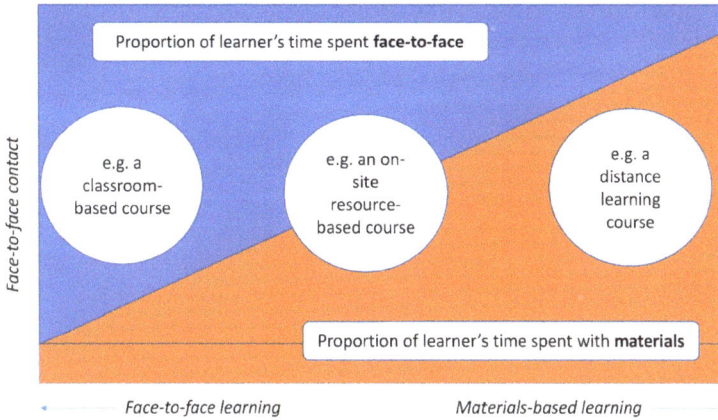

Figure 2.4: Balancing face-to-face contact with materials. Adapted from Rowntree (1997).

This approach has had various names, and there have been changes over time. The OU for some time used the label of "Supported Open Learning". This emphasised the support and contact component, as differentiating the approach from a correspondence based approach, and acknowledged the core role of the tutor in providing greater resilience and the ability to cope with the individual differences in the needs of the learners. A further label that has been given is of "Materials-based learning' (Rowntree, 1997). This emphasises the use of materials in place of contact that is designed to share knowledge. The concept of material based learning is one end of a continuum (see Figure 2.4 – based on the introductory figure given by Rowntree, 1997) that goes from traditional classroom based instruction through to learning at a distance from materials. Note that in Rowntree's model the contact does not fall to zero in how he considers materials, i.e. he is assuming that some contact will always be part of the teaching process.

The balance between a structured approach to the design of teaching and the dialogue and freedom to consider ideas was considered by Michael Moore during his time at the OU in the 1970s and 1980s and was described later under the label of *Transactional Distance* (Moore, 1993). This contained a rethinking of the distance element of distance education away from physical distance to measure instead how close the approach was to being able to transact the education through dialogue. In this model low transactional distance would be achieved through free-flowing dialogue between the learner and the educator which gave considerable autonomy to the learner. Higher transactional distance would be constrained provision of ideas in a tight structure that did not allow for the learner to take control. In conventional teaching, high transactional distance would occur in a content heavy lecture that offered little expectation of questions, low transactional distance in a one-to-one personal tutorial that allowed open discussion. The theory did not make any judgement as to which was the better approach, rather it highlights for distance education that the challenge is to develop ways to vary the transactional distance and understand how these can operate in combination to benefit the learner.

For the OU the challenge of course design recognised that the learner needed to be able to be supported so that materials guided them to achieve the original intentions stated in the Planning Report to address the "limited opportunities for education, determined by social, economic and political factors" (HMOS, 1969, p.2).

The role of evidence

The fourth component of the Beyond Prototypes model is evidence. This, perhaps more than anything, is how The Open University differentiated itself from other universities when it was formed and it has remained a key part of the OU's approach. Evidence of the impact of teaching was needed to show that new approaches resulted in a university that met quality requirements. This meant developing understanding of the processes of the university and how they could be justified, monitoring the performance of its students, and finding out what was the students' own view of their experience. This last component was very much an innovation and was supported through a process that included large scale surveys, which in turn influenced the development of the National Student Survey adopted in the UK (Richardson, Slater and Wilson, 2007). The Institute of Educational Technology has played a central role in the gathering of relevant research, in the application of that research to cases inside and outside the OU and in addressing the challenge of communicating an evidence base.

An evidence-based approach to decision making has often been advocated. Arguably this has been less apparent in education and in particular higher education where status and tradition can dominate over innovation and evidence. The revolution provided by the OU meant that it pushed against that tradition and needed to show that it could function, and meet similar quality measures to other universities, while working with a broader body of students and at a larger scale than other universities. The starting points rethought the approach away from contact-based teaching to one where content and support could operate together to provide the learners with all that they needed. As discussed in McAndrew (2010), a useful metaphor for the time (1960s) was of being able to support the lighthouse keeper who was physically remote from many resources, though with access to communications technology in the form of television and telephone.

Data wranglers

One of the challenges of gathering large amounts of data is the time and expertise required to interpret it. A focus on understanding the impact of different media on students had been part of the remit of IET first through an Audio Visual Media Research Group and then a more targeted Programme on Learner Use of Media, established in 1990 (Weinbren, 2015). In 2009 the focus moved from considering media to looking at data itself. At that time the Student Statistic and Survey Team had achieved a partial success in making available summarised date and then giving online access to data for deeper inspection. This was supported by training and opportunities to request further analysis. Even with careful planning the reality was that use of data was not uniform across the OU and there was a perception that data was more often used to consider the local concerns of an individual module rather than the priorities of the university or faculty. While the module will always be a key element of experience, common challenges such as retention and student performance required a more coordinated approach.

An academic team was created that would work in a targeted way both within faculties and across faculties on shared priorities. The focus on data was recognised in the chosen name for the team, Data Wranglers (Clow, 2014), and in initial targets, to make sure that clearly communicated reports that highlighted the key metrics needed by all parts of the university were provided. These developed over time to also include comparisons between different parts of the university and easy to interpret indicators of relative performance, one example being thumbs-up/thumbs-down signs to quickly show differences between different parts of the university for measures of student performance and satisfaction.

A role that developed out of the Data Wrangling approach, and linked to their typical position as academics also carrying out research inside and outside the university, was the provision of thematic reports initiated in 2016 (Rienties et al., 2016). These reports have covered a mix of OU-specific topics, such as understanding the different registration points a student passes through while studying, and wider issues, such as the role of summative and formative assessment and approaches to feedback.

Summary

In this chapter the Beyond Prototypes model, developed to analyse the processes of innovation in technology-enhanced learning and consider what can help enable successful TEL innovation, has been applied to one of the largest on-going educational technology projects, The Open University itself. The chapter has shown how the four aspects of innovations in the Beyond Prototypes model (the TEL complex, persistent intent, bricolage and evidence) can be successfully applied to The Open University. McAndrew has argued that complexity was a fundamental aspect of starting The Open University. In going beyond a correspondence approach, the original concept of "the University of the Air", with broadcasting playing a key role, was viewed very broadly and in developing an ambitious and complex structure for the OU, its planners learnt from relevant work in the US. So the first section considers how complexity was addressed by those working to bring The Open University together as they thought through how teamwork, and the role that educational technology needs to play could work in practice.

A clear example of persistence, the second component of the model, is continuing open entry, requiring support for entry into study. In discussing this aspect of the university, OU data was drawn on which shows it is only at the beginning of a student's study trajectory that their likely success can be judged from their background and or earlier achievements. Once a student's journey is underway the best predictor of success is previous successful study in the OU.

The chapter has also illustrated how the OU had to take an experimental approach, (applying the third factor, bricolage) from the very beginning; partly to address the complexity challenge: in working out how to operate at such scale; how to structure itself; how to remain innovative in a changing world and how to make best use of technology for educators and for students. Examples include providing online virtual learning environments, online conferencing and remote connections, and making changes to assessment. One of the innovations in the design of OU courses is that content is closely supported by feedback to the learner, and in this context, the chapter has shown how feedback operates both through the design of the learning experience and in how support is provided.

Evidence is the fourth aspect of the framework and this is shown to be a particularly important part of the OU's approach and significant in the distinctiveness of the OU. In this respect IET work has been key and has collected evidence on student learning and attitude from the very beginning. One example of the role of evidence is the use of 'Data Wranglers'.

A model for now

The Open University was intended to be different; to try out new ideas and go beyond prototypes to operate at scale. The OU of fifty years ago was a challenge to a model of limited access to university. Now such a model seems even more unsuited for the situation we are in. Wider access to education has not led to equal access with participation from those disadvantaged remaining behind on several different measures such as POLAR, and ethnicity. Passing on costs to the learner in the form of expensive loans has also created pressure on those who are already earning, in particular leading to a fall in the numbers of those studying part-time.

Taken together this means that there is a greater need to consider the ways in which we can effectively operate a larger scale, lower cost, university system for those who have a wider background of prior qualifications. This is the current challenge facing the whole sector. It also characterises the challenge that the OU has faced for 50 years.

Many aspects of this challenge, and how it is being addressed, are discussed in the following chapters. In particular, the next chapter, Chapter 3, considers the future of teaching and learning at scale.

References

Birch, D.M. and Rienties, B. (2014). Effectiveness of UK and international A-level assessment in predicting performance in engineering. *Innovations in Education and Teaching International*, 51(6) pp. 642–652.

Butcher, J., Clarke, A., Wood, C., McPherson, E. and Fowle, W. (2018). How does a STEM Access module prepare adult learners to succeed in undergraduate science? *Journal of Further and Higher Education*. 43(9) pp. 1271–1283.

Clow, D. (2014). Data wranglers: human interpreters to help close the feedback loop. In: *LAK '14 Proceedings of the Fourth International Conference on Learning Analytics And Knowledge*, ACM Press, pp. 49–53.

Coughlan, T., Pitt, R. and McAndrew, P. (2013). Building open bridges: collaborative remixing and reuse of open educational resources across organisations. In: *2013 ACM SIGCHI Conference on Human Factors in Computing Systems 'changing perspectives' (CHI 2013)*, 29 Apr – 02 May 2013, Paris, France, pp. 991–1000.

Dearing (1997). *Report of the National Committee of Inquiry into Higher Education*. [Online] https://www.leeds.ac.uk/educol/ncihe/natrep.htm

Finegold, D. (2006). *The Roles of Higher Education in a Knowledge Economy*. [Online] http://www.heart-resources.org/wp-content/uploads/2015/10/The-Roles-of-Higher-Education-in-a-Knowledge-Economy.pdf?e4e997

Guardian (2017). *Almost half of all young people in England go on to higher education*. [Online] https://www.theguardian.com/education/2017/sep/28/almost-half-of-all-young-people-in-england-go-on-to-higher-education

Hattie, J. (2008). *Visible Learning: A Synthesis of Over 800 Meta-Analyses Relating to Achievement*. Routledge Taylor & Francis Group.

Hills, L., Clarke, A., Hughes, J., Butcher, J., Shelton, I., and McPherson, E. (2018). Chinese whispers? Investigating the consistency of the language of assessment between a distance education institution, its tutors and students. *Open Learning: The Journal of Open, Distance and e-Learning*, 33(3) pp. 238–349.

HMSO (1969) *The Open University: Report Of The Planning Committee To The Secretary Of State For Education and Science*. London: Her Majesty's Stationery Office.

Law, P., McAndrew, P., Law, A., Warner, K., Runyon, J., Lascu, D., and Muramatsu, B. (2012). A bridge to success. In: *Cambridge 2012: Innovation and Impact – Openly Collaborating to Enhance Education, a joint meeting of OER12 and OpenCourseWare Consortium Global 2012*, 16–18 Apr 2012, Cambridge, UK.

Law, P. (2016). Digital badging at The Open University: recognition for informal learning. *Open Learning: The Journal of Open, Distance and e-Learning*, 30 (3): 221–234.

McAndrew, P. (2010). Defining openness: updating the concept of "open" for a connected world. *Journal of Interactive Media in Education*, 2010(10) pp. 1–13.

Moore, M.G. (1990). International Aspects of Independent Study, in *The Foundations of American Distance Education: A Century of Collegiate Correspondence Study*, Watkins, B and Wright S.J. (Eds), Kendall/Hunt, Dubuque, Iowa, pp. 287–386.

Moore, M.G. (1993). Theory of transactional distance In D Keegan (ed) *Theoretical Principles of Distance Education* pp. 22–38 Routledge, New York.

OfS (2019). *National Student Survey results spreadsheets 2019: 2019 NSS summary data.* [Online] https://www.officeforstudents.org.uk/advice-and-guidance/student-information-and-data/national-student-survey-nss/get-the-nss-data/

Open University (1970). *Proposal for the Institute of Educational Technology.* Paper to Senate, S/II/8. Milton Keynes: Open University.

Open University (1979). *Open Forum 41 1979: The First Ten Years.* Transcript available from [Online] https://www.open.ac.uk/library/digital-archive/exhibition/53/theme/2/page/3

Perry, W. (1969). *Establishment of an Applied Educational Science Unit*, Council Paper C/II/3. Milton Keynes: Open University.

Perry, W. (1977). *The Open University: History & Evaluation of a Dynamic Innovation in Higher Education.* Open University Press, UK.

Pitt, R., Ebrahimi, N., McAndrew, P. and Coughlan, T. (2013). Assessing OER impact across organisations and learners: experiences from the Bridge to Success project. *Journal of Interactive Media in Education*, article no. 17.

Richardson, J.T.E.; Slater, J.B. and Wilson, J. (2007). The National Student Survey: development, findings and implications. *Studies in Higher Education*, 32(5) pp. 557–580.

Rienties, B., Edwards, C., Gaved, M., Marsh, V., Herodotou, C., Clow, D., Cross, S., Coughlan, T., Jones, J., and Ullmann, T. (2016). *Scholarly insight 2016: a Data wrangler perspective.* Open University UK.

Rogers, E.M. (1995). *Diffusion of Innovations.* Free Press; 4th edition.

Rowntree, D. (1997). *Making Materials-based Learning Work.* London: Routledge Falmer

Scanlon, E., Sharples, M., Fenton-O'Creevy, M., Fleck, J., Cooban, C., Ferguson, R., Cross, S. and Waterhouse, P. (2013). *Beyond prototypes: Enabling innovation in technology-enhanced learning.* Milton Keynes: Open University.

Weinbren, D. (2015). *The Open University: A History.* Manchester: Manchester University Press.

CHAPTER 3

Teaching and Learning at Scale: Futures

Rebecca Ferguson

In this chapter, Rebecca Ferguson considers recent work toward the vision 'Teams can successfully teach any number of students at a distance', showing how a substantial body of TEL research work can be built up over time, responding to changes in society. In particular, she demonstrates how continuing work towards this vision relates to the emergence of massive open online courses (MOOCs) and, more broadly, to teaching and learning at scale. She shows how the different elements of the Beyond Prototypes framework, and its emphasis on bricolage and persistent intent, can be used to support the development of a research agenda that supports practice worldwide. She also looks at current and future work in this area, identifying key areas where work is still needed – learning design, educator teams, widening access, approaches to assessment and accreditation, and new forms of pedagogy.

Introduction

In 2015, world leaders attended a United Nations Sustainable Development Summit in New York, where they formally adopted a new sustainable development agenda, setting goals to transform our world. One of these goals is quality education, and a target to be achieved by 2030 is to 'ensure equal access for all women and men to affordable and quality technical, vocational and tertiary education, including university'.

How to cite this book chapter:
Ferguson, R. 2019. Teaching and Learning at Scale: Futures. In: Ferguson, R., Jones, A. and Scanlon, E. (eds). *Educational Visions: Lessons from 40 years of innovation.* Pp. 33–50. London: Ubiquity Press. DOI: https://doi.org/10.5334/bcg.c. License: CC-BY 4.0

This is an ambitious goal, particularly in the light of the numbers involved. Three years before the world summit, Daniel looked at the rapidly increasing demand for education in a world where, today, more than a quarter of the population is aged under 15 (The World Bank, 2018)

> *there are 165 million people enrolled in tertiary education [...] Projections suggest that participation will peak at 263 million [...] in 2025. Accommodating the additional 98 million students would require more than four major campus universities (30,000 students) to open every week for the next 15 years.* (Daniel, 2012)

This hasn't happened. Major campus universities aren't opening every couple of days. However, a phenomenon that grabbed the world's attention seemed to be the answer – massive open online courses (MOOCs). What had begun as a Canadian experiment in teaching and learning (Cormier, 2008), suddenly hit the headlines. These online courses, often from top-ranked universities, were openly available, which typically meant that they could be accessed free of charge by unlimited numbers of learners. The *New York Times* declared 2012 The Year of the MOOC, observing that 'more than 150,000 signed up for Dr Thrun's "Introduction to Artificial Intelligence" last fall, starting the revolution that has higher education gasping' (Pappano, 2012).

The stated aims of early MOOC providers related to the challenge of extending access to education. The original MOOCs had been designed to increase participation in lifelong learning (McAuley, Stewart, Siemens, & Cormier, 2010). The mission statement of the Coursera platform was 'to empower people with education that will improve their lives, the lives of their families, and the communities they live in'. The founder of the Udacity platform was

> *against education that is only available to the top one per cent of all students. I am against tens of thousands of dollars of tuition expenses. I am against the imbalance that the present system brings to the world. I want to empower the 99 per cent'* (Leckhart & Cheshire, 2012).

World-class teaching available, free of charge, for everyone, everywhere in the world? It seemed too good to be true – there had to be a catch.

In fact, there were several. The most widely publicised was the drop-out rate. The percentage of enrolled students who completed a MOOC varied widely but, typically, about seven students of every eight who signed up for a course did not reach the end (K. Jordan, 2015). This isn't necessarily a problem – a MOOC can be regarded as a resource, like a newspaper, that most people will never complete (Downes, 2014). However, the wide variation in completion rates – from a low of less than one student in forty to a high of more than half of students – suggested that there were other factors at work (K. Jordan, 2015).

There were other problems as well. Problems with funding – good quality MOOCs turned out to be expensive to produce. Problems with revenue generation – even the original low-budget MOOCs based on connectivist principles required server space and staff time. Problems with pedagogy – enormous class sizes hit the headlines but offered no clear benefits for learners. Problems with technology – even in the affluent west, not everyone has access to personal computing devices and the Internet. In fact, there were problems to be addressed that related to every element of the *Beyond Prototypes* framework: policy context, environment, funding, revenue generation, educator community, technology community, learner community, researcher community, ecology of practices, technical context, pedagogy and technology (Ferguson, Sharples, & Beale, 2015; Scanlon et al., 2013).

It was apparent that MOOCs – or, more broadly, learning at scale – didn't offer a magic pill that could quickly remedy a chronic shortage of access to higher education. In fact, it wasn't clear that this was the vision that was guiding the development of most MOOCs. Universities were more interested in using them to enhance the reputation of the institution, to develop staff skills, or to add value to accredited courses (White, Davis, Dickens, León Urrutia, & Sánchez-Vera, 2015). In addition, studies of the first wave of MOOCs suggested that learners were mainly people with prior experience of higher education, and found little evidence that MOOCs were widening participation for those distanced from education (Cannell & Macintyre, 2014).

From the perspective of The Open University, MOOCs had the potential to align with its mission to be 'open to people, places, methods and ideas'. They also promised to be a way of achieving its goals of promoting educational opportunity and social justice. The vision that 'Teams can successfully teach any number of students at a distance' was already an intent that the university had been pursuing persistently for decades. Making the connection with this intention meant that researchers at The Open University were able to build on previous work, using MOOCs as a way of working towards that goal.

Persistent intent

'Teams can successfully teach any number of students at a distance' was initially a vision for one university. The scope of the vision expanded as increasing numbers of learning institutions worldwide adopted online and distance learning. The possibilities opened up by new technologies led to further expansion, taking into account the growth of open educational resources, social media, and open learning on platforms such as YouTube and iTunesU.

This experience meant that researchers at the OU did not approach MOOCs as a completely new phenomenon. Instead, they were able to engage in a process of bricolage, bringing in their experience of investigating open learning, large-scale citizen science projects, and the use of data to support learning and teaching. The new feature offered by MOOCs was not that they were open, or online, or courses. The new feature was that they were massive.

'Massive' needs some explanation in the context of a university with decades of experience of teaching many thousands of students on the same course at the same time. MOOCs were massive in that they were designed to be accessed by unlimited numbers of students. In some cases, tens of thousands enrolled, and in some cases only tens, the 'massive' label was determined by design rather than by enrolment figures. Platforms and media tended to present this scale in terms of potential economic benefits. Large numbers of people could be exposed to the same curated set of resources and gain access to teaching materials assembled by well-known universities. Fewer trained educators were, potentially, required to educate greater numbers of learners (Sharples & Ferguson, 2014).

This brought a new perspective to the vision that 'teams can successfully teach any number of students at a distance'. Previous research in this area had focused on distance education at university level, in a context where students either paid for their education, or had that education paid for. Taking on more students meant taking on more staff to act as tutors, mentors, facilitators, assessors, and examiners. In a setting where learners could complete a course free of charge, new approaches to pedagogy were required, as well as attention to learner and educator communities, and the ecology of practices around MOOCs.

Pedagogy at scale: conversational learning

Many approaches to teaching and learning – such as sports coaching and personal tuition – are designed to work with a limited number of learners and do not scale. Only a few pedagogies can be used with cohorts that may range from tens of learners to tens of thousands. Lecturing is one such approach. As long as learners are able to hear the lecturer and see the presentation, the experience is broadly similar for any number of students. However, students gain little by being part of a large cohort and are unlikely to be able to ask questions to increase their understanding.

Another approach is the OU's model of supported distance learning (Price & Petre, 1997). As learners work through their studies, they are supported by many teams of academic and administrative staff, as well as by associate lecturers who provide personalised study support and feedback. This model scales successfully, and opens up opportunities for collaborative and social learning, but providing this level of support is expensive.

An alternative approach is conversational learning. This not only works at scale, the conversations become richer as more learners are involved.

The FutureLearn MOOC platform was set up in 2012–13, based on a conversational learning pedagogy that draws on decades of work within the OU. Learning through conversation relates to the theory of how learning takes place that was developed by Pask (1976). Pask provided a scientific account of how interactions enable a process of coming to know by reaching mutual agreements. This is more than an exchange of knowledge – it is a process in which participants share and negotiate differences in understanding with the aim of constructing new knowledge and reaching agreements. These conversations may involve other learners or may take the form of internal reflections. In order for either to happen, 'learners must be able to formulate descriptions of their reflections on actions, explore and extend those descriptions, and carry forward the understanding to a future activity' (Sharples & Ferguson, 2019).

Laurillard (2002) built on Pask's work when she developed her influential Conversational Learning framework. Discussions take place at two levels: actions and descriptions. Learners need to agree on clear goals and objectives at both levels.

- At the level of actions, discussion relates to a practical activity or model of the world. Learners ask 'how' questions, sharing their experiences and interpretations.
- At the level of descriptions, learners ask 'why' questions, putting forward and questioning interpretations in order to reach agreement.

The educator plays an important role throughout the process: suggesting goals, designing relevant activities and models, facilitating discussions, and encouraging reflection.

These understandings of how learning takes place, and how it can be enriched at scale, were built into the FutureLearn platform from the beginning and continue to inform technical and organisational developments. For example, a distinctive element of the platform is that, except in the case of assessment, every piece of learning material has an associated area for conversation. Because conversation takes place alongside content, it becomes part of the learning materials, rather than a separate activity that requires extra work to access and is likely to be disregarded. Some steps are designed as discussions, providing opportunities for learners to explore differences in conception and reach agreements. These discussions can be set up by educators in ways that encourage learners to share perspectives, synthesise new knowledge, and reach agreements.

Pedagogic research community

Using decades of research to support the development of a platform that currently has more than ten million registered learners worldwide was a very positive outcome for this line of work but was not the end of the process. More research was needed – and with learning taking place on a grand scale, a larger pedagogic research community was needed to support and develop the process. This requirement led to the formation of the FutureLearn Academic Network

(FLAN), an association of people carrying out MOOC-related research at FutureLearn's partner institutions (by mid-2019, FutureLearn had more than 160 partners around the world, including universities, specialist organisations, and centres of excellence).

A 2016 review of research work by a sub-section of these – FutureLearn's UK university partners – covered 109 publications and identified priority areas for future research. These included:

- develop educator teams
- identify and share effective learning designs
- support discussion more effectively
- widen access
- develop new approaches to assessment and accreditation
- develop appropriate pedagogy for learning at scale.

The following sections consider each of these research areas and relate them to the vision that 'teams can successfully teach any number of students at a distance'.

Develop educator teams

The educators responsible for leading work on MOOCs are typically university faculty members. Despite their expertise in research and in face-to-face teaching, they may have little or no experience of teaching at a distance, online, or at scale. Nevertheless they are faced with a series of difficult educational decisions and need research evidence that can help them to make decisions about issues as diverse as assessment, engagement, motivation, design, and accreditation.

While tackling these questions, educators are also adapting to a new role. They are likely to become increasingly aware that their traditional role has been 'unbundled' and that the tasks of designing a course, locating resources, presenting a course, assessing students' work, and supporting the students are carried out by a variety of people with different skills. Research-based evidence has the potential to help them make that move from lone educator to part of a distributed team.

Broadly speaking, teaching roles on FutureLearn fall into three broad categories: educators, mentors and collaborators (Papathoma, 2019).

- **Educators** typically work in academic roles at a university. Whatever their substantive job, they are likely to be involved in a MOOC because of their subject-matter expertise.
- **Mentors** are sometimes described as facilitators. This is a role that is often assigned to doctoral students. There may be an assumption that mentors have less experience and less subject matter expertise than educators. They

are likely to be involved in a MOOC in order to engage in learner discussion in some way.

- **Collaborators** support learning activity but are not expected to be directly involved with learners. Collaborators are typically not faculty members but are likely to work in academic-related jobs as, for example, learning designers, librarians, or managers of learning teams.

Each group brings different skills and perspectives to their teaching role on the MOOC and faces different sets of challenges. Ideally, individuals in each role work together seamlessly, drawing on each other's expertise. However, this way of working does not come automatically and is difficult to develop when time is limited, and team members do not necessarily meet each other or interact frequently.

Teams involved in course development need access to both practical and academic expertise. They must be aware of the team's responsibilities and the constraints under which both it and its individual members are working. To develop a course effectively, teams have to be willing to agree ways to negotiate these constraints. This means that professional learning 'is a critical component of the ongoing improvement, innovation and adoption of new practices that support learning at scale' (Papathoma, Ferguson, Littlejohn, & Coe, 2016, p1).

Successful teams involved in teaching on MOOCs (Papathoma, 2019) give explanations for aspects of teaching, developing shared vocabulary and understanding of the teaching process. They reflect on the process and explain aspects to each other, building new, shared knowledge that can be structured and recorded to support the development of subsequent MOOCs. If these opportunities are not built into the process, individuals have to deal with uncertainty and are forced to spend their time solving problems, searching for individuals with relevant expertise, and looking for helpful examples of previous practice.

Identify and share effective learning designs

Previous practice in learning design is an aspect of professional knowledge that can be shared between academic departments and institutions. As Chapter 7 will explain in more detail, learning design provides a way of sharing teaching ideas in order to improve student learning, helping educators to become more effective in their preparation and facilitation of teaching and learning activities. Design patterns provide a way of showcasing successful learning activities and design innovations, as well as making clear which approaches do not work.

Design patterns also provide ways of sharing solutions to problems that are commonly encountered when designing MOOCS. For example, Wintrup, Wakefield & Davis (2015) note that dropout is a concern with MOOCs, and that there is a need to identify measures that can be put in place to reveal what aspects of a course engage learners, and how particular activities engage different types of learner. Part of the solution might be to make an up-to-date recap of each MOOC available at any time so that new joiners can catch up with others (Nazir, Davis, & Harris, 2015). Another part of the solution might be to minimise distractions that do not support design objectives by organising resources, enabling creative expression in tasks, automating mundane tasks, supporting scale and sustainability, and focusing on learning (Celina, Kharuffa, Preston, Comber, & Olivier, 2016).

A review of published research from FutureLearn partners in the UK (Ferguson, Coughlan, Herodotou, & Scanlon, 2017; Ferguson, Herodotou, Coughlan, Scanlon, & Sharples, 2018) identified design patterns that appeared promising or had proved successful in the context of MOOCs. Some of these were brought together by Wintrup and her colleagues: providing guidance about ways to apply new knowledge to 'real world' problems can be helpful in deepening and sustaining understanding and promoting creativity, including and eliciting learners' own ideas and projects is also a way of developing greater involvement, games provide a useful way of introducing difficult concepts to learners (Wintrup et al., 2015).

Liyanagunawardena, Kennedy and Cuffe (2015) organised a series of workshops to explore MOOC design principles. In particular, they considered the challenge of promoting peer discussion and interaction when the size and diversity of a cohort and its patterns of participation mean that discussions become difficult to navigate and are likely to remain superficial. They identified seven design narratives that captured and interpreted the experience of MOOC designers. They then drew on these narratives to create design patterns that offered solutions to challenges commonly encountered when designing MOOCs. For example, the 'Look and Engage' design pattern provides a solution to the problem of 'How to structure peer communication and collaboration to support the sharing of ideas to stimulate meaningful dialogue and interaction among large, diverse groups' (p12). The pattern involves creating 'an individual collaborative task around a digital artefact to stimulate meaningful dialogues among large, diverse groups' (p10). 'Look and Engage' draws on three design narratives that deal with scaffolding interaction, easy co-construction, and sharing views.

Hatzipanagos (2015) went a step further, not only identifying design patterns used in MOOCs but also relating these to patterns used elsewhere, beginning to build the links between designs that can reveal underlying similarities between courses. For example, he related the pattern 'Computer-mediated communication media (fora)' to a previously identified 'crowd bonding' pattern, summarised as 'forming discussion groups to facilitate interaction for learning'. By making connections in this way, he demonstrated ways in which patterns could be used to access previously developed guidelines, advice, and practical examples.

Work on identifying and sharing effective learning designs demonstrates how TEL innovations are built over years, pulling together available resources in a process of bricolage. Educators around the world face similar challenges. How can dropout be reduced? How can peer communication be structured to support meaningful dialogue? They explore solutions in different contexts with different student populations. Researchers identify and publish solutions, but these are distributed across a wide range of literature and not easy to access. Research groups, such as the FutureLearn Academic Network, then work to pull together the challenges and solutions.

A different stream of work, on learning design, provides a way of structuring these challenges and solutions as design patterns that can be brought together and shared. At the same time, work on opening up research and education makes it increasingly acceptable to share work openly, rather than restricting it to journals hidden behind paywalls. As a result of these separate strands of work, the European bizMOOC project was able to create and openly share its *MOOCBook,* which brings together 50 key lessons, 25 key recommendations, and 20 good practices derived from extensive empirical research (BizMOOC, 2019).

Support discussion more effectively

One of the challenges when designing MOOCs is how to provide effective support for discussion. This is crucial when a course design is based on conversational learning. It is also more broadly applicable. The earliest distance education courses, which relied on published or posted material, offered little or no opportunity for discussion. They were based on a transmission model of education, which assumes an existing body of knowledge that can be transferred from one person to another, with assessment providing opportunities to check that the transfer has been completed successfully.

One problem with relying on a transmission model alone is that separating learners and teachers in time and space creates a space of potential misunderstanding, or 'transactional distance' (Moore, 1973, 1993) as noted by McAndrew in Chapter 2. The possibilities for reducing this space for misunderstanding increased when new communication technologies made it possible for distance learners to interact with each other and with educators. Most of this interaction was asynchronous, with no expectation that participants in a discussion would all be engaging at the same time. These new technologies, such as forum discussion, opened up opportunities for learners to engage in the active construction of knowledge together, as well as working to understand existing content.

However, online and offline interaction are not the same. Some types of interaction that commonly take place in the classroom are much rarer online, even though they shape learners' expectations of how interactions with teachers will take place. For example, a typical exchange between teacher and student in a face-to-face classroom involves initiation, response, and follow-up (Sinclair &

Coulthard, 1975). The teacher asks a question, students recognise that this is not a request for knowledge but a test of their own knowledge, one or more of them responds, and the teacher evaluates or extends those responses. Learners who expect educational discussions to take this form often struggle to see the value of conversations in forums or MOOCs where there is no teacher evaluating or extending their contributions.

Conversations in online environments share several characteristics that distinguish them from face-to-face conversations. Some of these are negative. It isn't necessarily clear who is taking part in the conversation, who is reading without posting, how much of the conversation any one person has read, and in what order they encountered it. Some students find online discussion intimidating and are nervous about contributing (Ferguson, 2010). On the positive side, asynchronous communication offers time to reflect before contributing, a transcript of the entire discussion, interaction at a distance, and opportunities to share direct quotations, references, and links to external resources (Ferguson, 2009).

With research on the benefits and challenges of social learning and online discussions already in place, MOOC researchers were able to focus on the practicalities of involving people in discussions. As a significant percentage of learners in any MOOC will not have studied online before, it's important to encourage good practices through providing guidance and examples. Good practices include the use of inclusive language, treating different viewpoints with respect, and encouraging social interaction that will support learning (Murray, 2014; Wintrup, Wakefield, & Davis, 2015; Wintrup, Wakefield, Morris, & Davis, 2015).

More detailed work is now being carried out to investigate ways of supporting interaction. The large number of comments posted in many MOOC discussions can disguise the fact that relatively few meaningful conversations are taking place. Many learners receive no response to their comments, which means they are unable to take part in the development of shared understanding. To some extent, the likelihood of response is based on the time of posting and on the nature of discussion. However, keyword analysis has shown that there are also linguistic factors at work. Posts that receive responses are often phrased as questions. They use non-specific pronouns such as 'anybody' or 'anyone'. They also hedge rather than making definitive statements, using words such as 'perhaps' and 'seems' (Chua, 2018). Work like this can be used to support guidelines for MOOC participants, and the models of interaction provided by MOOC educators.

Adult learners and educators typically have extensive experience of how educational interactions work in a face-to-face environment but may have little or no experience of how this can be done effectively online. Different strands of work, relating to appropriate pedagogies, learning design, and discussion can be combined to develop best practice, based on research and experience.

Widen access

Best practice is needed, because MOOCs do not currently provide learning opportunities that are suitable for everyone. Although we are making good progress towards the goal, 'Teams can successfully teach any number of students at a distance', more work is needed on inclusion and accessibility. This is particularly important, given that the original vision for MOOCs was that they could open up high-quality education to groups who had previously had no means of accessing it.

One aspect of widening access is reaching learners in areas that currently offer few opportunities for higher education. However, online learning is not necessarily the answer when some four billion people around the world still do not have access to the Internet. Global access would need to include regions that have poor infrastructure, low digital capability, unreliable electricity supplies, limited digital capability, and that currently lack capacity to train all teachers to a high standard. It would also have to take on the challenge of providing equal access to resources in countries that have multiple official languages and diverse ethnic communities (Littlejohn & Hood, 2018).

These are not new problems. Two long-term projects have investigated some potential solutions. The Teacher Education in Sub-Saharan Africa (TESSA) project launched in 2005 at the request of teacher education institutions throughout the region, and its success led to the creation of a sister programme, TESS-India. Both projects have at their heart resource banks of materials to support teacher education. These take into account the cultural diversity of the regions involved, and are available in multiple languages, in both printed and digital formats, online and offline (Wolfenden, 2008).

The TESS-India MOOC, which ran on the EdX MOOC platform, was able to build on more than a decade of research and experience. It was designed to introduce the idea of open educational resources (OER), and particularly the TESS-India OER to teacher educators. The rationale for working with this group was that these professionals have the opportunity to initiate significant changes in teaching and learning across the region if they have access to relevant training and resources (Stutchbury, 2016).

Due to the low bandwidth for internet connections across much of India, the TESS-India MOOC was not run wholly online. It included weekly contact classes in all the project's target states. This face-to-face contact supported the development of local communities of practice (Stutchbury, 2016). As a result, community members were able to support each other to extend and implement what they had learned. The learning design was also successful in supporting retention. The MOOC ran in English in late 2015 with over 10,000 people registered. Of these, 51% completed the course, with 81% of completers from the states where face-to-face support had been available. A second iteration the following year in Hindi attracted over 33,000 participants, of whom 52% completed the course (Wolfenden, Cross, & Henry, 2017).

Even when MOOCs are available in a relevant language, culturally appropriate, and suited to available technology and infrastructure, problems remain. MOOCs offer few opportunities for personalised interaction with an educator, which means that most people who sign up for MOOCs are responsible for regulating their own learning. Self-regulation requires a set of skills that take time to develop – many of which students are typically not expected to demonstrate until university level. These skills include time management, help seeking, strategic planning, goal setting, reflection, and self-evaluation. Most people initially find it challenging to apply this set of skills to their learning. This is particularly true when they are used to a teacher doing much of this work for them and they have not been supported to develop these skills for themselves.

Some of the variety of learning behaviours of MOOC participants relates to their ability to regulate their own learning (Littlejohn, Hood, Milligan, & Mustain, 2016). For example, those who score low on a measure of self-regulated learning focus their goals on traditional performance measures such as passing assignments and completing the course, while those who score higher are more interested in developing relevant knowledge and expertise. Participants with low scores are likely to be focused on the MOOC and its requirements, while those with higher scores for self-regulation are more interested in how they will use what they have learned (Littlejohn et al., 2016). This suggests that if teams want to be able to 'successfully teach any number of students at a distance' then they need to make sure that those students are prepared to take an active role in regulating their own learning.

They also need to make sure that the courses they offer are accessible. There are four key aspects to MOOC accessibility: learning design, technical elements, user experience, and overall quality (Iniesto, McAndrew, Minocha, & Coughlan, 2019). Universal design, an approach that considers how to meet the needs of all learners through design, provides a helpful starting point (McGuire & Scott, 2006). Technical accessibility can be shaped using the Web Content Accessibility Guidelines (WCAG) published by the World Wide Web Consortium, the main international standards organisation for the Internet. These guidelines focus on whether material is perceivable, operable, understandable, and robust. From a user-experience perspective, the activities within any MOOC need to be feasible for learners with a range of accessibility needs. More broadly, a quality audit can be used to scrutinise accessibility in terms of staff and student support, as well as curriculum design, course design and delivery, and assessment (Iniesto et al., 2019). Accessibility more generally in educational technology is discussed in the next chapter.

Develop new approaches to assessment and accreditation

Assessment and accreditation have a role to play in widening access to education, so they are important aspects of supporting learners in large-scale environments. MOOC participants who already have degrees or even post-graduate qualifications may enjoy informal study for the love of learning, but some form of accreditation for study is particularly important for those who do not already have the qualifications that will help them to acquire a job or develop a career.

In order to cover costs, many MOOC providers now charge for credentials and certification and do not make the entire learning experience freely available. This modified approach retains an open element – MOOC participants have the opportunity to study material without charge – but credit for that study comes as an optional extra that requires payment. Another shift away from openness is that the major MOOC platforms now offer courses that are only available to those who pay, challenging notions that an open course offers access for all or free education (Littlejohn & Hood, 2018).

Following a review of research by MOOC-providing institutions across the UK, Ferguson and her colleagues (2017) recommended that MOOCs should provide transparent information about accreditation to learners, institutions and employers; that MOOC providers should consider ways of supporting credit transfer; and that providers should also supply guidance to MOOC learners for recognition of non-formal learning, as awareness of the available options is currently limited.

Badging is one way of supporting the route from assessment to accreditation (Law & Law, 2014) without a charge to the learners. Open badges have two elements: an online image containing a hyperlink to course criteria, and online evidence that these criteria have been met (Cross, Whitelock, & Galley, 2014). Badges can be used as incentives to continue study, as a way of marking progress, as an informal means of accreditation, or as staging posts on the journey to more substantial learning goals (Hauck & MacKinnon, 2016). They can be used to reward achievement at marked points on a learning journey, to reward effort in terms of hours put in or activities completed, or they can reward exploration and deeper learning (Cross & Galley, 2012). Not simply a means of accreditation, badges can function as motivator, meaning maker, signifier of learning objectives, low-cost or low-effort option. They can be used as a way of valuing certain forms of engagement, a symbol of identity, a means of association, or an element of empowerment. They also have roles to play in encouraging engagement and limiting withdrawal (Hauck & MacKinnon, 2016).

Closely associated with accreditation is assessment, which plays a crucial part in learning and teaching. Expert feedback is a valuable part of the learning process, but it takes effort to produce. Skilled assessors come at a cost and their availability is limited. Together, these factors make assessment a particularly challenging aspect of learning at scale. Producing high quality feedback is not an activity that scales easily. MOOCs therefore need to make use of the full range of computer-based assessment options. These currently include selected responses (such as multiple-choice questions); constructed responses (in which learners construct their own responses); essays and short-answer questions; peer assessment; and online tools that can be used to showcase work, including e-portfolios, blogs and wikis (Jordan, 2013). None of these options is new, but as these forms of assessment play an important part in learning at scale, more work is needed to explore how they can best be implemented and validated.

Peer review offers a way of providing feedback on student work that cannot be assessed automatically. It also provides a learning experience for the reviewer, who has to think carefully about the criteria and how they are applied. However, work on supporting and structuring peer review at scale in an international context is still in its early stages (Meek, Blakemore, & Marks, 2016; O'Toole, 2013).

Another form of assessment that is commonly used in MOOCs is the multiple-choice quiz. These can be helpful in providing formative assessment and helping learners to assess their understanding, as long as educators are skilled in their design and implementation. However, unless multiple-choice questions are underpinned by extensive question banks, there is the danger that answers will be shared online, making them unsuitable for summative assessment. There is a need to build on what we already know about e-assessment (Jordan, 2013), so that appropriate forms can be built into pedagogy at scale.

Develop appropriate pedagogy for learning at scale

As learning at scale is taken up more widely and in new contexts, appropriate pedagogies are required to support this work. Conversational learning is one pedagogy that has already been incorporated within MOOC teaching and MOOC platforms, but there are other pedagogies still to be explored, including adaptive teaching, experiential learning, game-based learning and inquiry-led learning (Sharples & Ferguson, 2019).

One reason for developing new pedagogies is the increasing use of MOOCs to support workplace training, job readiness, and continuing professional engagement. Workers are looking for forms of personalised learning that align with their specific learning needs. They also need to develop skills and strategies that enable them to deal with the ill-structured problems under various levels of uncertainty that they are likely to encounter in their workplaces (Littlejohn & Hood, 2018).

Pedagogies that have been developed in other contexts and could be adapted for use at scale include: social learning to share workplace knowledge, coached team learning to develop and practise skills, case-based learning for problem solving and decision making, experiential learning to capture and reflect on shared experience, and competency-based learning to achieve and demonstrate mastery. Once again, there are opportunities to build on extensive previous work and to make use of recognised good practice.

Conclusion

'Teams can successfully teach any number of students at a distance' is one of the visions that has guided educational research at The Open University for the past forty years. As this chapter and the previous one have shown, over that time great progress has been made towards that vision. Online courses at The Open University and other institutions have successfully taught hundreds, even thousands, of students on formal courses for over two decades. Over the last fifteen years, the availability of open educational resources, and informal learning opportunities such as OpenLearn and iTunesU, have increased their scale and scope. Citizen science projects involving hundreds of thousands of people run on an international scale, providing opportunities to learn about the scientific method and to put it into practice to generate new knowledge.

The arrival of MOOCs on the scene was part of this expansion of educational opportunities, and researchers were immediately able to start making connections between this new format and previous decades of experience. The landscape of learning at scale continues to change. New providers emerge, their business models associated with new challenges and opportunities. By looking beyond the different formats and models to a vision of what can be achieved in the future, it is possible to identify and work towards objectives that make that vision achievable, focusing on teams, learning design, access, assessment, accreditation and, perhaps most important, the pedagogy that shapes these opportunities.

Bibliography

BizMOOC. (2019). *MOOC Book*. https://mooc-book.eu/index/insights/.

Cannell, P., & Macintyre, R. (2014). *Towards open educational practice*. Paper presented at the EADTU Annual Conference: New Technologies and the Future of Teaching and Learning (23–24 October), Krakow, Poland.

Celina, H., Kharuffa, A., Preston, A., Comber, R., & Olivier, P. (2016). *SOLE meets MOOC: designing infrastructure for online self-organised learning with a social mission*. Paper presented at the Designing Interactive Systems: DIS 2016 (4–8 June), Brisbane, Australia.

Chua, S.-M. (2018). *Why did nobody reply to me? A keyword analysis of initiating posts and lone posts in massive open online courses (MOOCs) discussions*. Paper presented at the 6th Conference on Computer-Mediated Communication (CMC) and Social Media Corpora (17–18 Sept), Antwerp, Belgium.

Cormier, D. (2008). The CCK08 MOOC – Connectivism course, 1/4 way (2 October). Retrieved from http://davecormier.com/edblog/2008/10/02/the-cck08-mooc-connectivism-course-14-way/

Cross, S., & Galley, R. (2012). MOOC Badging and the Learning Arc. (16 November). Retrieved from http://www.olds.ac.uk/blog/olds-moocbadgingstrategy

Cross, S., Whitelock, D., & Galley, R. (2014). The use, role and reception of open badges as a method for formative and summative reward in two massive open online courses. *International Journal of e-Assessment, 4*(1).

Daniel, J. (2012). Dual-mode universities in higher education: way station or final destination? *Open Learning: The Journal of Open, Distance and e-Learning, 27*(1), 89–95.

Downes, S. (2014). Like reading a newspaper (21 March). Retrieved from http://halfanhour.blogspot.co.uk/2014/03/like-reading-newspaper.html

Ferguson, R. (2009). *The Construction of Shared Knowledge through Asynchronous Dialogue.* (PhD), The Open University, Milton Keynes. http://oro.open.ac.uk/19908/ Retrieved from http://oro.open.ac.uk/19908/

Ferguson, R. (2010). Peer Interaction: the experience of distance students at university level. *Journal of Computer Assisted Learning, 26*, 574–584. DOI: 10.1111/j.1365-2729.2010.00386.x

Ferguson, R., Coughlan, T., Herodotou, C., & Scanlon, E. (2017). *MOOCs: What the Research of FutureLearn's UK Partners Tells Us.* Retrieved from Milton Keynes: http://intranet6.open.ac.uk/learning-teaching-innovation/main/quality-enhancement-report-series

Ferguson, R., Herodotou, C., Coughlan, T., Scanlon, E., & Sharples, M. (2018). MOOC development: priority areas. In R. Luckin (Ed.), *Enhancing Learning and Teaching with Technology: What the Research Says.* London: Institute of Education Press.

Ferguson, R., Sharples, M., & Beale, R. (2015). MOOCs 2030: A Future for Massive Online Learning In C. J. Bonk, M. M. Lee, T. C. Reeves, & T. H. Reynolds (Eds.), *MOOCs and Open Education Around the World*: Routledge.

Hatzipanagos, S. (2015). What do MOOCs contribute to the debate on learning design of online courses? *eLearning Papers*(42).

Hauck, M., & MacKinnon, T. (2016). A new approach to assessing online intercultural exchanges: soft certification of participant engagement. In R. O'Dowd & T. Lewis (Eds.), *Online Intercultural Exchange. Policy, Pedagogy, Practice* (pp. 209–234). Abingdon, UK: Routledge.

Iniesto, F., McAndrew, P., Minocha, S., & Coughlan, T. (2019). *Auditing the accessibility of MOOCs: a four-component approach.* Paper presented at the EC-TEL 2019 (16–19 September), Delft, Netherlands.

Jordan, S. (2013). E-assessment: past, present and future. *New Directions for Adult and Continuing Education, 9*(1), 87–106.

Jordan, K. (2015). Massive open online course completion rates revisited: assessment, length and attrition. *International Review of Research in Open and Distributed Learning, 16*(3), 341–358.

Laurillard, D. (2002). *Rethinking University Teaching* (2nd ed.). London: RoutledgeFalmer.

Law, P., & Law, A. (2014). Digital badging at The Open University: recognition for informal learning. Paper presented at The Open and Flexible Higher

Education Conference 2014: 'New Technologies and the Future of Teaching and Learning' (23–24 October), Krakow, Poland.

Leckhart, S., & Cheshire, T. (2012). University just got flipped: how online video is opening up knowledge to the world (May 2012). *Wired, 5: May 2012*. Retrieved from http://www.wired.co.uk/magazine/archive/2012/05/features/university-just-got-flipped?page=all

Littlejohn, A., & Hood, N. (2018). *Reconceptualising Learning in the Digital Age: the (Un)democratising of Learning*. Singapore: Springer.

Littlejohn, A., Hood, N., Milligan, C., & Mustain, P. (2016). Learning in MOOCs: motivations and self-regulated learning in MOOCs. *The Internet and Higher Education, 29*, 40–48.

Liyanagunawardena, T. R., Kennedy, E., & Cuffe, P. (2015). Design patterns for promoting peer interaction in discussion forums in MOOCs. *eLearning Papers, 42*(7).

McAuley, A., Stewart, B., Siemens, G., & Cormier, D. (2010). The MOOC model for digital practice. http://davecormier.com/edblog/wp-content/uploads/MOOC_Final.pdf. Retrieved from http://davecormier.com/edblog/wp-content/uploads/MOOC_Final.pdf

McGuire, J. M., & Scott, S. S. (2006). Universal design for instruction: extending the universal design paradigm to college instruction. *Journal of Postsecondary Education and Disability, 19*(2), 124–134.

Meek, S. E. M., Blakemore, L., & Marks, L. (2016). Is peer review an appropriate form of assessment in a MOOC? Student participation and performance in formative peer review. *Assessment and Evaluation in Higher Education (early view)*.

Moore, M. G. (1973). Towards a theory of independent learning and teaching. *The Journal of Higher Education, 44*(9), 661–679.

Moore, M. G. (1993). Theory of transactional distance. In D. Keegan (Ed.), *Theoretical Principles of Distance Education* (pp. 22–38). London and New York: Routledge.

Murray, J.-A. (2014). Participants' perceptions of a MOOC. *Insights: The UKSG Journal, 27*(2), 154–159.

Nazir, U., Davis, H. C., & Harris, L. (2015). First day stands out as most popular among MOOC leavers. *International Journal of e-Education, e-Business, e-Management and e-Learning, 5*(3), 173.

O'Toole, R. (2013). *Pedagogical strategies and technologies for peer assessment in Massively Open Online Courses (MOOCs). Discussion Paper*. University of Warwick. Coventry.

Papathoma, T. (2019). *MOOC Educators: Who They Are And How They Learn*. (PhD), The Open University, Milton Keynes.

Papathoma, T., Ferguson, R., Littlejohn, A., & Coe, A. (2016). *Making the production of learning at scale more open and flexible*. Paper presented at the L@S '16: Third ACM Conference on Learning @ Scale, Edinburgh, UK.

Pappano, L. (2012). The Year of the MOOC. *New York Times (2 November 2012)*. Retrieved from http://www.nytimes.com/2012/11/04/education/edlife/massive-open-online-courses-are-multiplying-at-a-rapid-pace.html

Pask, G. (1976). *Conversation Theory: Applications in Education and Epistemology*. New York: Elsevier.

Price, B., & Petre, M. (1997). *Large-scale interactive teaching via the Internet: experience with problem sessions and practical work in university courses.* Paper presented at the ED-MEDIA 97 and ED-TELECOM 97, Calgary, Alberta, Canada.

Scanlon, E., Sharples, M., Fenton-O'Creevy, M., Fleck, J., Cooban, C., Ferguson, R., . . . Waterhouse, P. (2013). *Beyond Prototypes: Enabling Innovation in Technology-Enhanced Learning.* Retrieved from London: http://beyondprototypes.com/

Sharples, M., & Ferguson, R. (2014, 16–19 September 2014). *Innovative Pedagogy at Massive Scale: Teaching and Learning in MOOCs.* Paper presented at the EC-TEL 2014.

Sharples, M., & Ferguson, R. (2019). *Pedagogy-informed design of conversational learning at scale.* Paper presented at the ECTEL, Delft, NL (16–19 September).

Sinclair, J. M., & Coulthard, R. M. (1975). *Towards an Analysis of Discourse: The English Used by Teachers and Pupils.* Oxford: Oxford University Press.

Stutchbury, K. (2016). *Moving forward with TESSA: what is the potential for MOOCs?.* Paper presented at the 3rd International Conference of the African Virtual University, (6–8 July) Nairobi, Kenya.

The World Bank. (2018). Population ages 0–14 (% of total). Retrieved from https://data.worldbank.org/indicator/SP.POP.0014.TO.ZS?view=chart

White, S., Davis, H. C., Dickens, K., León Urrutia, M., & Sánchez-Vera, M. d. M. (2015). MOOCs: what motivates the producers and participants? In S. Zvacek, M. T. Restivo, J. Uhomoibhi, & M. Helfert (Eds.), *Computer Supported Education: 6th International Conference, CSEDU 2014, Barcelona, Spain, April 1–3, 2014, Revised Selected Papers* (pp. 99–114). Cham: Springer International Publishing.

Wintrup, J., Wakefield, K., & Davis, H. C. (2015). *Engaged learning in MOOCs: a study using the UK Engagement Survey.* Retrieved from York, UK.

Wintrup, J., Wakefield, K., Morris, D., & Davis, H. C. (2015). *Liberating learning: experiences of MOOCs.* Retrieved from York, UK.

Wolfenden, F. (2008). The TESSA OER Experience: Building sustainable models of production and user implementation. *Journal of Interactive Media in Education, 2008*(3), 1–16.

Wolfenden, F., Cross, S., & Henry, F. (2017). MOOC adaptation and translation to improve equity in participation. *Journal of Learning for Development* 4(2), 127–142.

CHAPTER 4

Accessible Inclusive Learning: Foundations

Tim Coughlan, Kate Lister, Jane Seale,
Eileen Scanlon and Martin Weller

As a foundation to understanding how to be accessible and inclusive in TEL research, this chapter explores different conceptualisations of 'openness' and 'accessibility'. Using a range of examples, we then highlight how research projects take a particular orientation towards inclusiveness through their goals, methods and platforms. Technical accessibility, and opening up the potential to access education, are essential to an inclusive approach, but alone they rarely provide the basis for equitable learning. The examples therefore provide particular insights into how technological innovations need to be considered in concert with pedagogy. We then explore how our research has identified gaps and factors in digital inclusion for particular groups, and has been orientated towards designing for diverse audiences in response. An emphasis on processes and practices has emerged in both the accessibility and open education spaces, and we describe a practical example in which the OU has successfully embedded research-informed institutional practice through the Securing Greater Accessibility (SeGA) initiative.

How to cite this book chapter:
Coughlan, T., Lister, K., Seale, J., Scanlon, E. and Weller, M. 2019. Accessible Inclusive Learning: Foundations. In: Ferguson, R., Jones, A. and Scanlon, E. (eds). *Educational Visions: Lessons from 40 years of innovation.* Pp. 51–73. London: Ubiquity Press. DOI: https://doi.org/10.5334/bcg.d. License: CC-BY 4.0

The vision: Learning is accessible for everyone

One of the most persistent themes in discussions around technology in education is the idea that technology can affect access to learning. This can be seen as positive or negative, and it is often more complex than it seems. If computers can convert the text in a web page into spoken word, or the spoken words on a video into captions, have we made the learning accessible to deaf or blind students? Most likely we have made an important step in the right direction, but this might be only one challenge in the wider pedagogy and student experience. If MOOCs can teach thousands for free without any cost or entry requirements, does that mean they are increasing access? Perhaps, but are they also creating barriers for some through the pedagogical and technical design? In this chapter we will unpack how these issues have been tackled through research.

What do we mean by accessibility and openness?

'Accessible' can mean different things to different people in different contexts. Similarly, when we say that something is 'open', we have a broad sense of what this entails, but open to whom, when, and how? While it can be unhelpful to get bogged down in definitions, we should consider what these terms can mean. Hopefully this avoids some confusion that might otherwise arise, but it also gives us a starting point to think about what we are trying to achieve.

Let's begin with the model of open access education provided by The Open University (OU). This was developed to tackle the issue of supporting people to enter higher education who are traditionally excluded from it. What makes it 'open access' is the removal of entry requirements and the flexibility provided by support for study at variable levels of intensity, part time, and at a distance. It has been remarkably successful, with the OU's approach adapted in many institutions in countries around the globe. The model was enabled by technology and services from the very beginning. Radio, television, the postal service, printed materials, videos, DVDs, and the Internet have all been essential.

This model also presents an ongoing challenge. As the aim is to be 'open to all', and to provide opportunities for those otherwise excluded from education, the open access model had to include a focus on making learning accessible for people with disabilities, with the recognition that traditional higher education included barriers that might prevent them from studying. Being open to all created requirements for being accessible to an extent and scale that might not otherwise have been considered necessary, particularly in the past, when inclusion was not a major concern for most educational institutions.

How does this compare to a different model of openness? Let's consider Open Educational Resources (OER), including offshoots of this such as Open Textbooks. Here, openness is not just about access, but about the freedom for educators and for students to share and reuse or adapt resources to their needs,

Figure 4.1: Sharing your materials is an important part of OER – Image by Bryan Mathers reprinted under creative commons license.

free of charge. OER are free to use as long as the licence conditions are not breached. This provides a legal definition of openness, not just an educational or social one. It is also notable that the use of OER are intended to open up opportunities for educators as much as it is intended directly for students, since the benefits may be harnessed by educators and then benefit both their practice and their students' learning.

A different, less-defined model of openness is found in MOOCs and similar forms of online open learning at scale. These tend to be free or have lower costs involved than other forms of post-secondary education, and like the OU, they avoid entry requirements. But unlike OER, there are often limitations on the rights of learners and educators to make use of the materials. Anyone can create and share OER, but MOOC platforms may not be open in the sense that they will only publish certain courses or work with particular institutions. They may argue that being closed in this way supports quality control, but this approach could also be seen as exclusive rather than inclusive.

The focus of the MOOC agenda has been on producing platforms and content that can be accessed at large scale with low barriers. However, the need to keep costs low often means limited support for learners is available. In the OU, and in most traditional educational institutions, there are teachers and student-facing support staff to guide students and to adapt the learning to their needs. These forms of individual support do not generally exist within the MOOC approach.

Another less well defined (but often discussed) use of 'open' is that of Open Educational Practices. In this case, the individual or institution aim to reduce any boundaries surrounding them. Rather than teaching solely their own students within a VLE, an open practitioner could potentially teach through conversing and sharing their work on a multitude of platforms, and by working with others from around the globe. Open practices involve an open attitude towards mixing the role of institutions, resources, and platforms.

Like openness, the term 'accessible' is used in several different ways. In this chapter we mainly focus on accessibility in relation to disablement. This provides a specific focus to which persistent intent can be applied to make a difference to learners. However, the notion of whether something is 'accessible' can be used to focus attention for other populations too. For example, whether the language used in a course is accessible to particular audiences, or is too complex such that it might make the learning inaccessible to them (Rets et al., 2019; Coughlan & Goff, 2019).

As with 'open', there are technological and legal influences working alongside ideology and theory. Most technical consideration of online accessibility centres on whether resources and platforms meet specific criteria laid out by the widely-used Web Content Accessibility Guidelines (WCAG). But accessibility research also explores how a particular technology or service can be designed to enable or exclude particular users. Accessibility and assistive technology research has tended to emerge from the computing disciplines and technology companies.

An alternative perspective to this can be primarily pedagogical, asking whether specific learning activities or outcomes are taught in ways that exclude particular individuals. A focus on the aims for learning experiences and outcomes can then support exploration of how to achieve these outcomes in an accessible way.

We can also take a broader perspective to ask what barriers are experienced when a person tries to access education, and who may be missing out. Research through this approach can be driven by reports or observations from learner perspectives, or by data that highlights the relative gaps in engagement or attainment with education by particular groups.

Finally, we can conceive of accessibility as a quality achieved by the ways in which organisations, as combinations of people, systems, and processes, work together. This perspective recognises the holistic nature of support for accessible learning that cannot be reduced to a single technology or job role.

In the rest of this chapter we will explore how examples of these conceptions, or combinations of them, has driven research and produced greater understanding of what it means to make learning accessible to all.

How can we make learning experiences available to all?

In taking a pedagogical perspective on accessibility, we noted above that particular types of learning activities create specific barriers. In this section we describe how a persistent intent on enabling access to STEM laboratory and field work has driven research over many years. In this, researchers have looked to harness the cutting edge technologies of the day and envision how these can become embedded in mainstream teaching and learning.

It has been argued that science, technology, engineering, and maths (STEM) subjects raise some very particular and stubborn challenges for access in the areas of practical work, such as laboratory and field activities (IOP 2017). The impact of inaccessible field or lab activities can also be exacerbated as many STEM qualifications are accredited by professional bodies, and these bodies often list practical work as a requirement for accreditation. However, the challenges have attracted sustained attention and persistent intent to widen opportunities (Pearson et al., 2019a).

Traditionally, laboratory work requires students to be present in a lab to manipulate apparatus. The requirements to be in a particular location and to perform particular physical activities with apparatus can present accessibility challenges. In response, remote laboratories aim to provide manipulation or control of real apparatus through interfaces at a distance. Such approaches can expand access to important science learning experiences for students with disabilities, and for all students studying at a distance from laboratory facilities.

The Practical Experimentation by Accessing Remote Laboratories (PEARL) project explored ways in which computers could be used to give high quality learning experiences in science and engineering education by bringing the teaching laboratory to the students, giving flexibility in terms of time and location. The tools and activities created in the project were also designed to be accessible to disabled students using assistive technology, such as screen readers.

A model of collaborative working underpinned the learning activities, with students working with peers and receiving comments from tutors. The complex system which was developed provided a structure which combined tools for collaboration with technology to control the equipment, network server and interface technologies, and streaming media, video cameras, and microphones to provide the means of observation and communication.

As one of a number of explorations in different institutions, the project involved a re-versioning of an introductory Open University science experiment usually performed by students co-located at a residential school, to allow remote operation of a spectrometer to measure wavelengths. Scanlon et al., (2004) describe the interface through which students working at a distance could take part in this experiment. Evaluations with disabled students confirmed that they could use the interface effectively. While the remote approach was found to be a different experience, sufficient equivalence with the original laboratory experiment could be achieved.

Students and academics were supportive of the PEARL approach, which has continued to develop. Cooper and Ferriera (2009) summarized the lessons learned about the design and implementation of remote laboratories based on these experiences, stressing the importance of having a well-defined pedagogic strategy, of removing accessibility barriers, and the need for ease of automation and remote control.

Deployment of these ideas at scale then became the focus. In 2013 the OU, with support from the Wolfson Foundation, launched the OpenScience

Laboratory. This virtual lab allows students to carry out experiments online, bringing interactive practical science to students anywhere and anytime they have Internet access. As with PEARL, the aim is to provide access to real physical instruments and equipment through robotically controlled experiments, but the laboratory platform also provides a basis for interactive screen experiments; virtual instruments and labs; immersive 3D experiments; virtual field trips; and mass participation 'citizen science' networks (Garrow et al., 2013; Villasclaras- Fernandez et al., 2013).

This initiative led to the development of the OpenSTEM laboratories, a suite of distinct labs incorporating the OpenScience Lab, the OpenScience Observatories and the OpenEngineering Lab. The OpenScience Observatories provide access to two remotely operated optical telescopes based in Tenerife, and a radio telescope based at the OU campus in Milton Keynes. The OpenEngineering Lab allows practical lab-based teaching at a distance covering engineering, electronics, control, materials and robotics. Together these connect students to instrumentation, data and equipment for practical enquiries over the Internet, where time and distance is no longer a barrier.

In these developments it is important to maintain consideration of the physical and social aspects of the laboratory activities. Experiences that connect students to the on-campus labs allow students to acquire and practise lab-based skills. Lab casts provide an interactive experience by connecting students and lecturers via web streaming in a way that provides a live social experience at a distance.

Another activity that can often be inaccessible to learners, but is a recognised component of science and many other subjects is fieldwork. In subjects such as geology or biosciences, study in the field is seen as essential and is known to support conceptual and practical understanding (Elkins & Elkins, 2007; Scott et al., 2012). The terrain and location of many field sites of interest present barriers to those with mobility challenges. A persistent intent through research spanning more than a decade has led to greater understanding of how remote access to field work can be achieved.

The Enabling Remote Activity (ERA) approach was first prompted as a response to an enquiry from staff and a student who was using a wheelchair and studying earth sciences. They highlighted the possibility of using audio and video to communicate with students unable to reach a particular field site. From this, the wider issue of remote access to fieldwork was tackled through the development of a flexible toolkit (Collins et al. 2016).

The right field site may be expensive and time consuming to reach, so issues of access arise not only for students with mobility challenges. Cost and availability are often prohibitive factors that exclude students from access to field experiences.

As with remote laboratories, technologies including networks, sensors and cameras offer the potential to create remote presence and interaction with a field site. However in fieldwork, variability in locations and the need for mobility in order to explore the field site create further challenges. Technical solutions to these have pushed at the boundaries of what can be achieved with

Figure 4.2: Enabling Remote Activity (ERA) field trials. Copyright Mark Gaved, The Open University.

mobile networking and portable technologies. Meanwhile, the practical and pedagogical approaches employed in remote fieldwork have been a particularly interesting focus for research.

Findings from ERA include the value of multiple communications channels, with voice providing an important direct link between individuals, video providing a sense of presence and live interaction, and photographs important for details. A combination of these are used according to the learning activity. Rapid deployment of equipment was also key in order to fit in with field trip schedules and avoid students being left behind. The ERA approach has focused on getting people as close to the field site as possible, such that they can gain from as much of the field experience as possible and only use technology to overcome the parts that are inaccessible. This attends to the argument that social and experiential aspects of fieldwork are important and could be lost, resulting in a further form of inequity (Collins et al., 2016). Further development of the ERA approach has led to the development of an accessible field trip in Connemara (part of the National Science Foundation funded Geopath Extra project, 2017) and an inclusive field course in Anglesey (part of the Office for Students funded IncSTEM project).

The value of a persistent intent in this area has been that we have developed and tested multiple designs for technology-enhanced learning activities. So where the value of having learners in close proximity to the field site was recognised in ERA, this could itself become a barriers as it might not always be possible to have the learners close by. As such, alternative designs for social and collaborative field activities were also explored. The 'Out There and In Here' (OTIH) project took the ERA findings in a different direction. It explored how to set up a 'command centre' in a classroom setting, where a group of remote students could learn through dialogue and collaboration with their field-based peers. Trials and evaluations looked to find ways to design for balance, such that all students involved could have an equitable and valuable learning

Figure 4.3: Classroom (top) and field-based students in an 'Out There and In Here' remote fieldwork trial. Copyright The Open University.

experience (Coughlan et al., 2010). The outcomes showed that there are different strengths to each situation – a field-based student can capture data, but a classroom setting may be better suited to analysing or identifying it. There are also different challenges to each experience – the field-based student or teacher can feel pressured to provide material to their remote peers, who require this for the experience to be effective (Coughlan et al., 2011).

These examples of designing and evaluating remote laboratory and remote fieldwork experiences show how research can utilise technology to enable access to specific activities that are commonly inaccessible. While these experiences are not an exact replication, they can be designed to offer learning outcomes that would otherwise be lost. They can also prompt thinking about new pedagogical approaches and help to unpick what the aimed-for learning is, which may be otherwise implicit or taken for granted. Research in this area used cutting edge technologies and overcame a lack of suitable technologies to explore potential solutions in advance of these approaches reaching mainstream use. At the same time, it requires an awareness of the social and experiential aspects of learning to really evaluate how equitable, accessible learning can be achieved.

Broadening our understanding of accessibility from availability to equity

The multiple conceptions of openness and accessibility, and the examples of research that aims to make field and lab work accessible, both show that making learning accessible is not a simple endeavour. For example, the PEARL evaluation raises the notion of whether an accessible remote experience is similar or equivalent to that in the lab, and the ERA and OTIH projects highlight the importance of less formal aspects, such as the shared social experience of being on a field trip, in a particular place and in the company of fellow students.

These issues can impact on the learner but would not be captured by a narrow definition of accessibility. In this section we delve further into this sense that making learning available is not sufficient. The Beyond Prototypes framework highlights the importance of evaluation and evidence to drive TEL innovation. In this area, there is a wealth of evidence of persistent gaps in access, attainment, and experience of learning at scale. A review of this suggests that a simple notion of educational access (i.e. that a person was technically able to join a course of study) results in significantly different outcomes for learners with different characteristics. We then consider how it is possible to respond by understanding the needs of particular groups, in order to facilitate their equitable access to education.

Analysing data on registration, completion, and attainment in post-secondary study, the picture that emerges challenges simplistic visions of making learning accessible or open to all. Richardson has conducted a number of analyses in this area looking at specific groups such as categories of disability or ethnicity. The findings with regards to disabilities show a complex picture, including that students with declared autistic spectrum disorders studying at The Open University were just as likely to complete, pass, and obtain good grades in their modules as students without any declared disabilities (Richardson, 2017), and that students who are deaf or hard of hearing were more likely to complete their modules than their non-disabled peers (Richardson, 2015a). While students with dyslexia or other specific learning difficulties were just as likely to complete their module as students without declared disabilities, they were less likely to pass or to obtain good grades (Richardson, 2015b). In contrast, students with declared mental health difficulties, or with visual impairments, were less likely to complete their modules, and less likely to pass them (Richardson, 2015c; Richardson, 2015d).

Richardson's work highlights that considering all people with declared disabilities together as a meaningful group is problematic, since it hides differences that become visible when we look at particular sub-groups of 'disabled students'. The types of barriers to equitable learning faced by students with dyslexia, and the technologies and support actions that would enable equitable learning for them, are not the same as those faced by a person with mental health difficulties. At the same time, these analyses also highlight the importance of accounting for intersectionality, where multiple characteristics of a person may impact on the accessibility of learning. Richardson finds substantial proportions of students declare multiple disabilities, and that these groups tend to be less likely to succeed. Focusing on disability in isolation could be problematic, since other factors such as prior educational qualifications and ethnicity can also be shown to correlate with student success.

With regards to ethnicity, persistent and ubiquitous gaps in attainment for ethnic minority students have been identified in UK higher education when compared to white students. A particularly interesting finding from the perspective of making learning accessible is that these gaps are only partly explained by entry qualifications. One analysis extrapolates that around half of the attainment gap in higher education can be explained by poor attainment in earlier stages of education, but that the other half cannot be explained by this measure of academic ability. This may be occurring due to unknown factors within the higher educational experience, which could include discrimination or more subtle processes through which these students are not supported to perform (Richardson, 2015e). We do not fully understand where and why these gaps occur, but this work suggests that a simple notion of accessibility in education – that a person can manage to register, engage, and complete a course – does not necessarily lead to equitable educational outcomes. We need to consider the experience as a whole and identify elements of teaching that a person might find inaccessible or which might lead to inequality that impacts on outcomes.

Richardson's findings draw on data about students taking part in formal open access education at The Open University. But what about OER and MOOCs? Arguments have been made that these approaches could lead to greater inclusion in higher education by lowering barriers of cost and flexibility (Lane, 2008). However, as Farrow et al. (2015) report, non-formal users of OER are likely to already hold a degree, or to be currently studying on a formal higher education course. This is not to say that OER are not supporting some widening of access, but it suggests that they may be primarily useful to those who are already benefiting from formal study. MOOC platforms have been found to have substantial failings with regards to accessibility for disabled learners, and those involved in the production and presentation of MOOCs are still developing strategies to provide disabled learners with a good study experience (Iniesto et al., 2016). OER are often derived from existing formal course materials and so can replicate some of the barriers for non-traditional audiences that exist in these, while removing the active support and encouragement of learners that would perhaps support them to succeed in a formal educational setting (Lane, 2008; Coughlan & Goff, 2019).

Richardson (2015e) notes that we can struggle to identify the causes of inequity for particular groups, even where we can see the results in quantitative analyses. A range of studies have provided richer insights into ways in which educational provision can be problematic for particular groups, or can be designed with recognition of these problems. Having established these issues, how can we move from a notion of accessible or open as equating to 'available', to something more equitable? What might we need to understand in order to design to close these gaps? The next section addresses these issues.

Responding to the diversity of contexts and individuals

We have already introduced some examples where new uses of technology create a basis for educational opportunities and increased access. In this section we will focus further on ways of designing for audiences and contexts.

An important point to start with is that while the focus of our attention is often rightly on pedagogy, there may be practical and social issues that impede access to education and which need to be understood and adapted to any specific context. For example, working to design educational technology solutions for the context of refugee camps, Alain et al. (2018) argue that issues such as prior and current disruption to formal education, language barriers, and the availability of teachers, need to be considered if technology-based interventions are to effectively engage children. Each refugee camp will have different social, physical, and technological resources and limitations that can be employed to create informal educational opportunities in these settings, and further distinct challenges are faced in situations where refugee children are to be integrated into local school systems. However there has been a tendency for initiatives around refugee education to design for scale in an homogeneous way, with a lack of awareness or potential to adapt to these contextual differences.

The move towards greater online and hybrid learning has enormous potential for making access to education easier for many populations. However, when this results in the removal of other means of study it can create new forms of exclusion. A prime example of this is in education for students in secure environments. A study of universities across four different countries highlighted that prisoners found it increasingly difficult to access distance education, with risk-averse correctional systems prohibiting or restricting access to the Internet and to computers (Farley et al., 2016). Solutions can be used that present an offline digital version of materials, or printed versions can be provided. However, it is important that these solutions are designed in such a way that they provide the intended learning experience and do not become an afterthought.

More subtle barriers to online learning are present for people who lack skills or confidence in ICT. Concepts related to digital inclusion or exclusion have been described and debated to highlight the increasing reliance on digital technologies across society and the impacts this can have. While it was appealing to think that younger generations of 'digital natives' had different expectations and skills with technology when compared to older 'digital immigrants', research by Jones and Shao (2011) refuted such a simple age-based dichotomy. They also found that many of the new technologies discussed in educational research, such as virtual reality, wikis, or blogs, were not ones that students made use of or expected to be used. At the same time, there were clear signs of the rising general use of social media, mobile technologies, and online multimedia. Where these become key to learning – perhaps as part of open educational practices – there are further possibilities to include or exclude.

It is therefore important to understand and critique the factors that mediate the relationships between digital technologies and learners. Seale (2014) argued that it is necessary to look beyond a simplistic notion of accessibility in order to understand the factors impacting on disabled students. If we focus only on whether technologies are available and if the person can access them, there is a risk that the complexity of the relationship that disabled students have with their technologies and their educational institutions will be ignored. We need to avoid a situation where we only consider the relationship between student and institution as one of receiver and provider of resources.

How then can we think more broadly about accessibility in terms of the relationships between students, resources, and educational institutions? Drawing on the ideas of digital inclusion researchers such as Eynon (2009) and van Dijk (2005) who talk about the resources that people need in order to be citizens of a digital society, Seale (2014) identified a range of factors that potentially mediate the relationship between students and their institutions:

> *Temporal Resources:* The time available to disabled students to invest in learning how to use new technologies. Time can be limited and insufficient due to the additional study burden that disabled students experience – particularly if their courses have not adopted an inclusive approach to teaching or made reasonable adjustments.
> *Mental Resources:* The knowledge, awareness and skills that disabled students possess that means they are confident and competent in using a wide range of technologies and have created a wide range of strategies for using their technologies to support their learning.
> *Social Resources:* The range of formal and informal support networks such as academic peers, tutors, friends and family that disabled students can draw on.
> *Cultural Resources:* A climate or environment where disabled students are perceived as legitimate technology users, where there is an

expectation that they (along with everyone else in the community) can and should be using technology.

Material Resources: Access to a range of generic and assistive technologies, some of which disabled students may personally own, some of which are provided by the institution.

In this case, the access to technology (material resources) is just one aspect of a broader view. Even in considering these material resources, we should note that only some of what a disabled student might use to learn is provided by the institution.

Building on this framework, Seale (2013) and Seale et al. (2015) apply a 'Digital Capital' framework to the understanding of the relationship between disabled students, their technologies and the institutions in which they study. Drawing on the ideas of earlier research (Bourdieu, 1997; Putnam, 2000, Selwyn, 2004) two key concepts were proposed: 'Digital Cultural Capital' and 'Digital Social Capital'.

The acquisition of digital cultural capital is exemplified by individuals investing time in improving their technology knowledge and competencies through informal or formal learning opportunities, as well as a socialization into technology use and 'techno-culture' through family, peers and media.

Digital social capital is developed through, for example, the networks of 'technological contacts' and support that people have, which can be face to face (e.g. family, friends, tutors) or remote (e.g. online help facilities).

Seale (2013) used this digital capital framework to analyse data collected from 30 disabled students regarding their experiences of using technology to support their learning. Results indicated that disabled students possessed a significant amount of digital cultural capital and a fair amount of digital social capital. Seale observed however that for some disabled students, this cultural and social digital capital did not appear strong enough. For example, some disabled students appeared to be affected by the extent to which using specialist technologies marked them out as different. Seale et al. (2015) also applied the digital capital framework to analyse the experiences of 175 students with declared disabilities regarding their use of technology to support their learning. Results suggested that while these students do have access to social and cultural resources; sometimes these resources are not appropriate or effective (e.g. school-based ICT qualifications) or disabled students are not drawing on all the possible resources available to them (e.g. non-institutional based support or support from disabled students). This means that disabled students can lack the 'right' kind of digital capital to enable them to succeed within higher education environments.

Using an analytical framework that goes beyond a simple conception of accessibility, this research suggests that higher education institutions may need to conceptualise and organise technology related support services for disabled students differently. There is a need to think beyond simplistic notions of access, availability and skills training.

To summarise, for learning to be accessible to all means more than for it to just be available, because inequitable situations arise through a lack of consideration of how contexts and individuals are related to the resources and support for learning. Analyses of student data can highlight inequalities of engagement or attainment, and qualitative studies offer understanding of the challenges faced in particular contexts. To build on this, we look in the next section at procedural and practice-based approaches to understanding and achieving accessible learning.

Consider process and practice, not just artefacts and outcomes

In research and scholarship around openness and accessibility, there has been a growing recognition of the need to consider process and practice, rather than only artefacts and outcomes. This makes sense to educational technology in particular for a variety of reasons. For example, if we think in terms of process and practice it is easier to explore how we could adapt technological artefacts to be better suited to particular contexts, and support individuals to be aware and able to use them. If we consider the experience of a student as a process that includes multiple events that could have short and long term impacts on their learning and attainment over time, we are better placed to identify why gaps in attainment might appear.

The importance of taking a process view of accessibility has emerged more recently with the suggestion that any artefact can only be considered accessible in relation to a particular person trying to use it; or as Cooper et al. (2012) put it: "The focus of WCAG (Web Content Accessibility Guidelines) is on the technical artefact – i.e. the "web page", not on users and user goals" (pg.1), yet "accessibility is a property of the relation between the user and the resource in the context of how that is mediated; not a property of the resource" (pg. 2). While WCAG is very important in defining characteristics of a resource that should support it to be accessible, it is not sufficient to ensure equitable experiences because it gives no sense of how it is used in practice by particular audiences and (for example) the mental, social, temporal and cultural resources that Seale (2013, 2015) explores in her analyses of disabled student experiences.

There is a related trend in open education research. Much effort has been focused on tasks such as defining what an open educational resource should be in terms of legal or technical infrastructure, and in devising implementations of this such as Open Textbooks. But until recently, it has been less common to conduct research to understand how people do, or could, engage in practices around using these resources (Weller et al., 2015).

In both cases, the original focus on artefacts could be attributed to a desire to build a broadly applicable basis for change at scale – the wide use of WCAG standards to evaluate web page accessibility, and of Creative Commons licences for sharing of OER are clearly influential developments that have achieved widespread impact. But the move towards practice and process is prompted by the understanding raised in the previous section, that truly providing access means responding to individual contexts and needs that are subject to change over time.

A focus on practices in open education helps us to understand the benefits that stem from sharing resources under open licences, and the barriers that could prevent these from being realised. For example, when Pitt (2015) explored educator perceptions on the impact of introducing OpenStax College open textbooks, they found a range of responses. A key driver for openly-licensed texts was the need to serve students for whom the expense of proprietary textbooks was a barrier, and to save money for cash-strapped institutions. Cost savings were certainly a theme in responses, but when asked what the main impact of introducing the textbooks was on their teaching practice, the most common responses were that it had made teaching easier (29%), or had led to innovations in their teaching practice (25%). These educators reported that they could build on the text, adapt it to suit their classes and students, feel more able to combine it with other resources, and be creative in a way that a closed proprietary text would not support. One stated that with open licences that support adaptation of content "the book is my servant, I am not its servant" (pg. 148).

At the same time, reusing and adapting OER can be challenging. Educational resources are produced for a particular context and audience, and it can be problematic to reuse these with other audiences. Research in this area has analysed processes of reuse to highlight how participation in remixing can improve the relevance of resources to particular audiences, while maintaining the original objectives of the material. In the 'Bridge to Success' project, courses designed by The Open University as an introduction to study for those with limited prior educational experiences, were released as OER and remixed for use with US audiences of underserved learners. The collaborative approach engaged US-based authors in adapting the content to the needs of their own students. Changes were made at various levels including to find appropriate language, or to increase content in areas that were more important for the intended US pre-college audience, when compared to the original UK audience. These included, for example, fractions in mathematics. In addition, promotional activity to introduce the courses, and to work with educators to find ways in which it would be best integrated into their teaching, was essential to gaining uptake across a range of settings. Although intended to be useful to colleges, the resources were also used in unexpected contexts, such as charitable organisations who worked with underserved groups (Coughlan et al., 2013; Coughlan et al., 2019).

Given that open online courses are not necessarily reaching underserved audiences, related practices of targeted collaboration in the creation and use of OER have been applied in other projects. When creating courses with the intent of reaching a particular underserved audience, our research identified ways in which collaboration with a 'Learner Representative Partner' could be beneficial. The research analysed the processes of creating a suite of six open online courses in collaboration with different organisations, and each aimed at encouraging engagement with higher education from an identified target audience, for example those working in healthcare assistant roles, or looking to start their own business (Coughlan & Goff, 2019). The partners informed the design of the courses, including the reuse of their own resources and media, and in deciding on appropriate language and content for the audience. The partners facilitated the courses to embody student-centred strategies, influenced the language used in the course materials, provided authentic case studies from people similar to the audience, and acted to highlight areas of 'decoupling' where academic practices did not fit with the desire to widen participation.

An interesting example of research that recognises the need to consider process, practice, and particularly people, is the EU4All (European Unified Approach for Assisted Life-long Learning) project, which took place between 2006 and 2011. The project involved 13 European partners and aimed to research and develop ways to make life-long learning at higher education level accessible to disabled people. This involved wide stakeholder engagement, individualised design approaches and extensive evaluation; it resulted in the creation of a model of 'professionalism in accessibility' (McAndrew et al., 2012) and a learner-centred framework for personalisation of content and service. Other, less tangible outputs from the project include key lessons learned about operationalising accessibility; it became clear in the EU4All project that accessibility cannot be achieved in an educational institution if it is viewed only as a technical consideration. Understanding user needs, experience and preferences is critical if accessibility is to be embedded. As accessibility frequently means different things to different stakeholders, human engagement through a multi-faceted, multi-stakeholder approach is an essential part of this process.

The EU4All project drew on work by Seale (2006) that explored adopting a holistic view of the stakeholders and activities involved in achieving accessible learning. Seale had investigated the perspectives of different stakeholders, including their issues and concerns, in an attempt to amplify these diverse voices and provide a cross-sectional view of accessibility. Drawing on personal experience, Seale stresses that for accessibility to be realised, a range of stakeholders need not only to be involved but to actively form strategic partnerships, and that this "cannot happen successfully unless each stakeholder understands the different perspectives of each of the other stakeholders" (2006, pg. 4). The EU4All researchers modelled their work on Seale's, ensuring all Seale's identified stakeholders had a voice in the EU4All project, as well as adding other stakeholder groups. The resulting 'model of professionalism in accessibility' placed strong emphasis on a 'holistic view of accessibility' with stakeholder engagement and human beings 'in the loop' (McAndrew et al, 2012).

These lessons became part of Open University practices through the development of the SeGA (Securing Greater Accessibility) initiative. In 2010 it was becoming clear in The Open University that there was a disconnect between student support teams and academic staff, which was resulting in academics not being aware, when designing learning content, of feedback about what students were finding inaccessible. This frequently resulted in costly, retrofitted reasonable adjustments being made by student support units that could have been avoided through inclusive design. Pockets of good practice did exist, but responsibility for supporting disabled students was dispersed across a number of academic and non-academic units and information was difficult to find; the good practice that existed was not systematised and was 'decoupled' (Meyer and Rowan, 1977) from institutional strategy, policy and business as usual.

Acknowledging these issues, several stakeholders in different areas joined forces to lobby for a change; an initiative that would begin to address these issues and operationalise accessibility in a way that was systematic, consistent and sustainable. This would be a whole-institution and whole-product and service life-cycle approach, with stakeholders from both academic and support units. The SeGA initiative was launched with the objectives of:

- Clarification of responsibility and accountability for leading on and delivering accessibility.
- Improved access to the curriculum for disabled students.
- Improved understanding of staff roles and responsibilities regarding accessibility.
- Improved documentation of how the reasonable adjustments offered to students have been arrived at.
- Reduced overall cost for providing adjustments to disabled students.
- Improved organisational knowledge of enabling accessibility best practice.
- Improved visibility of the levels of accessibility afforded to students within courses and programmes.

(Cooper, 2014)

In its conception, SeGA drew heavily on Seale (2006) and the EU4All findings and resulting model of professionalism in accessibility (McAndrew et al, 2012). It also incorporated aspects of Communities of Practice theory (Lave and Wenger, 1991) and the social model of disability (Oliver, 1983). Initially it worked to clarify responsibilities, processes and systems, and, through a network of accessibility coordinators and champions, to ensure information was easily available to people who needed it. It acts to bring different stakeholders together and to empower the voice of students and other stakeholders in operationalising accessibility. In short, to be the 'humans in the loop' (McAndrew et al, 2012).

SeGA is embedded in the processes of teaching through 'Accessibility Coordinators', members of staff who take responsibility to advocate for accessibility in the teaching in their faculty and school areas (Pearson et al., 2019b). SeGA supports the Accessibility Coordinators with regular training events, and coordinates a working group through which Accessibility Coordinators can share

Figure 4.4: Securing Greater Accessibility.

their current practices and challenges, and take part in projects to improve the accessibility of learning and teaching at an institutional level. Recent projects have included creating guidance for external assessors and critical readers of module material, and embedding this guidance in the Curriculum Management System; changing university systems so that all undergraduate modules are required to have an 'accessibility statement' available to prospective students on the university website (as well as coordinating the writing of these statements); and refining the reasonable adjustment process so that examples of reasonable adjustments are recorded in a way that makes it easier to apply similar adjustments for future students.

As the project became business as usual, SeGA expanded its reach beyond the curriculum to include other aspects of learning provision, for example it now includes representation from staff responsible for the production of OER, staff involved in the development and production of online learning tools and resources, and staff from areas such as Careers, the Library, Marketing and IT. A coordination group brings together representatives from across the university to identify and discuss key areas for attention, and a referrals panel brings together expertise to inform decision making on complex individual cases and course-level decisions that could impact on accessibility for students.

SeGA also increasingly plays a conduit role between research and practice, working to implement research findings into practice through training and staff networks, and ensuring current concerns and issues are shared with research group channels to inform investigation. This acts to facilitate and empower ongoing persistent intent to make learning opportunities accessible to disabled learners.

Conclusions

This chapter started by considering that 'accessible' and 'open' are terms that can be defined and interpreted in different ways. They are often conceived of through technical definitions of licenses and web accessibility standards, or more broadly, that something is available and free or low in cost. However, making educational activities available is only a starting point to producing equity. Persistent intent to utilise TEL to widen access to field and lab-based activities has produced solutions which have been reused and adapted in teaching practice. At the same time, many of the interesting findings from these studies were pedagogical in nature. These technologies provided a positive learning experience where previously there was none available, but this needed to be approached with a sensitivity to social elements of the experience, roles, and the nature of different environments.

The Beyond Prototypes framework emphasises that innovations should be driven by evaluation and evidence. By compiling detailed understanding of uptake, completion and attainment by students with different characteristics, we can see that different issues exist for these groups in the Open University's open access model. Inequity is also found in the wider sector, and in the uptake of OER and MOOCs.

These quantitative findings provide a starting point to motivate and target research on inclusion, and lead to participatory and qualitative approaches to develop richer findings that address the 'why' behind these gaps, and to develop effective and appropriate interventions with audiences. In the past, it has not always been clear to TEL researchers that they should be cognisant of issues such as learner confidence or organisational risk aversion. However, these have come to the fore as factors that can create inequity with TEL.

There are difficulties in moving between TEL research and mainstream practice, and the Beyond Prototypes framework encapsulates the complexity of this. However, there have been encouraging results in moving research and innovation on inclusion into organisational practice. A shift of focus in research beyond creating assistive technologies, and assessing the accessibility of artefacts, towards conceptualising accessibility as process that must include a range of stakeholders, informed the development of the Securing Greater Accessibility (SeGA) initiative which then became embedded in business as usual practices. Similarly, creating and using OER to widen participation have moved from a niche innovation to an established practice at the OU. Open-Learn now provides learning opportunities to millions of people every year, and Chapter 2 of this book provides further examples of practice-based projects to create inclusion through open learning at scale. In the next chapter, we explore how these foundations are expanding to harness new ideas and technologies.

References

Alain, G., Coughlan, T., Adams, A., and Yanacopulos, H., (2018). A Process for Co-Designing Educational Technology Systems for Refugee Children. In Proceedings of British HCI 2018, Belfast, Northern Ireland, UK.

Bourdieu, P. (1997). The forms of capital. In Education: Culture, economy, society, Edited by: Halsey, A., Lauder, H., Brown, P. and Stuart-Wells, A. 46–58. Oxford: Oxford University Press.

Collins, T., Davies, S., and Gaved, M. (2016). Enabling remote activity: widening participation in field study courses. In: D. Kennepohl (ed.) Teaching Science Online: Practical Guidance for Effective Instruction and Lab Work. Sterling, VA, USA: Stylus Publishing, 183–195.

Cooper, M. (2014). Meeting the needs of disabled students in online distance education – an institutional case study from The Open University, UK. Distance Education in China, 2014(12) pp. 18–27.

Cooper, M., Sloan, D., Kelly, B., and Lewthwaite, S. (2012). A challenge to web accessibility metrics and guidelines: putting people and processes first. In *Proceedings of the international cross-disciplinary conference on Web accessibility*. ACM.

Cooper, M. and Ferreira, J. M. M. (2009). Remote laboratories extending access to science and engineering curricula. *IEEE Transactions on Learning Technologies*, 2(4) pp. 342–353.

Coughlan, T., Pitt, R., & Farrow, R. (2019). Forms of innovation inspired by open educational resources: a post-project analysis. *Open Learning: The Journal of Open, Distance and e-Learning,*. Taylor & Francis.

Coughlan, T., & Goff, J. (2019). Creating Open Online Courses with Learner Representative Partners to Widen Participation in Higher Education. *Journal of Learning for Development, 6*(2).

Coughlan, T., Pitt, R., & McAndrew, P. (2013). Building open bridges: collaborative remixing and reuse of open educational resources across organisations. In *Proceedings of the SIGCHI Conference on Human Factors in Computing Systems*. 991–1000. ACM.

Coughlan, T., Adams, A., Rogers, Y., and Davies, S., (2011). Enabling live dialogic and collaborative learning between field and indoor contexts. In: *The 25th BCS Conference on Human Computer Interaction*, British Computer Society. 88–98.

Coughlan, T., Adams, A., & Rogers, Y. (2010). Designing for balance: Out there and in here. In *Proceedings of the 24th BCS Interaction Specialist Group Conference*. British Computer Society. 468–473.

Elkins, J. T. & Elkins, N. M. L. (2007). Teaching Geology in the Field: Significant Geoscience Concept Gains in Entirely Field-based Introductory Geology Courses, *Journal of Geoscience Education (55)* 2. NAGT. 126–132.

Eynon, R. (2009). Mapping the digital divide in Britain: implications for learning and education. *Learning, Media and Technology, 34* (4), 277–290.

Farley, H., Pike, A., Demiray, U., & Tanglang, N. (2016). Delivering digital higher education into prisons: the cases of four universities in Australia, UK, Turkey and Nigeria. GLOKALde, 2(2), 147–166.

Farrow, Robert; de los Arcos, Beatriz; Pitt, Rebecca and Weller, Martin (2015). Who are the Open Learners? A Comparative Study Profiling non-Formal Users of Open Educational Resources. *EURODL (European Journal of Open, Distance and E-Learning), 18*(2) pp. 50–74.

Garrow, K., Braithwaite, N., Richardson, B., and Swithenby, S. (2013). The OpenScience Laboratory: a globally available online lab at the cutting edge of practical science teaching. In: *ED-MEDIA 2013: Conference on Educational Multimedia, Hypermedia & Telecommunications*, AACE.

Iniesto, F., McAndrew, P., Minocha, S., & Coughlan, T. (2016). Accessibility of MOOCs: Understanding the Provider Perspective. *Journal of Interactive Media in Education, 2016*(1).

IOP (2017). Building momentum towards inclusive teaching and learning. Institute of Physics. http://www.iop.org/publications/iop/2017/file_69353.pdf

Jones, C. & Shao, B. (2011). The net generation and digital natives: implications for higher education. Higher Education Academy, York.

Lane, A. (2008). Widening participation in education through open educational resources. *Opening up education: The collective advancement of education through open technology, open content and open knowledge, 149*–163.

Lave, J. and Wenger, E. (1991). Situated Learning: Legitimate Peripheral Participation. Cambridge: Cambridge University Press. ISBN 0-521-42374-0

McAndrew, P., Farrow, R. and Cooper, M. (2012). Adapting online learning resources for all: planning for professionalism in accessibility. *Research in Learning Technology*, 20(4) pp. 345–361.

Meyer, J. and Rowan, B. (1977). Institutionalized Organization: Formal Structure as Myth and Ceremony. *American Journal of Sociology*, 83, 340–363. https://doi.org/10.1086/226550

Oliver, M. (1983). 'Social Work with Disabled People' Basingstoke: Macmillan

OpenLearn (2019). Free badged courses from the Social Partnership Network. https://www.open.edu/openlearn/spn-courses

Pearson, V., Lister, K., McPherson, E., Gallen, A., Davies, G., Colwell, C., Bradshaw, K., Braithwaite, N. S. & Collins, T., (2019a). Embedding and sustaining inclusive practice in online and blended learning, *Journal of Interactive Media in Education*. 2019(1).

Pearson, V., Lister, K., & Coughlan, T., (2019b). Accessibility coordinators: a model for embedded, sustainable change towards inclusive higher education, *Proceedings of 12th International Conference of Education, Research and Innovation (ICERI 2019)*. IATED.

Pitt, R. (2015). Mainstreaming Open Textbooks: Educator Perspectives on the Impact of OpenStax College open textbooks. *The International Review of Research in Open and Distributed Learning (IRRODL) 16*, (4) 133–155.

Putnam, R. D. (2000). Bowling alone, New York: Simon & Schuster.

Rets, I., Coughlan, T., Stickler, U. & Astruc, L., (2019). Accessibility of Open Educational Resources: how well are they suited for non-native English readers? *Under review.*

Richardson, J. T. E. (2017). Academic attainment in students with autism spectrum disorders in distance education. *Open Learning: The Journal of Open and Distance Learning, 32*(1) 81–91.

Richardson, John T. E. (2015a). Academic attainment in deaf and hard-of-hearing students in distance education. *Open Learning, 30*(2) 164–177.

Richardson, J. T. E. (2015b). Academic attainment in students with dyslexia in distance education. *Dyslexia, 21*(4) 323–337.

Richardson, J. T. E. (2015c). Academic Attainment in Students with Mental Health Difficulties in Distance Education. *International Journal of Mental Health, 44*(3) 231–240.

Richardson, J. T. E. (2015d). Academic attainment in visually impaired students in distance education. *British Journal of Visual Impairment, 33*(2) 126–137.

Richardson, J. T. E. (2015e). The under-attainment of ethnic minority students in UK higher education: what we know and what we don't know. *Journal of Further and Higher Education, 39*(2), 278–291.

Scanlon, E., Colwell, C., Cooper, M. & Di Paolo, T. (2004). Remote experiments, re-versioning and re-thinking science learning. *Computers & Education 43.* 153–163.

Scott, G. W., Goulder, R., Wheeler, P., Scott, L. J., Tobin, M. L., & Marsham, S. (2012). The Value of Fieldwork in Life and Environmental Sciences in the Context of Higher Education: A Case Study in Learning About Biodiversity. *Journal of Science Education and Technology, 21*(1), 11–21. DOI: 10.1007/s10956-010-9276-x

Seale, J. (2006). Disability and e-learning in higher education: Accessibility theory and practice. 1st Edition. Routledge, Abingdon.

Seale, J. (2014). Disability and e-learning in higher education: Accessibility theory and practice. 2nd Edition. Routledge, Abingdon.

Seale, J. (2013). When digital capital is not enough: reconsidering the digital lives of disabled university students. *Learning, Media and Technology, 38*(3), 256–269.

Seale, J., Georgeson, J., Mamas, C., & Swain, J. (2015). Not the right kind of 'digital capital'? An examination of the complex relationship between disabled students, their technologies and higher education institutions. *Computers & Education, 82*, 118–128.

Selwyn (2004). Reconsidering political and popular understandings of the digital divide. *New Media & Society*, 6(3): 341–62.

Van Dijk, J. (2005). The deepening divide: Inequality in the information society, London: Sage.

Villasclaras Fernandez, E., Sharples, M., Kelley, S., and Scanlon, E. (2013). nQuire for the OpenScience Lab: supporting communities of inquiry learning. In: Scaling up Learning for Sustained Impact, *Lecture Notes in Computer Science*, Springer, pp. 585–588.

Weller, M., de Los Arcos, B., Farrow, R., Pitt, B., & McAndrew, P. (2015). The impact of OER on teaching and learning practice. *Open Praxis, 7*(4), 351–361.

CHAPTER 5

Accessible Inclusive Learning: Futures

Tim Coughlan, Kate Lister, Jane Seale,
Eileen Scanlon and Martin Weller

The previous chapter on Accessible Inclusive Learning: Foundations outlined some key approaches and challenges when conducting research that seeks to make learning accessible to all. Here, we explore newer trends that are directing our current research and practice in this area. These promising directions include devising models for global networks, the potential to collect and use data to understand learning experiences in new ways, and new opportunities arising through artificial intelligence. By exploring current and recent projects around these areas, we also highlight some emerging tensions. Finally, we return to thinking about how we conduct research, considering how concepts of bricolage and guerrilla research are important in our methodological palette.

The trajectory of the vision: Learning is accessible for everyone

At The Open University (OU), we aim to be open to all in our ethos for teaching, and we look for similar approaches in our research. This means seeking to engage groups who are currently underserved in education, such as refugees or people from low socio-economic backgrounds who may not traditionally

---

How to cite this book chapter:
Coughlan, T., Lister, K., Seale, J., Scanlon, E. and Weller, M. 2019. Accessible Inclusive Learning: Futures. In: Ferguson, R., Jones, A. and Scanlon, E. (eds). *Educational Visions: Lessons from 40 years of innovation*. Pp. 75–91. London: Ubiquity Press. DOI: https://doi.org/10.5334/bcg.e. License: CC-BY 4.0

access higher education. It also means we want to be open to engaging with people who have expertise and knowledge to offer, regardless of where or who they are. It means sharing and discussing our work through networks in ways that allow others to easily engage with it, or build on it (Weller, 2011).

We begin by considering how institutional practices and research can be enhanced or driven by global and local collaboration. We follow this by exploring how new approaches to data gathering and analysis are required to realise the practice and process based views of accessibility described in the previous chapter. We then explore how research can broaden its audience, and broaden its impact, by moving from particular audiences and bricolage towards mainstream use.

Working together through global and local networks

We have argued in the previous chapter that understanding and adapting to the specific contexts of individuals, and of particular populations, is essential to create accessible education. At the same time, the advantages of working together around the world, and creating an impact at scale through mutual interest and discussion, are particularly visible in this area.

Global collaboration has led to the Web Content Accessibility Guidelines (WCAG) that provide a common standard and criteria (W3C, 2018). The widespread application of this in education and elsewhere provides a means to promote and define expectations of accessibility that any website should be able to achieve.

The development of Open Educational Resources (OER) also benefited from collaboration from stakeholders around the world, (e.g. Cape Town Open Education Declaration, undated). It has provided a well-defined means for anyone to share educational content and courses which supports other educators or students to reuse and adapt these (Creative Commons, 2016). OER provides a great example of the power of working together over time in a loosely-coupled way. This means that institutions, projects and individuals have declared enough consensus on their aims, and developed and adopted shared principles and models, such as the use of Creative Commons licencing.

Because anyone can become involved in open education, and the collaborations can be loose or sporadic, it can be hard to understand what people are doing and the impact it is having. The OER World Map project tackles this issue and offers an example of working differently in the open, alongside insights into the way in which such a service can be designed to garner and sustain interest. The platform is designed to collect and visualise data on actors and activities in the open education space, providing a means to understand what initiatives, people and resources are available to engage with. While global in scope, it does not ignore local requirements. Tailored, country-specific maps can be produced, which provide insight that might be of specific interest to

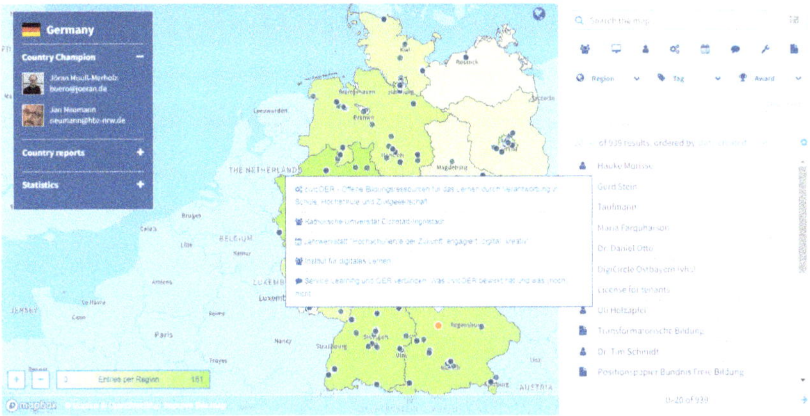

Figure 5.1: OER World Map – screenshot of Germany portal from https://open-educational-resources.de/karte/.

practitioners in a particular region. There is functionality to display 'Country Champions' who are members engaged with the project in a particular region. The project combines a bottom-up approach to engage end users to contribute, alongside work to develop worldwide partnerships and strategic alignment to priorities. As OER becomes a mainstream approach for education, the availability of information about resources and actors will become even more valuable (Neumann & Farrow, 2018).

In some contrast to the OER World Map, the Global OER Graduate Network (GO-GN) is focused on supporting the development of individual PhD researchers in a global context. Doctoral candidates are joined by experts, mentors, and interested parties to form a community of practice. The network uses online webinars and face-to-face meetings to raise the profile of research in open education, offer support to students conducting research in the area, and to develop openness as a process of research. Because of the relative novelty of OER research, expertise and support for a doctoral researcher at their own institution may be limited, and connecting with other students and experts offers potential for greater impact. Furthermore, the network can provide a community where openness in the process of research is valued (de los Arcos et al., 2016).

Networks such as GO-GN are not designed to be the exclusive 'home' of a researcher. People involved in GO-GN often belong to other networks and act as a bridge between these and GO-GN. For example, GO-GN has been an important further network for students who form part of the Leverhulme Trust funded Open World Learning (OWL) initiative. This initiative was devised to bring together diverse perspectives, with doctoral researchers coming to study at The Open University from all around the world (Institute of Educational Technology, 2018). Many of these projects explore inclusion in OER and MOOCs, including how MOOC learning varies by geo-cultural and socio-economic factors, with differences identified in how learners behave based on location and prior education (Ritzi et al., 2019); and how OER presented in English may not be suitable for those for whom English is a second language, with the potential for language simplification to tackle this (Rets et al., 2019).

A further model of global collaboration is found in the Ed-ICT network. This explores the role that ICTs can play in creating or removing disadvantages for students with disabilities in post-compulsory education. The approach taken here has been for themed workshops to be hosted in five different countries (Canada, Germany, Israel, UK, and USA). A core team formed from each country attends each event to create coherent understanding across the workshops, but local practitioners, researchers, and students play an essential role in each workshop by sharing their perspectives and developing ideas and knowledge that are grounded in the local context. This is a wider instantiation of the ethos argued for by the network partners in their own work, which highlights the importance of student voice in research and technology development (e.g. Fitchen et al., 2014; Seale et al., 2013).

The network brings to attention similarities and differences between the ways in which different countries approach accessibility and the factors that influence these, such as government and institutional responsibilities, or common models of practice. Links can be drawn between prior research conducted in different countries and student populations, alongside practice-based issues.

One example of this, which became the focus of an Ed-ICT workshop, is transitions. This can encompass situations such as the transition between school and post-compulsory education, transitions between different modules, institutions, or years of study, and transitions from study to employment. In each case, there are challenges for disabled students as the support mechanisms, strategies, and expectations placed upon them may change. The design of technology and technology-related support can be a pivotal factor within this (Burgstahler, 2003). Examples of challenges raised included the removal of assistive technology that was loaned or supplied by one organisation as the person transitions into the remit of another, or the incompatibility of workplace systems with the assistive technologies and strategies that the person has developed as a student.

Attention should be drawn to resolving these types of gaps that emerge as a person moves through a transition. At the same time, it was argued that it is essential to support the development of self-advocacy – an individual's skills and capacity to describe their requirements, and the confidence to know their right to reasonable adjustments to support them. The experiences of network members, and prior research, both highlight that developing a persons' capacity for self-advocacy plays a pivotal role in successful transition, because there is often no single consistent entity supporting them across the transition.

By bringing together students, practitioners and researchers, complex issues can be unpicked with discussion across stakeholders. One issue in which all voices are required to build understanding is the adoption or rejection of technologies by students. In many countries or institutions, resources are spent on making specific assistive technologies available for students and providing training for these. However, research by network members has found substantial disparities between the technologies that experts suggest are useful and those students consider useful (Fitchen et al., 2013). Other work by network members has explored related issues, such as how mainstream and specialist assistive technologies can both be useful in making learning accessible (Seale & Cooper, 2010). In the Ed-ICT approach, students presented their views of which technologies were useful to them and how they chose and used these. Practitioners, including those supporting disabled students in education and technology developers, expressed their perspectives on how they supported students, and researchers presented findings and provocations. The proceedings of these workshops then became a basis for balanced analysis and agenda-making for continued work that includes all these perspectives (Ed-ICT, 2017; Ed-ICT, 2018a, Ed-ICT, 2018b). Proposals for further research or practice-based innovations can emerge that combine the different potential, resources, and expertise of multiple local contexts.

Each of the approaches outlined in this section – The OER World Map, GO-GN, OWL, and the Ed-ICT Network – provides a different example approach to how collaboration can respond to the potential for both global and locally situated research. They each build on an awareness that local context matters in terms of the available support for accessing learning opportunities, and in the ways in which research can have an impact. They also harness the value of openness through global networks.

Harnessing data to understand barriers and improve support for learning

While the increase of interactions with technology creates the potential for ever more data to be collected and analysed, this does not necessarily lead to greater understanding of the needs of learners.

Prioritising openness and accessibility does present challenges to big data or analytical research approaches. For example, in the Bridge to Success initiative introduced in the previous chapter, it was noted that if we aim to create a situation in which anyone can access and use a course or resource in flexible ways, we cannot then put restrictions on them such as requiring them to fill in details about themselves. Neither can we necessarily gain access to institutional data about students in order to use this to contextualise and understand their learning (Pitt et al., 2013). In Bridge to Success, we worked closely with some partner colleges to evaluate the impact of introducing the OER into particular classes in their institutions, but in other scenarios, OER can be adopted and used with very little trace of this activity having occurred, or a sense of its impact on learners.

Equally, supporting the flexibility required for disabled learners can also challenge analytics approaches. For example, if a learner requires their learning materials in an alternative format, they may not produce data through their interactions with a Virtual Learning Environment (VLE) in the same way that other learners would. If a research method uses data on VLE interactions, such as measurements of student logins or page views, are students using alternative means of access and engagement represented in the data? These issues need attention for the benefit of both the students who engage through these means to ensure they are not excluded, but also for the validity of the research, which might otherwise inaccurately suggest a lack of engagement with the learning materials where actually these are being delivered by alternative means.

While these problems need to be considered, data-driven approaches, which are explored in Chapter 7, can also be used to understand the accessibility of courses, and to identify where potential problems might exist. Cooper et al. (2016) conducted an analysis using a large data set spanning five years of module-level data on student retention. By analysing the proportions of students with declared disabilities who completed each particular course or module, they could identify discrepancies where disabled students were performing more poorly than could be expected, using odds ratios of the likelihood of completing a module when compared with students who had not declared a disability.

Cooper et al. (2016) note that this approach only identifies modules where there may be accessibility problems. It does not tell us what the causes of these lower completion rates in these modules are. Therefore, they also explore the use of student feedback to augment the approach. Feedback is commonly collected from students on all modules through end of module surveys. If this contains free text responses, and if the responses within this data that relate to access issues can be isolated, this feedback offers a means to create improvements which follows the notion that accessibility should be considered as a process (Coughlan et al., 2017). For Cooper et al. (2016), their analysis of student survey feedback highlighted a different set of courses that may contain accessibility issues to the ones they identified through the comparison of completion rates. This suggests that multiple approaches to evaluating course accessibility are complementary rather than providing similar results.

A focus on one particular variable, such as whether or not a student has declared a disability, offers potential for insights such as those found for course accessibility by Cooper et al. (2016). However, students and the challenges they face are not one-dimensional. The concept of intersectionality – that multiple aspects of discrimination co-exist and interact – should also be considered in analytical strategies. By analysing multiple intersecting data points about a student (for example, gender, disability, socio-economic status and race), we can harness data to identify and explore the combined effects (Borden & Coates, 2017). Encouraging research and evaluation with an intersectional approach is now an explicit focus for the Office for Students, the body responsible for Higher education provision in the UK (Office for Students, 2019).

Noting that most prior research had focused only on one or two demographic variables, Rizvi et al. (2019) set out to analyse the relative effects of six demographic variables on the attainment (distinction, pass or fail) of students who had completed one of four OU courses. These variables comprised geographical region; socio-economic status via the Index of Multiple Deprivation (IMD) for the student's postcode; highest level of previous education; age, gender and disability. Using a Decision Tree analysis approach, they identify that the geographic and socio-economic factors had the largest impact of all these factors for these students. Analysis such as this is important to ensure a broad understanding of factors impacting on attainment.

End-of-module surveys and data collected through student behaviour and assessment are the current materials available for learning analytics, but there could be better methods for students to self-report their experiences in ways that provide further insights. Prompted by the desire to support disabled students to represent the challenges they faced and the impacts of these on their studies, the Our Journey tool (https://ourjourney.ac.uk/) has been developed with the participation of students and other stakeholders to provide a structured approach to capture the diverse journeys our students take (Coughlan et al., 2019a). By creating a series of 'cards' that represent important events for the student and their emotions at the time, combined with free text to further contextualise the event, we can create a different means of representing the student experience.

The representation of a journey taken over time helps to unpack the ways in which series of events and the development of the person combine in both the challenges and achievements of study, and the impacts other areas of life may have on study. Our Journey aims to capture the experience of each student, but we are exploring how this can be combined with other forms of analytics data and events. In this way, adding additional context and narrative that

Figure 5.2: Our Journey card creation interface.

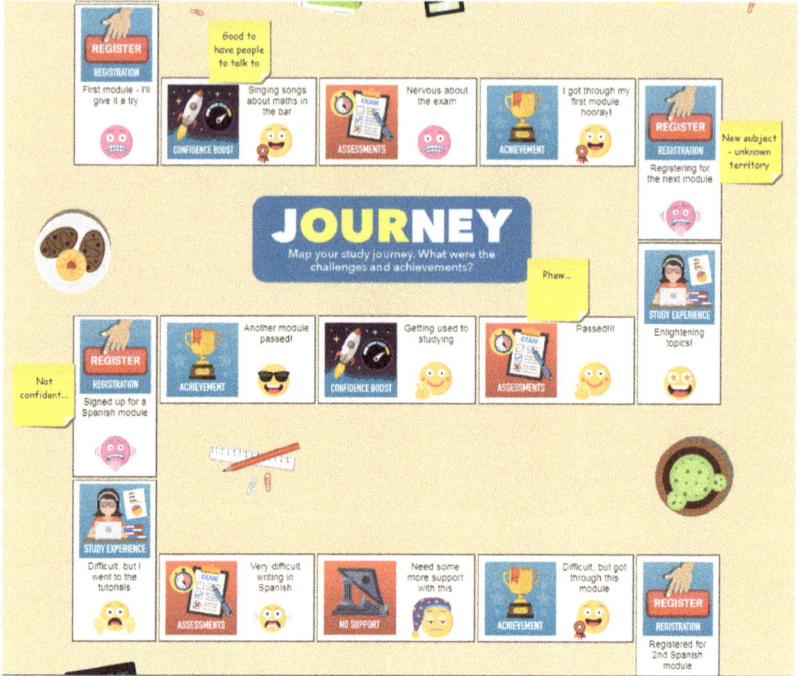

Figure 5.3: A student journey representation created in the Our Journey tool.

is structured by the student rather than the institution. Furthermore, unlike a survey, Our Journey is designed to be engaging and enjoyable for the student, with the potential to underpin reflective learning activities around study skills. Finally, options are being explored to integrate the tool, with prompts for guidance and support. We continue to iteratively refine the design, and to trial the tool in a variety of ways, in order to develop an evidence base and improvements.

Our Journey is being developed with continual input from students and staff, and was informed by our prior research around the challenges that disabled students face and the impacts of these (Coughlan & Lister, 2018). One particular area that was highlighted in this process was the importance of the emotional effects of events in the student journey. For example, that having to complete arduous administrative processes is a cause of stress and potential exacerbation of mental health challenges. As such, the application of Our Journey to understand student mental health and wellbeing is an important direction in our work. Because students report an emotion in relation to each event, and the patterns in this over time can be studied, the tool has the potential to uncover patterns and types of events around emotional wellbeing.

More broadly, there has been a wave of activity around student wellbeing and mental health in recent years. This has been prompted by data showing increased disclosure of mental health conditions, and high-profile cases of student suicide. As well as providing new understanding at scale of student mental health, analytics and other technologies could underpin preventative approaches that respond to students with relevant guidance and prompts to support (Jisc, 2019). However, the complexity of practically measuring or engaging with student mental health requires qualitative, co-produced approaches to the design of strategies (Piper & Emmanuel, 2018; Piper & Byrom, 2017).

Future advances in our capacity to understand our students and the challenges they face as they access education may depend on our ability to combine analytics drawn from university systems with the participation of students and other stakeholders to give context.

Innovation for inclusion benefits everyone

Rather than inhibiting innovation, a focus on inclusion is key to directing innovation towards human-centred outcomes that are useful for all people. By embedding accessibility from the start of the process, and by working in the open, we create greater opportunities for people to use and build on our work.

The 'Our Journey' tool described above provides a reminder of this. The project developed because we recognised a need for disabled students to be able to communicate the challenges they face, as well as a difficulty for educators, researchers and support staff to understand these challenges.

However, we now see that Our Journey could be useful for all students, and that the underlying concept has potential for a wide range of scenarios. This is because most students face some challenges and could benefit from representing and reflecting on these, as well as their successes. Equally, institutions lack rich understanding of their students in general, so could benefit by understanding the journeys of all their students. There is wider interest in applying the Our Journey concept even further from this starting point, by using the activity of creating a journey as a way to capture and learn from personal experiences in a range of different domains. The tool and graphics are openly licenced, which can simplify and enable adaptations of the tool to different types of activities and contexts.

This doesn't mean that the project has become detached from the original purpose – we maintain the involvement of disabled students and will still use the tool to create greater understanding of their experiences. But rather than suggesting that accessibility and inclusion constrain innovation, projects like Our Journey identify needs or goals by working with a particular population, and direct innovation towards it (Coughlan et al. 2019a). In doing so, it is often the case that the goal which is particularly apparent to this population is actually more widely applicable. By aiming for a mainstream audience, a tool that is inclusive by design is no longer a specialised solution. Instead we have empowered the underserved audience such that they are directing innovation in the mainstream.

It is argued in the Beyond Prototypes framework that "TEL involves complex systems of technologies and practices" (Scanlon et al., 2013, pg. 7). Because inclusive innovation projects are grounded in tackling real problems, they are usually open minded towards combinations of technological and practice-based solutions. For example, the 'Returning to STEM' Badged Open Course (BOC) was based on research that explored the challenges for women returning to STEM careers after an extended break (e.g. because of child care). The project identified strategies that had been successful for women returning to their careers. BOCs are a model for free courses designed to support independent study (Law, 2015). The 'Returning to STEM' BOC was created by drawing on the project research and through a partnership with Equate Scotland - an organisation that works towards the advancement of women in STEM careers. However, a key lesson learned was around the effectiveness of a blended learning approach, which combined the BOC with face-to-face workshops and individual meetings (Herman et al., 2019). While there is a tendency to focus on the online experience of OER, it can be at their most useful when combined with face-to-face teaching and support. As Cannell and Macintyre (2017) argue, partnerships that provide for physical, face-to-face activities to introduce learners to OER and build confidence are important because there is a danger that if we only make online learning opportunities, we are likely to reinforce digital and educational divides.

Where technological advances are developed to improve inclusion, these often go on to underpin mainstream advances. Captions and transcripts for online videos provide a useful example. Back when online learning was still relatively new, Colwell et al. (2005) described the development and evaluation of a video player to identify requirements for deaf students. This supported existing transcripts to be displayed alongside the relevant video, and for software-generated transcripts to be produced where there was no transcript available. We now find that many students benefit from such transcripts in situations where they cannot easily listen to audio or prefer to read (e.g. reported in Coughlan et al. 2013). More broadly, the technologies that developed for speech to text (speech recognition), and text to speech (screen readers) as an essential component of assistive technologies now find both in pervasive use in mainstream technologies from smart speakers such as Amazon Echo, smartphone-based assistants such as Apple's Siri, and in automated telephone answering services.

The value of innovation also flows in the opposite direction, with mainstream technologies having the potential for specialist assistive uses. If properly harnessed, virtual assistants, smart home devices, and other Internet of Things technologies can be beneficial for inclusion. Technology companies, such as Microsoft, now recognise that Artificial Intelligence (AI), combined with pervasive mobile computing, has many potential applications to accessibility (Microsoft, 2019). An example of this is the 'Seeing AI' app, which provides visual recognition of objects and reading of text in the environment using a smartphone camera (Microsoft, 2018). By focusing on the development of an innovation that supports blind or low vision people, they provide a grounded and important challenge for the underlying technology to be applied to. There is, however, a perennial concern that if these new technologies are not designed with consideration of accessibility, they may instead exclude by design. The development of standards through global networks is again important here (Abou-Zahra et al., 2017).

While some AI innovations will be specialist assistive technologies, the integration of accessibility with mainstream technologies means that people are not segregated or left out of activities. Live automated captioning of lectures or other presentations is being integrated into mainstream presentation software such as Microsoft Powerpoint. It seems likely that more teachers will use this technology than if a specialist tool needed to be purchases and installed. The Android Live Transcribe app offers immediate speech to text conversion as a means for deaf or hard of hearing learners to communicate as equals with peers in collaborative activities, just using a standard smartphone (Android, 2019).

Taking this idea further, AI is being applied to overcome communication barriers of all kinds for all people, automatically translating audio and text between any language that is spoken, including sign languages (Ahmed et al., 2018; Wolfe et al., 2016). We are at the point where it is possible to translate, for example, British Sign Language into written Spanish and vice versa. To achieve this, sensors to convert gesture into data, text to speech, translation services, speech to text, and virtual reality technologies to enact a signing avatar would be used in concert. As these various technologies mature, the potential to create online learning that is more global and inclusive of all groups becomes a realistic and exciting prospect.

Some people may expect innovation to work best when unconstrained by the hassle of having to produce results that work for everyone. But meaningful innovation should identify and work to tackle real issues. In our current research, we are working with Microsoft to explore how an AI-based assistant could support people through the processes of communicating about their disabilities and getting effective support in study and everyday life. Research grounded in the participation of students identified these issues (Coughlan & Lister, 2018), and now provides an inspiration for us as we explore how to harness and innovate with these technologies.

Having argued that the results of inclusive innovation projects are likely to be useful to wider audiences, we want these to be adaptable and easily available to others to use. This leads us back to importance of an open approach. The tool and graphics are openly licenced, and our discussions about adapting the tool to different types of activities and contexts are made easier because of this.

Taking advantage of opportunities: bricolage and guerrilla research

In the previous chapter, we described persistent strands of research in the areas of virtual laboratories and remote access to fieldwork. These pushed the possibilities of technology at the time, and there was value in conducting these experiments to produce a close approximation of what would become more achievable in time. Taking available opportunities to use cutting edge technologies in new ways allowed for the investigation of pedagogical possibilities, in advance of these becoming a mainstream reality. We use what is available now to create and learn things that should be important later.

Taking these opportunities as they arise is important to the bricolage approach. As Scanlon et al. (2013) put it, bricolage 'involves bringing together and adapting technologies and pedagogies, experimentation to generate further insights, and a willingness to engage with local communities and practices.' (pg. 7). Key features of the approach are that a project may start by reviewing what tools and resources are available and how they could be innovatively used; and that the use of theory to underpin research is balanced with engaging communities and grounding innovation in practice. Attention is paid to the constraints of a situation and how these can be overcome or compensated for.

Bricolage can be particularly pertinent to work around inclusion because of the pressing need to address and have an impact on real problems faced by people. Also, exclusion often occurs through restrictions and constraints within particular situations, so attending to these is often an effective starting point and continued interest for any project.

We also see the value of bricolage in the more recent IncSTEM project (Embedding and Sustaining Inclusive Practices in STEM). This built on and scaled up existing examples of inclusive practice in STEM at a range of levels, including teaching activities, institution-wide systems and policy and sector-wide accrediting bodies (Pearson et al, 2019). In order to do this, IncSTEM has sought the voices and involvement of staff and student stakeholders from across the university and the sector, adopting a diverse range of methodologies and a collaborative approach (McPherson et al, 2019). The aim here is to systematically take opportunities to review, refine, and spread innovations for which there is evidence that they could make a difference to inclusion.

The potential of open approaches to support and help to spread innovations widely in education is commonly alluded to, but as noted in the Beyond Prototypes framework, such processes need to be viewed longitudinally, which is problematic when projects are only funded for short periods. In a retrospective analysis of Bridge to Success, which returned to interview stakeholders in the three years following the completion of the project (Coughlan et al. 2019b). Through this we found instances where the introduction of the OER to new audiences led to wider change, such as embracing the idea of providing free and openly licenced materials for all students studying with the institution, rather than expensive proprietary texts. Equally, enthusiasm for OER by individuals could be tempered over time by a lack of organisational buy-in, and the withdrawal of the support that the project funding could enable. We must conclude that sustainability is an essential focus that can be hampered by the project and innovation focused world of TEL research. Once again a persistent intent in an area means that successive projects build on each other.

The concept of bricolage can also help us to understand how an open resource can become a basis for innovation. In the case of Bridge to Success, the original course materials, such as 'Starting with Maths', were designed to support learners new to higher education with support from a tutor. Years after their original production, these course materials were openly-licenced and remixed for self-directed use, predominantly for a US audience. This created 'Succeed with Math'. Additional elements such as quizzes were added which supported independent use of the materials, and further revisions of these resulted in 'Succeed with Maths' Parts 1 and 2. These were some of the first set of Badged Open Courses (BOCs) referred to earlier. This potential for reuse and remixing of tried and tested educational content in new contexts helped to make innovation a reality (Coughlan et al. 2019b).

If we consider what openness offers as part of an approach to bricolage, there is also a sense of supporting opportunities to arise and taking advantage of the increasing resources that are freely available to use. Valuable research projects can be constructed using open data, open source tools, platforms and people who can engage, or openly-licenced materials.

Arguing for the value of harnessing this, Weller (2014) describes the notion of 'guerrilla research', as an alternative to the common template of an academic research project. The key notion is that in many situations where we identify a research question, there are open resources that provide opportunities to do interesting research right away, for ourselves, and without extensive costs and planning. Guerrilla research can have the following characteristics:

- It can be done by one or two researchers and does not require a team.
- It relies on existing open data, information and tools.
- It is fairly quick to realise.
- It is often disseminated via blogs and social media.
- It doesn't require permission.

These characteristics can be seen in initiatives to harness open data as a means to social change. A nice example of this has been the School of Data initiative, which has created structures to enable small and large projects around the world that develop data literacy among journalists and NGOs, and lead to practical results by exploring and creating publicly available data (School of Data, 2019).

While longer term plans and funding are important for many research projects, these may become barriers that prevent progress being made in the development of knowledge. One of the great things highlighted by this approach is the way in which it promotes the notion that anyone can conduct research at any time, we just need an idea or question that matters to get us started.

Conclusions

Continual change in technology and in education mean that inclusion requires constant re-evaluation and discussion. In this chapter we have explored some of the practices and trends that are important to the present and future of our work in accessibility, openness and inclusion.

We have highlighted how global networks can support sharing of research and practice and work towards shared goals. In the modern age these networks are always likely to have a digital foundation, and these networks can embody and exemplify how open practices enable wider participation and inclusivity. However, these networks should still be designed to account for individual and local matters. Networks based around principles of openness and inclusion have created global standards, but they also help localised activities gain traction, and provide individual researchers with homes and communities that benefit their research and enhance the impact of it.

From the early foundations, data analysis has been used to identify gaps in participation, completion and attainment for particular groups. More recently, the trajectory of innovation in data gathering and analysis has been to embrace complexity by looking at wider ranges of variables and intersections between these, and to develop means to capture and analyse events in the student journey and their impacts over time. These analyses often lead to more questions, and there is still much that we do not know about the mechanisms of exclusion. But we are embracing new opportunities, including more data captured from learners interacting with online learning environments, data at scale from new platforms for open education, and new learning analytics tools and techniques.

We are also finding that our work to address audiences with particular needs leads to wider impact. There is increasing recognition that harnessing technologies such as AI to address problems identified by working with a minority group is an important means to create mainstream innovations. Rather than considering these outcomes as incidental, we can argue that inclusive research and innovation should be the norm. This is achieved by opening up our projects to participation at all stages, and making sure that the outputs of these are available to others to innovate with through their own bricolage and guerrilla research.

References

Abou-Zahra, S., Brewer, J., and Cooper, M. (2017). Web Standards to Enable an Accessible and Inclusive Internet of Things (IoT). *Proceedings of the 14th Web for All Conference on the Future of Accessible Work*. ACM.

Ahmed, M. A., Zaidan, B. B., Zaidan, A. A., Salih, M. M., & Lakulu, M. M. B. (2018). A review on systems-based sensory gloves for sign language recognition state of the art between 2007 and 2017. Sensors, 18(7), 2208.

Android, (2019). Live Transcribe, retrieved from https://www.android.com/accessibility/live-transcribe/

Borden, V. M., & Coates, H. (2017). Learning analytics as a counterpart to surveys of student experience. New Directions for Higher Education, 2017(179), 89–102.

Burgstahler, S. (2003). The role of technology in preparing youth with disabilities for postsecondary education and employment. *Journal of Special Education Technology*, 18(4), 7–19.

Cannell, P., & Macintyre, R. (2017). Free open online resources in workplace and community settings–a case study on overcoming barriers. *Widening Participation and Lifelong Learning*, 19(1), 111–122.

Cape Town Open Education Declaration (undated), retrieved from https://www.capetowndeclaration.org/

Colwell, C., Jelfs, A., & Mallett, E. (2005). Initial requirements of deaf students for video: lessons learned from an evaluation of a digital video application. *Learning, Media and Technology*, 30(2), 201–217.

Cooper, M., Ferguson, R., & Wolff, A. (2016). What can analytics contribute to accessibility in e-learning systems and to disabled students' learning? In *Proceedings of the Sixth International Conference on Learning Analytics & Knowledge* (pp. 99–103). ACM.

Coughlan, T., Lister, K. & Freear, N. (2019a). Our Journey: Designing and utilising a tool to support students to represent their study journeys, *Proceedings of 13th annual International Technology, Education and Development Conference (INTED) 2019*. IATED.

Coughlan, T., Pitt, R., & Farrow, R. (2019b). Forms of innovation inspired by open educational resources: a post-project analysis. *Open Learning: The Journal of Open, Distance and e-Learning*. Taylor & Francis.

Coughlan, T. and Lister, K. (2018). The accessibility of administrative processes: Assessing the impacts on students in higher education. *Proceedings of the 15th International Cross-Disciplinary Conference on Web Accessibility (Web4All 2018)*, ACM.

Coughlan, T., Ullmann, T. D., & Lister, K. (2017). Understanding Accessibility as a Process through the Analysis of Feedback from Disabled Students. In *Proceedings of the 14th Web for All Conference on The Future of Accessible Work*. ACM.

Coughlan, T., Pitt, R., & McAndrew, P. (2013). Building open bridges: collaborative remixing and reuse of open educational resources across organisations. In *Proceedings of the SIGCHI Conference on Human Factors in Computing Systems*. 991–1000. ACM.

Creative Commons (2016). What is OER? Retrieved from https://wiki.creativecommons.org/wiki/What_is_OER%3F

de los Arcos, B., Farrow, R., Weller, M., & Pitt, R. (2016). Global OER Graduate Network: Raising the Profile of Research into Open Education. In The Online, Open and Flexible Higher Education Conference. 554–557

Ed-ICT (2017). Proceedings of the Ed-ICT International Network Symposium One: Effective Models, Frameworks, and Approaches. Retrieved from http://ed-ict.com/wp-content/uploads/2017/06/Symposium-Effective_models_frameworks_and_approaches_0.pdf

Ed-ICT (2018a). Proceedings of the Ed-ICT International Network Montreal Symposium: Stakeholder Perspectives. Retrieved from http://ed-ict.com/wp-content/uploads/2018/01/ConferenceProceedingsEdICTMontreal.pdf

Ed-ICT (2018b). Proceedings of the Ed-ICT International Network Israel Symposium: In Search of New Designs http://ed-ict.com/wp-content/uploads/2018/09/ProceedingsEd-ICTIsraelSymposium.pdf

Fichten, C. S., Asuncion, J., & Scapin, R. (2014). Digital technology, learning, and postsecondary students with disabilities: Where we've been and where we're going. Journal of Postsecondary Education and Disability, 27(4), 369–379.

Fichten, C. S., Nguyen, M. N., King, L., Barile, M., Havel, A., Mimouni, Z., Chauvin, A., Budd, J., Raymond, O., Juhel, J.C., & Asuncion, J. (2013). Information and communication technology profiles of college students with learning disabilities and adequate and very poor readers. *Journal of Education and Learning*, 2(1), 176.

Herman, Clem; Gracia, Rosaria; MacNiven, Lesley; Clark, Bernie and Doyle, Geraldine (2019). Using a Blended Learning Approach to support Women returning to STEM. *Open Learning: The Journal of Open, Distance and e-Learning*, 34(1) pp. 40–60.

Institute of Educational Technology (2018). OWL, retrieved from https://iet.open.ac.uk/projects/owl

Jisc, (2019). The mental health and wellbeing challenge in FE and HE, in *Horizons report on emerging technologies and education*, 37–47. Retrieved from http://repository.jisc.ac.uk/7284/1/horizons-report-spring-2019.pdf

Law, P. (2015). Digital badging at The Open University: recognition for informal learning. *Open Learning: The Journal of Open, Distance and e-Learning*, 30(3), 221–234.

McPherson, E., Lister, K., Pearson, V., Colwell, C., Gallen, A. & Collins, T., (2019). Embedding and sustaining inclusive practice in STEM, *Journal of Interactive Media in Education*.

Microsoft (2018). Seeing AI, retrieved from https://www.microsoft.com/en-us/seeing-ai

Microsoft (2019). AI for Accessibility: Featured Projects, retrieved from https://www.microsoft.com/en-us/ai/ai-for-accessibility-projects?activetab=pivot1%3aprimaryr2

Neumann, J. & Farrow, R. (2018). The OER World Map: Suddenly grown up – and now? In: *Proceedings of OE Global 2018*.

Office for Students (2019). Equality and Diversity: What do we mean by taking an intersectional approach?. Retrieved from https://www.officeforstudents.org.uk/about/equality-and-diversity/equality-and-students/

Pearson, V., Lister, K., McPherson, E., Gallen, A. M., Davies, G., Colwell, C., Bradshaw, K., Braithwaite, N., & Collins, T. (2019). Embedding and Sustaining Inclusive Practice to Support Disabled Students in Online and Blended Learning. *Journal of Interactive Media in Education.*

Piper, R. & Emmanuel, T. (2018). Co-producing mental health strategies with students: A Guide for the Higher Education Sector, Student Minds. Retrieved from https://www.studentminds.org.uk/co-productionguide.html

Piper, R. and Byrom, N. (2017). Student Voices Report. [Online] Student Minds. Retrieved from http://www.studentminds.org.uk/uploads/3/7/8/4/3784584/170901_student_voices_report_final.pdf

Pitt, R., Ebrahimi, N., McAndrew, P., & Coughlan, T. (2013). Assessing OER Impact across Organisations and Learners: Experiences from the Bridge to Success Project. *Journal of Interactive Media in Education.*

Rets, I., Coughlan, T., Stickler, U. & Astruc, L., (2019). Accessibility of Open Educational Resources: how well are they suited for non-native English readers? *Under review.*

Rizvi, S., Rienties, B., and Khoja, S. A., (2019). The role of demographics in online learning; A decision tree based approach. *Computers & Education,* (137) 32–47.

Scanlon, E., Sharples, M., Fenton-O'Creevy, M., Fleck, J., Cooban, C., Ferguson, R., Cross, S., and Waterhouse, P., (2013). Beyond prototypes: Enabling innovation in technology-enhanced learning. Open University, Milton Keynes.

School of Data (2019). Official website retrieved from https://schoolofdata.org/

Seale, J. K., Nind, M., & Parsons, S. (2014). Inclusive research in education: Contributions to method and debate. *International Journal of Research & Method in Education,* 37(4), 347–356.

Seale, J., & Cooper, M. (2010). E-learning and accessibility: An exploration of the potential role of generic pedagogical tools. *Computers & Education,* 54(4), 1107–1116.

W3C, (2018). Web Content Accessibility Guidelines (WCAG) Overview https://www.w3.org/WAI/standards-guidelines/wcag/

Weller, M. (2014). The Battle for Open: How openness won and why it doesn't feel like victory, London, Ubiquity Press.

Weller, M. (2011). The digital scholar: How technology is transforming scholarly practice. Bloomsbury Academic. London: UK.

Wolfe, R., Efthimiou, E., Glauert, J., Hanke, T., McDonald. J., and Schnepp, J. (2016). Special issue: recent advances in sign language translation and avatar technology, *Universal Access in the Information Society* 15 (4).

CHAPTER 6

Evidence-Based Learning: Foundations

Ann Jones, Bart Rienties and Canan Blake

This chapter discusses some of the Computers and Learning (CAL) research group's early work, focusing on our attempts to understand learners' practices so that teaching could be adapted to meet learners' needs. The chapter describes and discusses examples of CALRG research from the group's early days to the start of the 2000s. One reason for doing this is to explore the extent to which there has been continuity in the group's work over time. In the chapter we argue that the group's motivation, aims, ethos and overall approach have remained similar during its forty-year existence. The chapter draws on the Beyond Prototypes framework, described in Chapter 1 of this book, to frame some of the discussion, in particular focusing on policy and environment. Analysis of the case studies that led to the development of the framework suggest that Technology Enhanced Learning (TEL) needs to be understood as a 'complex', made up of a series of elements that need to be considered together. The chapter also uses the three themes of the group's first conference to provide an organising framework for the discussion. The three themes from that first conference are firstly, models of learning; secondly, methods for studying learning and thirdly, institutional research.

Introduction

As will be highlighted below, much early CALRG research was experimental, and ground-breaking at the time. While many students are now used to working

---

How to cite this book chapter:
Jones, A., Rienties, B. and Blake, C. 2019. Evidence-Based Learning: Foundations. In: Ferguson, R., Jones, A. and Scanlon, E. (eds). *Educational Visions: Lessons from 40 years of innovation.* Pp. 93–108. London: Ubiquity Press. DOI: https://doi. org/10.5334/bcg.f. License: CC-BY 4.0

with computers, smart-phones, and tablets, and may have only lived in an era where CAL was always around, it may be useful to remind the reader that 40 years ago most students did not have access to computers, let alone the Internet. For example, only 13% of households in the UK in 1985 had a home computer, and only in 2002 did a majority of households have at least one home computer (Office for National Statistics (UK), 2019) Similarly in an age of ubiquitous connection to the Internet, it seems hard to remember a time when people were not connected. In fact, in 1998 only 9% of UK households had access to the Internet, mostly using a slow telephone modem for those who remember. Only in 2005 did more than half of UK households actually have online access, which is nearly 25 years after CALRG was established. Therefore, some of the case-studies discussed will need to be interpreted in their historical context.

This chapter will discuss some of the research group's work, focusing on our attempts to adapt teaching to meet learners' needs. This will serve to illustrate and document some of the research that has taken place from 1979 to the 2000s. It will also support our argument for continuity in the group's work over time: that the motivation, aims, ethos and overall approach of the group during its forty-year existence have remained similar across the years. In discussing the work, we will draw on three aspects of the Beyond Prototypes framework (policy, environment and funding), and will also refer to the three themes of the group's first conference to provide one organising framework for the discussion. These three themes are firstly, models of learning; secondly, methods for studying learning; and thirdly, institutional research. The Beyond Prototypes framework developed by Scanlon et al. (2013), has been described in the first chapter of this book. The case studies that led to the development of the framework suggest that Technology Enhanced Learning needs to be understood as a 'complex', made up of a series of elements that need to be considered together, as represented in Figure 1 (Scanlon et. al., op. cit.) and reproduced in Chapter 1. In this chapter we will illustrate how the elements of the complex have been applied by the CALRG in our research into our students' learning and trying to meet their needs.

Models of Learning: a cognitive science approach to understanding the learner

As noted in the introductory chapter, during its first decade much of the CAL-RG's work was in the area of cognitive science. There was a strong interest in applying this to the OU context through considering how instruction could be designed to help improve student performance, so the relationship with teaching was strong. Alongside this was an interest in theory development, e.g. understanding how problem solving skills were developed. And again as described in the introductory chapter, one focus was on developing understanding of learners' practices through collecting student protocol data.

One example of this approach is Jones's doctoral research on novices learning programming (Jones, 1993). Four different programming languages in use at the OU were investigated, including high level and low-level programming languages. The first example is of learning SOLO: an AI programming language designed by Eistenstadt (1982, 1983), to introduce Open University cognitive psychology students to Artificial Intelligence as a tool for modelling human cognition. The aim was to make it easy for the user to get the system to do what they wanted it to without getting tangled up in trivial spelling and syntactic errors. SOLO was designed so that such unproductive errors could be trapped thus optimising productive interaction. The main component of SOLO is a language for manipulating a relational data-base, containing facilities for inserting descriptions into the database and for pattern matching against descriptions already in the database.

Eisenstadt (1982) explains the motivation behind SOLO in greater detail and also the project that included a "six year period of design, implementation, testing, and iterative re-design of a programming language, user-aids, and curriculum materials for use by Psychology students learning how to write simple computer programs" (Eistenstadt, 1982, p.1).

Thirteen participants took part in the SOLO case study, all of whom were studying the cognitive psychology course and had agreed to come into the OU psychology laboratory when they reached the part of the course where they were starting to learn SOLO.

The participants in the OU laboratory worked through the instructional materials in the SOLO book. They sat in a room on their own to work and were recorded talking aloud about what they were doing – the researcher would go in from time to time and ask how they were getting on. The task that students were engaged in was working through the instruction book and they reached the first activity that required them to produce some code, the so-called ASSESS problem. This problem was described in the course booklet as follows:

> *"Define your own procedure called ASSESS which prints out UNHEALTHY if someone (the node to which it is applied) either drinks whisky, on the one hand; or else if that person **both** smokes cigarettes and drinks beer. Using the NOTE procedure, add some descriptions of your own to SOLO's database, and try out your ASSESS procedure to get it working properly. You must decide for yourself how you are going to represent "drinks whisky" etc. in the database."* (Eisenstadt, 1983, p56.)

Some further context will be helpful to make sense of the protocol data. The SOLO primer which participants worked through provides two particular examples to illustrate how flow of control works in SOLO which is described in a section entitled 'Sequencing of programs'. (Eisenstadt, 1983, p.54). These examples are referred to as the 'weakassess' and 'strongassess' procedures.

So what I did was to combine the weakassess and strictassess type programs here, so, here we've got line 10 if drinks whisky, print unhealthy and exit. If absent continue. ...
That's the weakassess model.
The next two takes part of the strictassess model, so...: somebody has to smoke cigarettes and drink beer to be deemed unhealthy, so therefore line 20, check somebody smokes cigarettes if absent print healthy
I didn't know if it was right to do healthy and unhealthy, - it doesn't specify that.
So, if present continue and it goes to line 30, check drinks beer, if present print unhealthy because by definition if it's got to drinks beer it's had to have been smoking cigarettes as well. If absent continue and then at line 40 print healthy.

Figure 6.1: an example of protocol data from one of the students, Jane.

These examples are referred to by Jane, one of the participants, as she works on defining the ASSESS problem. Figure 6.1 shows part of Jane's explanation of working on the ASSESS procedure. She drew on examples in the book – e.g. referring to the 'weakassess model' here, and indeed she worked it out correctly.

Other students had more difficulties. These were particularly apparent when they were studied learning a different kind of programming language – an assembler language. This is a level of programming languages where there is a strong correspondence between the program's statements and the architecture's machine code instructions.

This study by Jones (1993) indicated the importance of data which provided information about how students interacted with and acted on the text, and the extent to which the design of instructional materials supported their learning. For some of the analysis programs were approached and viewed as a collection of plans, and this helped to identify the extent to which learners identified (or did not) and used (or did not) appropriate plans. For a researcher and teacher to observe directly how students react to materials that have been written, or technologies that have been developed is a very powerful experience.

A different, later approach to observing learners' behaviour and interactions with computers was the establishment of the data capture suite, many years later when more sophisticated technology could be deployed but with a similar aim. This was to observe and capture detailed learner interactions with media – although by this time the CALRG group was focussing on students' interactions with computers rather than text. One report is by Blake and Scanlon (2003) who used video data to analyse collaborative learning in what became known as the 'data capture suite'.

Learning design has developed considerably since the early work. The next chapter charts the development of the OU learning design initiative and discusses current research into the relationship between learning design, student behaviour, satisfaction, and performance. However, like the early work, there is still an emphasis on detailed information about student interactions with course materials.

In undertaking the observation work carried out in the data capture suite, Blake and Scanlon's overall enterprise was to the investigate *"the usefulness of technology-mediated collaborative problem-solving as part of an ongoing research programme."* (Blake and Scanlon, 2003, op. cit., p5.) For this series of studies, the emphasis had shifted away a little from The Open University's students, although the authors note how the work is associated *"with a desire to improve the experience of learning for our students"*, Blake and Scanlon, 2003, p.5. They also refer to their use of the CIAO! Framework, developed within the CALRG for evaluating CAL, and how it draws on a variety of sources, using both qualitative and quantitative approaches (Jones et al., 1999). In evaluating student use of computers, particularly collaborative learning, they argued for the need to observe students interacting with the educational innovation, and also note Issroff's holistic approach (Issroff, 1995) which in addition to recording interactions emphasises the importance of affective measures. Issroff et al., (1994) analysed students' collaborations over a number of sessions and the results showed developments over time. In their overview of this work Blake and Scanlon (op. cit., 2003, p.6) advocated the use of video data: *"Examining the interactions that students have with computers and with each other requires observational data, preferably supported by video data"*.
They note that the advantages of such an approach include:

- Its relative objectivity.
- That analysis can be carried out collaboratively by more than one researcher.
- Its use for either or both qualitative and quantitative data.
- That considerable amounts of data can be stored and analysed relatively easily by video-analysis software.

The data capture suite was developed to enable video capture of interactions and combined video data records of each participant with a synchronous record of their computer screen.

This approach was used to investigate a range of problem solving and learning tasks including: teenagers learning the laws of momentum (Whitelock and Scanlon, 1996), children learning about the phases of the moon (Whitelock et al., 1996); adults learning applied maths (Smith et al., 1989), and healthcare professionals using CoMET (Concept Modelling Environment for Teachers) to investigate the educational potential of a concept-based toolkit (Alpay and Giffen, 1998).

One study (Scanlon et al., (2000) investigated the problem-solving behaviour of pairs of adults working on a statistical problem. As in the earlier studies, protocol data was gathered, but additional video data made it possible to observe the subjects' non-verbal gestures. The video provided evidence about the degree of certainty with which the participants put forward their suggestions or solutions to each other and also recorded their reactions to their partner's suggestions. In comparison, a verbal protocol does not always contain clues about these behaviours. This example is part of a larger database with which the group explored the value of videoconferencing and eye contact during remote problem-solving. The study established that pairs who communicated with video which enabled eye-contact were more successful in their problem solving.

Later work, often led by CALRG research students, included an investigation of how newer technologies (newer at that time) might be employed for identifying learners' attention, recording real-time writing and sketching, and analysing multiple data feeds in an integrated way (San Diego et al., 2012). This was a study of learners' interactions with multiple representations to illustrate the advantages and disadvantages of digital approaches to collecting, coordinating and analysing observational data. In these investigations detailed gaze videos were obtained and were able to indicate the paths as well as 'fixations'. This allows researchers to study participants' attention in detail and how it changes over time (see San Diego and Aczel, 2007).

Other research used protocol analysis again combined with a more quantitative approach as a way of observing students using software via the internet (Hosein et al., 2007), thus providing remote observation. In this approach, students used a remote application facility on their own computer to connect to the researcher's computer: they were then able to interact with this computer and use software on it. Audio and video data, mouse clicks and keyboard entry were captured. A quasi-experimental design was used for collecting mainly quantitative data but by adding on talk-aloud strategies, interviews and videoing, qualitative data was also collected. As the researchers noted, this approach to understanding students' use of software for problem solving is not limited to studying students in a particular setting but to any student connected to the Internet in an environment where rich qualitative and quantitative data can be collected.

These studies, where there is an emphasis on the detailed analysis of interaction among learners, can be seen as having a learning analytics focus, although that field had yet to emerge.

Evaluating CAL programs: institutional research

Collecting protocol data was one method for studying student learning, which as noted above, was used over a long period of time. Other approaches were taken in the evaluation work that the CALRG conducted, and this is discussed in this section.

Early evaluation work in the CALRG was on understanding student use of particular CAL programs including CICERO, (Jones and O'Shea, 1982); Works Metallurgist, (Blake et al., 1996); MERLIN, CALCHEM and EVOLVE (Scanlon et. al., 1982). These CAL offerings were developed in response to student needs or challenges. For example, the CICERO CAL tutorials were a way of providing diagnostic feedback and additional help to students. The aim was to understand student behaviour and improve teaching. It is important to note that as courses were often in place for eight years or more, and the main component was printed text, it was not possible to make changes to the text following student feedback. However, it *was* possible to make changes to the CAL programs.

The evaluations aimed to understand the extent to which students used such CAL; benefits and challenges; how they used them and how the programs might be improved. Two case studies will illustrate the CAL evaluation studies, the first one conducted was the CICERO evaluation (Jones & O'Shea, 1982). After each case study summarising the research we will offer some brief reflections.

Case study 1: Tutorial CAL in the early 1980s

The first study focused on tutorial CAL: (Jones & O'Shea, 1981; 1982). The main aim of these programs was to provide diagnostic feedback, remedial help, and revision aid. The particular tutorial CAL program evaluated in this study was called CICERO, and first used on a psychology course in the Educational Studies faculty: "Personality and Learning", in 1977. Note that this was *before* the establishment of the CAL research group – and was one of the first, if not the first, evaluation studies carried out by the CALRG – motivated by a desire to understand more about student use, or lack of use, of CICERO.

CICERO was available at study centres across the four nations (where tutorials were held), and there was a less interactive postal version too. Study centres were not open all the time, so students needed to check that they would be open, and once there they would be using the tutorial via a terminal.

For each tutorial, diagnostic questions relating to a specific block of the course were sent to students to answer at home; the answers provided information about students' conceptual strengths and weaknesses related to the specific objectives of the block and course. These answers were taken to the study centre, the program accessed, and the answers typed in. Further questions might then be asked and according to the answers, advice and remedial help would be given. A 'postal' version was also available providing advice based on the students' performance on the diagnostic questions. The student would receive a printout a few days after posting the answer form.

Use of the system on three courses was rather low and dropped during the course of the academic year, so it was decided to evaluate the use on one course – the interdisciplinary course Biological Bases of Behaviour where 4 CICERO tutorials replaced 4 computer marked assignments. The study aimed to find out why students used or failed to use the tutorials and their beliefs about the educational benefits and practicalities. As the tutorials were optional, introduced no new material, and covered only a selected part of the course, there was no attempt to establish their educational effectiveness. The methods used consisted of an initial questionnaire; a questionnaire built into interactive tutorials and sent with postal tutorials; interviews with students and staff at summer school; final questionnaire to follow up answers to earlier open-ended questions and tutor questionnaires. Usage figures from the computing service records were also available.

Once students could access the tutorials the majority were satisfied and found they met their expectations, but the number of users fell rapidly throughout the year. What put students off? We found (as in many OU studies): an instrumental approach to this optional study; a fear of secret assessment; fear of using computers and embarrassment at the possibility of making mistakes in front of other students. Hence we asked about these issues in the final questionnaires and 22% (out of 100) reported 'bad computer experiences'. The most prevalent bad experience was difficulty in access; of these the most frequently reported were logging in difficulties; 12% (of 543) reported they were nervous of using the terminals and 13% (again out of 543) talked about embarrassment. Only a small percentage (16%) intended to definitely use CICERO again – the main obstacle was travelling and using it at the study centre. We ended up with a Chinese box of barriers, where each access issue is framed within the next: access to terminal (layer 1); access to program (2); quality of program and integration with the course. So students needed to negotiate a number of barriers, or layers, before engaging with the course tutorial itself. We noted that the real breakthrough would be in providing home access, and indeed the personal computing policy, described next, was set up many years later to provide such access.

Reflections on case study 1

Looking back at this study across nearly forty years, five elements struck us. Firstly, at a time when nearly all the focus of educational technology was on cognitive factors, affective issues were noted – students were concerned about secret assessment; fear of using computers and embarrassment at the possibility of making mistakes in front of other students. Secondly, in terms of 'analytics', although no sophisticated records of use were available we did have usage figures available from the computing service records. Thirdly, the barriers were such that many students did not use the tutorial CAL – or they did not persist in using it – hence there was little feedback that fed back into the design of the programme. Fourthly, the approach taken in tutorial CAL (diagnostic multiple-choice questions) was a forerunner of computer-based assessment that developed significantly later especially in the science faculty. Finally, in an elementary way we were able to include some built-in evaluation (e.g.the questionnaire at the end of the tutorial). The next section describes the university's response to the barriers to access that were found in this and in many other CAL evaluations: the personal computing policy.

The home computing policy evaluation project

As noted in case study 1, there were difficulties with accessing computers from study centres. Even so, use of the terminal access system expanded throughout the 1970s. It should be noted that most of the use was by students for whom access was a requirement. For example, from 1970, students on the mathematical foundation course were required to spend around five hours online to the mainframe computer. During that period, similar students in traditional universities were also using computers through online, time-shared terminal access but the equipment was usually in computer laboratories on campus. By 1980, students on 35 courses were using the OU system for some aspect of their study. This included computing courses, and courses began experimenting with various 'standalone' microcomputers at summer schools. Hence, Jones et al., (1993), referring to a period around the late 1970s, and the difficulties of access noted that: *"despite these problems, student computing at a distance was a success and there was pressure to expand"* (p.42).

This led to the development of the "Open University's Home Computing Policy" that both required students (on certain courses) to acquire their own computers and supported them in doing so. This was a large-scale innovation, affecting 17,000 students by 1992. Running alongside the policy development was a research project that evaluated the policy. The book describing this educational evaluation explains that *"We set out to investigate the effects of requiring students on particular courses...included in the policy, to make their own arrangements for acquiring a microcomputer"*. (Jones et al., 1993, Preface). In terms of the TEL complex, taking account of the ecology of practices and technical content is particularly salient in the Home Computing Policy (HCP) project.

The 'success' of student computing at a distance meant an increase in the number of courses that wanted to include some form of computer provision. Although terminals and the mainframe were updated, the university system could not even cope with student demand from existing courses. Courses began to experiment further with using 'standalone' micros at residential schools: the evaluation of one such experiment is reported in case study 2 described below. Different course teams adopted different solutions, including different computers, as there was no leading market standard or computer at the time. For example, one low population course found funds to buy computers in order to loan these to students. Student demand was also increasing: many students wanted to use a computer for their OU study – or were already using one and wanted guidance on what to use or buy:

> *"By 1984 the university was considering the feasibility of specifying one particular machine which would primarily serve the computer science courses, but would have the capacity to handle a variety of software applications"* (Jones et al., 1993, p.44).

In the end the direction taken was to define the equipment according to compatible software, thus developing a home computing policy which specified an operating system. A core policy team oversaw the project, and a large team of academics and staff from the student computing services collaborated with senior university managers to conduct studies of students' and tutors' practices, to run pilot projects, and capture student and tutor experiences. Twenty different reports were written over the period of the project (1988 – 1991); reporting on diverse aspects including the use of computer-mediated communication (Mason, 1988), computing on mathematics courses and tutor use of the home computing facility more generally (Kirkup and Dale, 1989). The pedagogical context of the university was particularly important given the OU's commitment to openness and accessibility. The wider context of what computers were available at the time was clearly crucial – and a policy was needed that could respond to changes in the wider environment. That was achieved by defining software requirements rather than hardware.

The development of the policy and its evaluation is a good example of the Beyond Prototypes model of the TEL complex in practice. The key features of the project that determined its success were:

- Commitment to the policy at a senior level in the OU, underpinned by the importance of providing access to computers which, given student and course team demand, was argued as being crucial to the university's core business.
- The idea originated with academic staff and 'spread upwards' (Jones, Kirkup and Kirkwood, 1993, p.148) so had strong champions who prepared the ground and developed the argument. This and the previous point show the importance of context.
- Key players included the chair of a very large population course, which needed access to a computer for the preferred design of the course to work.
- The policy aimed to provide affordable and accessible access for our students in line with the OU mission: 'to be open to people, places, methods and ideas' and to 'promote…educational opportunity and social justice'.
- Alongside a history of collecting evidence about our student learning lay a commitment to evidence-based research: so the evaluation findings had a ready audience in appropriate university committees.
- The evaluation took a broad approach. Issues highlighted by the evaluations included the students' social and physical context; issues of access and equal opportunities; teaching practical computing work at a distance; the design of learning materials and institutional support.
- The OU saw itself, and was viewed externally, as innovative.

One chapter in Jones et al.(1993) devotes itself to an analysis of why and how the university adopted the HCP. This adds an additional dimension to the features above, which is the political and economic context of the 1980s when a period of recessions and contraction began. There were a number of challenges to the institution, and the OU felt particularly under threat, and needed to find ways to cut production costs. The policy had powerful and persuasive champions who carefully laid the ground and made preparations for the final debate at the university's senate. The chapter concludes (see Jones et al. op. cit., p.148) that "one of the most interesting aspects of the HCP was that it was an idea that spread upwards from the academic staff who argued it through formal and informal channels in such a way that ownership of the idea became diffused throughout the institution."

Case study 2: Works Metallurgist (1996)
"The Works Metallurgist", (Blake et al., 1996), was an interactive tutorial designed to teach interpretations of phase diagrams and the Lever Rule (a method of calculating percentage of solid and liquid in an alloy at a given temperature from a phase diagram) to Open University students. It was developed for "Materials: Engineering and Science", a second-level course which ran from February until October and included a residential summer school. Course evaluations had shown that students had difficulties in interpreting and applying phase diagrams, and the program was specifically developed to help students in this area. It was in a game format, and students were given job titles ranging from Applicant for Apprentice Metallurgist to Works Metallurgist, according to their performance.

Students used the CAL programs during their laboratory work. The program had been designed for individual use, but students mainly worked in the laboratories in pairs, and usually chose to use the program in pairs too, and to discuss their answers with each other before typing them in. Three computers were also provided in the student hall for use at any time. The aim was to answer the following questions:

1. How do students use the program?
2. Does the software contribute to learning? and if so what do students learn?
3. How can it be improved?

The participants were 540 students who studied "Materials: Engineering and Science" in 1995. The researcher attended two weeks of residential school (out of seven) and conducted observations and interviews. The students had reasonable familiarity with computers, and were given a questionnaire, attitude scale, and knowledge pre-test, along with the evaluation disk (a special version of the program that recorded some usage information).

Forty-four sessions were observed; both in the laboratory and the student hall where the program was also available for use during summer school. Where appropriate the students were asked to supply reasons for their answers. The observer tried to minimize the disturbance to students' natural progress with the program, but was occasionally asked for help with the tasks, and this was used as an opportunity to ask probing questions. A two-stage question-naire was given to 60 randomly selected students, where stage 1 asked about previous OU courses, study of phase diagrams, and the students' computing background. This provided an attitude measure and a knowledge pre-test.

Stage 2 concerned the efficiency of the program, the quality and nature of students' interactions with it, their difficulties, their opinions of the program, and general comments. These 60 students were given a special version of the program which recorded usage information and were asked to return the disk after five weeks. This evaluation disk enabled us to see how much time students spent on the program, which sections took most time, and how much improvement in their understanding they made in that limited time. To measure their learning achievement students completed a knowledge pre-test along with the first part of the questionnaire, and they were tested again (using the same questions) after they had finished working with the program. Four more short questions covered the important concept of phase. Formal and informal interviews were conducted in the laboratories and in the computer suite in the student hall. Tutorials related to phase diagrams were also attended by the researcher, and students' attendance and activities during the tutorial were observed.

Observations revealed that The Works Metallurgist was the program used most during the 2 summer-school weeks. It was available for sale and most students who saw it decided to buy it, if they had access to an appropriate computer. The observations about its use and popularity were supported by the sales figures. Students reported that the program was very useful, and most could only suggest making minor changes to it. None of the students reported the program as being difficult to use, and they were easily able to use specific features such as Crosshairs, and the Draw Tie Line and Show Labels facilities. Evaluation disks returned showed that they spent a great deal of time using the program, ranging from 12 to 276 minutes with a mean of 128 minutes.

The pre-post test data showed little difference in their knowledge before and after using the program. At that time, we noted that the difficulties in using pre-and post-tests in CAL evaluation were known and documented and that such instruments are not sensitive to the complexity of the learning situation. Data from the evaluation disks showed that the errors made in each section decreased with time. The students also commented that the game-like nature of the program was motivating. We also had data from 29 students who were positive about having learnt from using the program and in particular felt that it had helped them in understanding phase diagrams.

Reflections on case study 2

As in case study 1 we did have usage data for the students that used the evaluation version of the program (but at a very small scale – 60 students). In addition to the questionnaires and interview used in this study as with case study 1, students were observed using the program and students also completed knowledge tests, although the pre-post test data showed little difference in their knowledge before and after using the program – a common result in CAL evaluation.

The main link between this work and learning analytics is that both are concerned with understanding student behaviour and use and improving teaching as a result – but that in our historical CAL evaluations we were focusing on one aspect of a course – the CAL component.

Summary and Conclusions

In this chapter we have described some very early work of the CAL research group, noting the influences on work in the late 1970s and in the '80s from research in cognitive science and Intelligent Teaching Systems. Thus the methods adopted for such work often focused on observations of student learning and collecting detailed data of students interacting with written texts of CAL or of whole models. Earlier studies often used protocol data in the laboratory: in later work, the CALRG 'data capture suite' provided video data of students working collaboratively. The commitment to a fine-grained understanding of student behaviour, use and learning with technology and improving teaching as a result is echoed in today's learning analytics work (see Chapter 7) although of course this focuses on the student experience throughout the course or module.

Major goals of our early work were to develop a better understanding of student behaviour, and to improve instructional design. Also, when the course materials consisted of texts that lasted a number of years, it allowed feedback to inform changes to CAL: this could be changed in a way that print could not. Some elements have persisted through time. One such element, the aspiration to have built in evaluation and data collection, was successful, although this was much more limited in the 1970s and early 1980s.

CAL evaluation: institutional research, was illustrated by two case studies of CICERO (tutorial CAL) and the Metallurgy works. One of the findings in the CICERO evaluation was that affective issues were important – as well of course as the importance of integrating any CAL closely with the course and providing good accessibility.

So, two main strands of work have been identified here; firstly a technology-focused approach influenced by AI and focusing on learner models, and secondly a focus on research that investigated what learners' needs actually are. In both these approaches, the OU was ahead of its time. We are now witnessing a ressurgence of interest in applying AI to education (see, e.g. Luckin and Holmes, 2016) but in 1978 it was unusual to teach AI as part of cognitive psychology. The university was also breaking new ground in researching into its own students: in collecting and analysing usage data of student CAL use, in trying out mixed-methods methodologies, exploring methods of data capture, in detailed analysis of interactions and in considering affect. Some of this research laid the ground for the current work on learning design and analytics which is described in the next chapter.

Some of the lessons learnt from this early work for meeting learners' needs are still valid and really important today:

- It is not possible to meet learners' needs without an understanding of pedagogy and how people learn;
- Context is vitally important and needs to be considered in different ways;
- Affect is very important: emotions such as fear and embarrassment have a significant effect on learning behaviours, yet it is only during the last fifteen years or so that this has been widely acknowledged and become part of mainstream educational technology research;
- Assessing how people learn and how they learn best is challenging because' of the nature of the learning situation.

The chapter has also considered a successful institutional innovation – the OU's Home Computing Policy – that was analysed at the time in terms of the economic and political climate, both at a local and wider level. However, the HCP is also a good illustration of the TEL complex in practice. One of the important components of the policy's access that was listed was the commitment to the policy at senior university level. This is not a novel argument or finding, but perhaps the fact that it was also 'bottom-up' and so had ownership amongst academic staff and our associate lecturers is significant.

References

Alpay, L. and Giffen, R. (1998). 'Investigating a concept-based tool to enhance the process of curriculum development: an example for healthcare education', in B. Cesnik, A.T. McCray and J.R. Scherrer (eds), Proceedings of MEDINFO' 98 (9th World Congress on Medical Informatics), Seoul, Korea: IOS Press, 781–4.

Blake, C; Butcher, P; Scanlon, E and Jones, Ann (1996). The Works Metallurgist: an evaluation of a CAL package on phase diagrams. *ALT-J: Research in Learning Technology*, 4 (1) pp. 55–57.

Blake, C. T. and Scanlon, E. (2003). Enriching accounts of computer supported collaboration by using video data. *ALT-J: Research in Learning Technology*, 11(2) pp. 5–13.

Eisenstadt, M. (1982). Design features of a Friendly Software Environment for Novice Programmers, in (Eds. Marc Eisenstadt, Mark T Keane and Tim

Rajan), Novice Programming Environments: Explorations in Human-Computer Interaction and Artificial Intelligence, Routledge, UK.

Eisenstadt, M. (1983). Units 3–4, Cognitive Psychology, Artificial Intelligence project: the SOLO primer. (2nd edition), Open University, Milton Keynes, England.

Hosein, A., Aczel, J., Clow, D., and Richardson, J.T. E. (2007). An Illustration of Students' Engagement with Mathematical Software using Remote Observation. In: 31st Conference of the International Group for the Psychology of Mathematics Education, 8–13 Jul 2007, Seoul.

Issroff, K. (1995). 'Investigating computer-supported collaborative learning from an affective perspective', unpublished Ph.D. thesis, Institute of Educational Technology, Open University, Milton Keynes.

Issroff, K.; Jones, A. and Scanlon, E. (1994). Case studies of children cooperating with computers: a time based analysis. In: Foot, H. C.; Howe, C. J.; Anderson, A.; Tolmie, A. K. and Warden, D. A. eds. *Group and Interactive Learning*. Southampton: WIT Press, pp. 73–80.

Jones, A and O'Shea, T. (1981). An evaluation of tutorial CAL at The Open University: the use of Cicero on SDT286. CAL research group Technical report no. 5. The Open University.

Jones, A and O'Shea, T. (1982). Barriers to the Use of Computer Assisted Learning. *British Journal of Educational Technology*, 13(3) pp. 207–217.

Jones, A. C. and Scanlon, E. (1981). A review of research in the CAL group: A report of the first annual conference, November 1981; Open University, UK.

Jones, Ann (1993). Conceptual models of programming environments: how learners use the glass box. *Instructional Science*, 21(6) pp. 473–500.

Jones, A., Scanlon, E., Tosunoglu, C., Morris, E., Ross, S., Butcher P. and Greenberg, J. (1999). Contexts for evaluating educational software. Interacting with Computers, Volume 11, Issue 5, May 1999, Pages 499–516.

Jones, Ann; Kirkup, Gill; Kirkwood, Adrian and Mason, Robin (1992). Providing computing for distance learners: a strategy for home use. *Computers & Education*, 18(1–3) pp. 183–193.

Jones, A., Kirkup, G., & Kirkwood, A. (1993). *Personal Computers for Distance Education. The Study of an Educational Innovation*. London: Paul Chapman Publishing Ltd.

Kirkup, G. and Dale, E. (1989). Home Computing Evaluation Project. M205: End of Year Report. Home Computing Evaluation Reports, Institute of Educational Technology, Open University.

Luckin, R; Holmes, W. (2016). Intelligence Unleashed: An argument for AI in Education. UCL Knowledge Lab: London, UK.

Mason, R. (1988). The Use of Computer Mediated Communication for Distance Education at The Open University. Home Computing Evaluation Reports, Institute of Educational Technology, Open University.

Office for National Statistics (UK). n.d. *Percentage of households with home computers in the United Kingdom (UK) from 1985 to 2018.* Statista. Accessed June 27, 2019. Available from https://www.statista.com/statistics/289191/household-penetration-of-home-computers-in-the-uk/.

San Diego and Aczel, James (2007). New approaches to researching the pedagogical benefit of representations and interactivity. In: Computer Assisted Learning (CAL '07), 26–28 Mar 2007, Trinity College Dublin, Ireland.

San Diego, Jonathan P.; Aczel, James C.; Hodgson, Barbara K. and Scanlon, Eileen (2012). Digital approaches to researching learners' computer interactions using gazes, actions, utterances and sketches. *Educational Technology Research and Development*, 60(5) pp. 859–881.

Scanlon, E., Jones, A., O'Shea, T., Murphy, P., Whitelegg, E. and Vincent, T. (1982). 'Computer assisted learning', in *Teaching at a Distance Research Supplement no. 1.*, pp59–79, Open University, Milton Keynes.

Scanlon, E., O'Shea, T., Smith, R. B. and Joiner, R. (2000). 'Technological mediation of synchronous collaboration: science and statistics in SharedArk and Kansas', in R. Joiner, K. Littleton, D. Faulkner and D. Miell (eds), Rethinking Collaborative Learning, London: Free Association Books.

Scanlon, Eileen; Sharples, Mike; Fenton-O'Creevy, Mark; Fleck, James; Cooban, Caroline; Ferguson, Rebecca; Cross, Simon and Waterhouse, Peter (2013). Beyond prototypes: Enabling innovation in technology-enhanced learning. Open University, Milton Keynes.

Scanlon, E., Blake, C., Joiner, R. and O'Shea, T. (2005). Technologically mediated complex problem solving on a statistics task. *Learning, Media and Technology*, 30(2) pp. 165–183.

Smith, R. B., O'Shea, T., O'Malley, C., Scanlon, E. and Taylor, J. (1989). 'Preliminary experiments with a distributed multimedia problem solving environment', Proceedings of the First European Conference on Computer-supported Cooperative Work (EC-CSCW '89), London, 13–15 September, 19–34. Whitelock, Denise; Scanlon, Eileen and Taylor, Josie (1996).

Whitelock, D. and Scanlon, E. (1996). 'Motivation, media and motion: reviewing a computer supported collaborative learning experience', in P. Brna, A. Paiva and J. Self (eds.), Proceedings of the European Conference on Artificial Intelligence in Education, Brighton: AIED.

Whitelock, D., del Soldato, T., Scanlon, E. and Taylor J. (1996). 'Moons and collisions: how different tasks influence collaborative problem-solving in science using information technology', paper presented at European Conference on Educational Research, University of Seville, Spain.

CHAPTER 7

Evidence-Based Learning: Futures

Using learning design and learning analytics to empower teachers to meet students' diverse needs

Bart Rienties and Ann Jones

With the introduction of learning design in early 2000 and learning analytics in 2012, the OU has led the way in how teachers make complex decisions to design interactive courses, and how students can maximise their learning potential. The next obvious steps would be to include AI, personalisation, and student-led learning analytics to provide learning opportunities that meet the unique needs of each learner, but whether this would be technically feasible and pedagogically desirable will be discussed. In this chapter we will look at recent and future developments concerning the "holy trinity" of learning design, learning analytics, and how teachers can help institutions like the OU to ensure that our current and future students' needs are met. Furthermore, we will reflect on the affordances and limitations of learning design and learning analytics to help teachers to adapt their teaching and learning practices to meet learners' needs.

Introduction

The Open University (OU) has been at the forefront of innovation in teaching and learning since its inception in 1969. As highlighted in the previous chapter,

How to cite this book chapter:
Rienties, B. and Jones, A. 2019. Evidence-Based Learning: Futures. In: Ferguson, R., Jones, A. and Scanlon, E. (eds). *Educational Visions: Lessons from 40 years of innovation.* Pp. 109–125. London: Ubiquity Press. DOI: https://doi.org/10.5334/bcg.g. License: CC-BY 4.0

even when most people did not have access to a computer, let alone a smart phone, the OU was actively experimenting and rolling out innovative ICT systems and applications to help support teachers to deliver exciting and relevant approaches to help students meet their needs. In this chapter, we will primarily reflect on major developments of innovative teaching practice since 2010 that have shaped the OU and wider environment, and vice versa. In particular, this chapter will focus on the holy trinity between learning design, learning analytics, and teachers.

Like many other institutions across the globe, as highlighted in Chapter 6 the OU continuously explores the opportunities information technology affords to provide a better, more consistent, and ideally more personalised service to its learners, teachers, and wider stakeholders (Herodotou et al., 2017; Hidalgo, 2018; Rienties & Toetenel, 2016; Tait, 2018). Globally (Dalziel, 2016; Hernández-Leo et al., 2018; Lockyer & Dawson, 2012; Mangaroska & Giannakos, 2018) as well as within the OU (Nguyen et al., 2017; Rienties et al., 2018a; Rienties & Toetenel, 2016; Toetenel & Rienties, 2016a; van Ameijde et al., 2018) there is an increased recognition that learning design is an essential driver for learning, as well as empowering teachers to meet students' needs. For example, using concepts originally developed by Conole (2012) the Open University Learning Design Initiative (OULDI) has been implemented on a large-scale within the OU (Cross et al., 2012; van Ameijde et al., 2018). An excellent example of this large-scale implementation comes from a review of 157 learning designs of OU modules, whereby Toetenel and Rienties (2016a) found a wide tapestry of interactive and unique learning designs, from more traditional constructivist designs to more socio-constructivist designs.

However, learning design by itself is just a useful approach to depict how teachers design a particular learning activity or a complete course. Only when learning design is combined with how students are actually engaging with these learning designs do we start to make real progress. One way to empower learning design is to use learning analytics data of students. As argued by a range of researcher and practitioners (Calvert, 2014; Ferguson et al., 2016; Hlosta et al., 2015; Toetenel & Rienties, 2016a; Wolff et al., 2013) *learning analytics* may empower distance learning institutions like the OU to provide near real-time actionable feedback to students and teachers about what the "best" next step in their learning journeys might be. For example, the OU uses learning analytics dashboards displaying learner and learning behaviour to our academic staff and associate lecturers (ALs) in order to provide more real-time, or just-in-time support for students. (Herodotou et al., 2017, 2019; Hlosta et al., 2015). Furthermore, some institutions like Universiteit van Amsterdam (Berg et al., 2016), University of Keele (de Quincey et al., 2019), and Maastricht University (Tempelaar et al., 2018b) have successfully experimented with providing learning analytics data directly to students in order to support their learning processes and self-regulation.

As also highlighted in Chapter 3, the role of teachers in making sense of these dynamic and complex systems is vital. In fact, how teachers are making sense of the teaching and learning practice, its students, and data arising from the complex interactions of students with learning resources, peers, and teachers, has become even more important in the last 5–10 years (Herodotou et al., 2017, 2019; Hidalgo, 2018; Rienties et al., 2016a; 2018a, 2019; Tait, 2018). As demonstrated by a range of projects within the OU as well as outside the OU (Guri-Rosenblit, 2018; Lawless & Pellegrino, 2007), the teacher is the key success factor in making pedagogy and technology work. As highlighted elsewhere in this book in Chapter 2, the OU has a relatively unique approach to teaching and learning, whereby typically central academic staff supported by TEL professionals design and produce high-quality online courses (Jones & Issroff, 2005; Jones et al., 1996). The actual implementation and "teaching" of these modules (i.e., courses) is done by a combined team of module academics and ALs, who typically would support around 20 students per group (Herodotou et al., 2017; Toetenel & Rienties, 2016a; van Ameijde et al., 2018). With current movements towards co-creation and integration of ALs and (former) students into module production and presentation, in this chapter we use the broader notion of a "teacher" to refer to a person working together with other experts to effectively design, implement, and/or evaluate the teaching and learning practices to meet students' needs (Olney et al., 2018; Rienties et al., 2013, 2019).

Using the Beyond Prototypes framework developed by Scanlon et al. (2013), which is described in Chapters 1 and 2, we will aim to illustrate how the holy trinity of learning design, learning analytics, and teachers can help institutions like the OU to ensure that our current and future students' needs are met. The Beyond Prototypes case studies that led to the development of the framework indicate that Technology Enhanced Learning (TEL) needs to be understood as a 'complex'. This 'complex' is made up of a series of elements that need to be addressed together, as reproduced in Figure 1.1 of Chapter 1 of this book.

The second to outer level of Figure 1.1 shows the different communities that are all involved in the TEL complex: the student community, pedagogic research community, teacher community and technical communities. These communities are all necessarily involved in our learning analytics work (Ferguson et al., 2016; Herodotou et al., 2019; Rienties et al., 2019). This work is being undertaken by a group of researchers within the Computers and Learning research group (CALRG). One aspect of that work is what we call data wrangling' (Ullmann et al., 2018) and includes iterative conversations with academics in the university who are responsible for developing our modules. Essentially the data wranglers team interpret the student data and then have conversations with academics about how changes might be made to the modules to improve student learning.

As illustrated in Figure 7.1, there may be inherent tensions between the three base layers of learning analytics, learning design, and teachers. Depending on

Students' needs

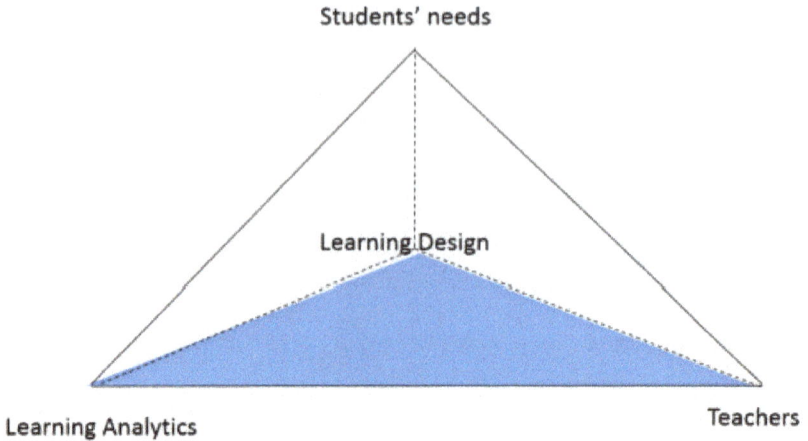

Learning Design

Learning Analytics   Teachers

Figure 7.1: Balancing learning design, learning analytics, and support by teachers to meet students' needs.

how effectively organisations are able to balance these three "forces", the more we can meet the unique and individualised students' needs (i.e., the higher or flatter the pyramid will become).

Learning Design

As highlighted by a systematic review of 43 studies on learning design by Mangaroska and Giannakos (2018) few institutions have implemented learning design on such a large scale as the OU. Conole (2012) started experimenting with mapping learning design processes, whereby they "developed an approach to using learning design as a methodology to guide design and foster creativity in concert with good practice in the creation of learning activities". Building on this initial work, the OU's learning design taxonomy was established as a result of the Jisc-sponsored OU Learning Design Initiative (OULDI) (Cross et al., 2012; Rienties et al., 2017), and was developed over five years in consultation with eight other Higher Education institutions. In contrast to instructional design, learning design is process based (Conole, 2012): following a collaborative design approach in which OU module teams, curriculum managers and other stakeholders make informed design decisions with a pedagogical focus, by using representations in order to build a shared vision. For a detailed description of the OULDI approach, we refer to work published elsewhere (Rienties et al., 2017; Rienties & Toetenel, 2016; van Ameijde et al., 2018).

In one of the first studies to visualise the complex decisions that OU teachers make when designing courses, Toetenel and Rienties (2016a) used the OULDI approach to classify 157 modules at the OU. As illustrated in Figure 7.2, substantial depth and breadth of learning designs is present at the OU, perhaps reflecting the unique and diverse nature of the disciplines and the creative people that work at the OU. A considerable number of OU modules had a relatively high focus on assimilative activities, as well as assessment. At the same time, some OU modules used a perhaps more innovative pedagogical design, whereby for example Module 94 had nearly 60% of productive activities (i.e., creating, building, making, doing) for students to work with, while nearly 40% of activities in Module 56 were experiential (i.e., practice, apply, mimic, experience). Perhaps surprisingly for an online distance institution, less than 5% of learning activities on an average of modules mapped in 2016 were devoted towards communication activities (i.e., student to student, staff to student, student to staff).

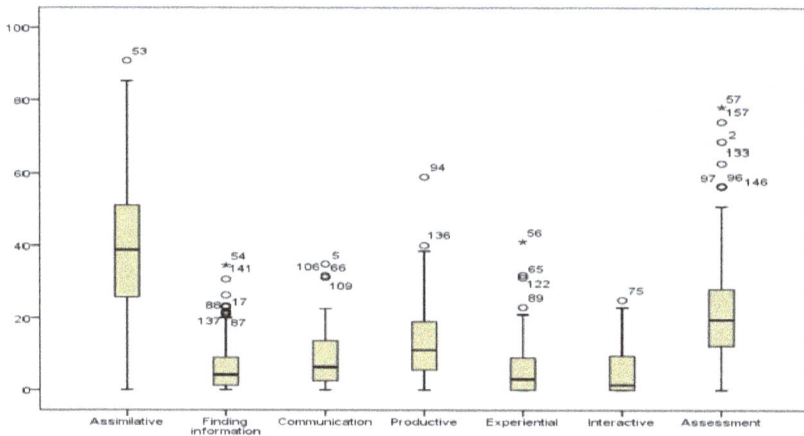

Figure 7.2: Learning design across 157 modules at the OU (activities in %). *Retrieved from Toetenel and Rienties (2016a).*

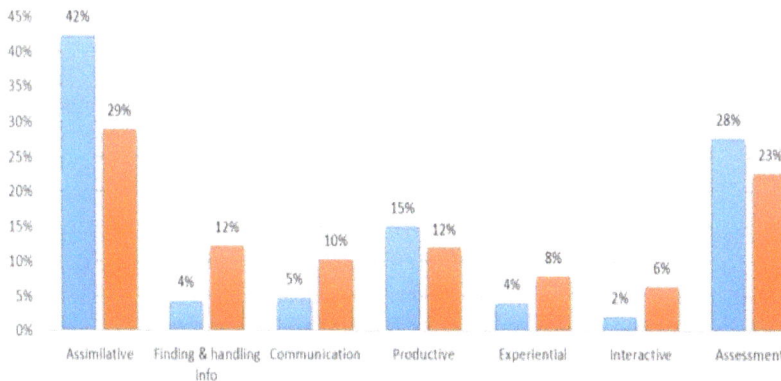

Figure 7.3: Changing OU teachers' learning design (before and after visualisations). *Retrieved from Toetenel and Rienties (2016b).*

In follow-up work of 148 learning designs by Toetenel and Rienties (2016b), the introduction of a systematic learning design initiative, consisting of visualisation of initial learning design and workshops, helped OU teachers to focus on the development of a range of skills and more "balanced" learning designs. As illustrated in Figure 7.3, when OU teachers were given visualisations of their initial learning design activities (i.e., orange) compared to teachers who were not given these visualisation (i.e., blue), they adjusted their designs towards more student-active activities, such as communication and finding information, while reducing the emphasis on assimilative activities.

Learning analytics

Although these above visualisations of learning design decisions made by teachers are an important advancement in terms of understanding our design practice, a next logical step would be to explore how these learning design decisions influence students' affect, behaviour, and cognition. One way to do this is to use learning analytics, which is commonly defined as "the measurement, collection, analysis and reporting of data about learners and their contexts, for purposes of understanding and optimizing learning and the environments in which it occurs" (Ferguson, 2012, p.307). As noted by Scanlon et. al. (2013, p.37) "learning analytics can provide actionable intelligence".

A considerable literature from the OU has emerged around both conceptual development (Clow, 2013; Ferguson, 2012; Ferguson & Buckingham Shum, 2012), how to evidence that learning analytics works (Ferguson et al., 2016; Ferguson & Clow, 2017; Rienties et al., 2016b), and how to design appropriate predictive learning analytics to effectively support different groups of OU students (Calvert, 2014; Herodotou et al., 2017; Rienties et al., 2019; Wolff et al., 2013). In fact, a recent bibliometric review of learning analytics has found that the OU is the most prolific institution in publishing about learning analytics (Adeniji, 2019).

With the arrival of fine-grained log-data and the emergence of learning analytics as a research field there are potentially more, and perhaps new, opportunities to map how students with different affective, behavioural, and cognitive learning needs want to engage with the OU (Nguyen et al., 2018a; Rienties et al., 2019; Rogaten et al., 2019). This is part of a commitment to investigate students' practices: part of our efforts to understand our learning ecology, an important layer of the TEL complex captured in Figure 1.1 in Chapter 1. As noted in Chapter 6, the CALRG's early work included a focus on affect. This was unusual at the time but this emphasis has continued. For example, with trace data on students' affect, the OU is currently exploring how emotional expression could be identified in written text, such as chat, discussion forums, or feedback from students (Aznar et al, 2016; Chua et al., 2017; Hillaire et al., Submitted; Ullmann et al., 2018). For example, Hillaire et al. (Submitted) showed that effective sentiment analyses approaches could be developed to identify positive, negative, and mixed emotions when 500+ students collaborated online in an interactive chat environment. Similarly, Ullmann et al. (2018) found, when using sentiment analyses of 51,000 student evaluation comments from 23 large OU modules, that substantial differences in lived and affective experiences could be identified.

Currently, experiments using techniques like eye gaze investigate how students are making sense of complex and simple texts (Rets, 2018). Furthermore, a range of studies within the OU have combined self-reported dispositions with how students are engaging with tasks over time (Tempelaar et al., 2012, 2015, 2018a). These affective data could be useful in providing more personalised feedback to students, such as giving automated hints to a "surface" learner with math anxiety that, say, engaging with a worked example on task 15 would help him to better understand this math problem and reduce his math anxiety, while for a "deep" but disengaged learner for the same task 15 providing a hint to read the theoretical modelling narrative could prevent her from being bored.

In terms of students' behaviour, substantial progress has been made over the last five years in terms of identifying and predicting effective behaviour (e.g., engagement, time on task, clicks). For example, our state-of-the-art predictive learning analytics system called OU Analyse has been providing effective support to hundreds of teachers across dozens of modules where students might need some additional support (Herodotou et al., 2017; Hlosta et al., 2015; Wolff et al., 2013). OU Analyse uses a combination of machine learning and artificial intelligence approaches to predict which students are doing well, and who might be at risk not submitting the next assignment. One remaining challenge for learning analytics research is to deliver "actionable feedback", which might be achieved by taking into account the context in which learners, teachers, and the respective learning data is situated (Chua et al., 2017; Herodotou et al., 2017; Hidalgo, 2018; Rienties & Toetenel, 2016).

Finally, in terms of students' cognition some substantial progress has been made in the OU to signpost students about what they could do next, and what might fit better with their learning needs. For example, several module teams have been experimenting with asking for real-time feedback from students. Similarly, several module teams have implemented Computer-Based Assessments (CBA), which give automatic feedback to students (Nguyen et al., 2017). Preliminary analyses across 74 modules seemed to indicate that these CBA have a positive impact on engagement of students, and on higher pass and retention rates (Nguyen et al., 2017).

At the same time, as argued by Rienties et al. (2019) in a recent review held during an interactive workshop of leading experts and users of learning analytics at the OU, many of the 42 participants indicated a strong need to further develop learning analytics approaches to allow for effective communication and personalisation with students, while at the same time providing the learning analytics tools as part of an integrated design that is based upon a solid evidence-base.

Linking learning analytics with learning design

In terms of linking learning design with learning analytics approaches, several substantial steps have been made by CALRG researchers in the last five years (Mangaroska & Giannakos, 2018; Rienties et al., 2017). For example, Rienties and Toetenel (2016) linked 151 modules taught in 2012–2015 at the OU followed by 111,256 students with students' behaviour using multiple regression models and found that learning designs strongly predicted Virtual Learning Environment (VLE) behaviour and performance of students, as illustrated in Figure 7.4. Findings indicated that the primary predictor of academic retention was how teachers designed their modules, in particular the relative amount of so-called "communication activities" (i.e., student to student, teacher to student, student to teacher).

In contrast, student satisfaction was negatively predicted by these communication activities, whereby students in particular preferred to work in modules following more traditional distance learning designs, such as constructivist learning designs. This may be an important finding as in particular in online learning there tends to be a focus on designing for individual cognition rather than social learning activities (Arbaugh, 2014; Koedinger et al., 2013), while recently several researchers have encouraged teachers and researchers to focus on the social elements of learning (Arbaugh, 2014; Ferguson & Buckingham Shum, 2012)

Building on this initial work, Quan Nguyen has made substantial steps towards more dynamic, temporal conceptualisations and empirical analyses linking learning design from a day-week-module perspective with how students are actually engaging (Nguyen et al., 2017, 2018a, 2018b) For example, a large-scale empirical study by Nguyen et al. (2017) on learning designs of 74 modules over 30 weeks revealed that the way teachers designed their

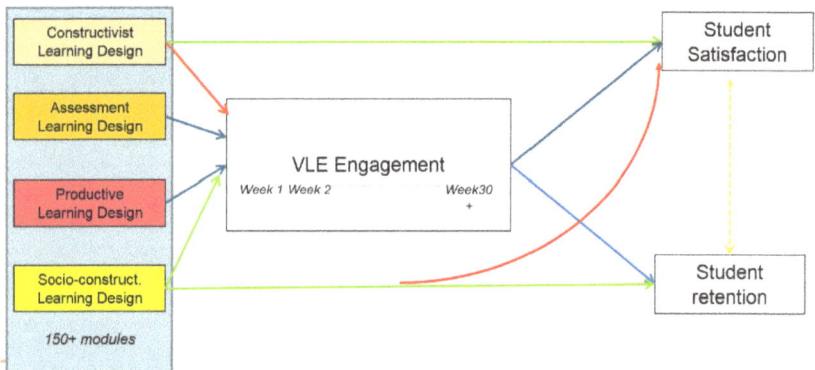

Figure 7.4: Learning design strongly influences student behaviour, satisfaction and performance (Adjusted from Rienties and Toetenel (2016).

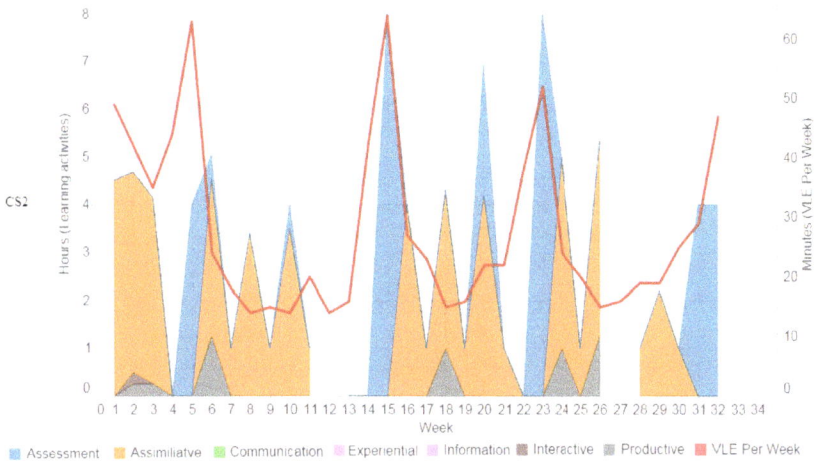

Figure 7.5: Longitudinal visualisation of learning design and student engagement. *Retrieved from Nguyen et al. (2017).*

learning designs could explain up to 69% of the variance in VLE behaviours. For example, the weekly workload of the seven learning design activities of one module is illustrated in Figure 7.5. As highlighted from this visualisation, there were substantial fluctuations in expected workloads on a weekly basis, whereby there were specific weeks with a relatively high workload, primarily links to assessment points. As indicated by the red line in Figure 7.5, the average VLE engagement of students on a weekly basis also fluctuated, and primarily peaked when assessments were due. In follow-up work looking at when and what students are engaging with in one fully online module, Nguyen et al. (2018a, 2018b); found that students made conscious decisions not to follow the course schedule, by either studying well in advance, or catching up after the course schedule.

Role of teachers in using learning analytics and learning design

Irrespective of the specific learning design and the learning analytics approaches used, teachers will always play an essential role in online and distance learning (Guri-Rosenblit, 2018; Lawless & Pellegrino, 2007; van Leeuwen et al., 2015). Several authors (Herodotou et al., 2017; Rienties et al., 2013, 2018a) have indicated that beyond designing learning activities and managing the learning process teachers have a social, personal counselling role, whereby teachers provide pedagogical support and evaluate learning progression and outcomes. With the advancements of learning design and learning analytics it is anticipated that teachers will increasingly receive unprecedented amounts of information, insight, and knowledge about their learners and their diverging needs. Learning analytics dashboards may provide teachers with opportunities to support learner progression, and perhaps personalised, rich learning (FitzGerald et al., 2018; Rienties et al., 2016b; Tempelaar et al., 2015). Indeed, two recent systematic reviews of 26 and 55 learning analytics dashboards studies (Jivet et al., 2018; Schwendimann et al., 2017) indicated that teachers and students will be able to obtain (almost) real-time information about how, where, and when to study.

Beyond providing just-in-time support (Daley et al., 2016; Herodotou et al., 2017), learning analytics may help teachers to fine-tune the learning design if large numbers of students are struggling with the same task (Hidalgo, 2018; Rienties et al., 2016a; Rienties & Toetenel, 2016). In line with the Beyond Prototypes framework, paying attention to the ecology of practices, one layer of the policy context is a key element of our approach to learning analytics, so teacher and learning practices and perceptions are investigated. Regarding teachers, a recent large-scale study by Rienties et al. (2018a) amongst 95 experienced teaching staff at the OU indicated that many teachers were sceptical about the perceived ease of use of learning analytics tools. Most teachers indicated a need for additional training and follow-up support for working with learning analytics tools.

These findings resonate with a recent study by Herodotou et al. (2017), who compared how 240 teachers made use of learning analytics predictions and visualisations in OU Analyse at the OU (Hlosta et al., 2015; Wolff et al., 2013). Herodotou et al. (2017) found that most teachers struggled to turn learning analytics predictions and recommendations into concrete actions for their students-at-risk. Follow-up qualitative interviews with five teachers who used OU Analyse indicated that they preferred to learn a new learning analytics system by experimenting and testing the various functionalities of learning analytics dashboards by trial-and-error (Herodotou et al., 2017; Herodotou et al., 2019). However, at this moment the OU does not actively track how teachers are making interventions, and what the best way could be to provide effective feedback for different groups of students.

Conclusion and future directions

In the last ten years universities and distance learning institutions like the OU have experienced unprecedented change. Beyond the "neo-liberalist waves" running through many universities, the affordances and limitations of technology to transform universities as exciting and relevant places of learning and teaching have fundamentally impacted the way universities are run, as indicated elsewhere in this book in Chapter 2 and Chapter 3.

The central message of this chapter is that learning design, learning analytics, and teachers together can support student success. With the emergence of learning design combined with learning analytics, there is an increased narrative developing that teachers should start to pro-actively think, reflect, and act upon data. While there is widespread evidence that learning analytics tools and predictive engines could accurately identify which students might need some additional support, there is mixed evidence (Ferguson et al., 2016; Ferguson & Clow, 2017; Herodotou et al., 2017; Rienties et al., 2018a) as to whether universities and teachers in particular are ready to engage with these tools and approaches.

As emphasised in the Beyond Prototypes framework: "In the TEL complex, practices include explicit aspects of teachers' practices...." (Scanlon, 2013, p.29), and it is increasingly evident that without an appropriate understanding of the context in which learners and teachers are learning, learning analytics may not be as effective as hoped (Ferguson et al., 2016). At the same time, our ground-breaking research (Nguyen et al., 2017, 2018a; Rienties et al., 2018b; Rienties & Toetenel, 2016) linking learning design (i.e., what do teachers design) and what, how, and when students are actually engaging with these learning activities could have a transformative impact on how we teach at the OU, and perhaps more importantly how we can develop, test, and implement new educational theories of effective learning design. Given the tremendous impact of learning design on what students do on a daily and weekly basis (Nguyen et al., 2017, 2018b;), we need a much better understanding of why teachers are designing particular learning activities, and how these learning activities relate to learners' needs.

Indeed recent research has highlighted that on a more micro-level learners at the OU have substantially different learning needs and ambitions (Law, 2015; Li et al., 2017), depending on a complex interplay of affective (Hillaire et al., Submitted; Tempelaar et al., 2018b), behavioural (Chua et al., 2017; Rets, 2018; Rizvi et al., 2018), and cognitive factors, as well as socio-economic and demographic factors (Richardson, 2015). Therefore, in the remainder of this chapter we will primarily focus on how to provide more personalised and individualised support for learning in the next 2–5 years.

Moving forwards

With the renewed and increased interest in *Artificial Intelligence* (Holmes et al., 2019; Luckin et al., 2016; Rizvi et al., 2018) there is an emerging narrative developing that universities should start to embrace some of the affordances of AI. In particular for some of the more mundane tasks that students and staff need to complete on a frequent basis (e.g., registering for a course, asking for an exception, replying to standard emails), providing automated responses using AI could provide some quick efficiency savings. Similarly, in providing automatic responses to standard or frequently asked questions, chat bots can learn to effectively support learners.

Personalisation (FitzGerald et al., 2018) and *student-led analytics* (Ferguson et al., 2017; Prinsloo & Slade, 2017) are two specific themes that are emerging from the literature that could start to play an important role for distance learning providers in the near future. Although distance learning theoretically can provide flexible options to learners depending on their needs, we continue to see many distance learning providers offering "one-size-fits-all" courses starting on say the 1st of October and finishing in June/July. Given that many learners do not necessarily want to follow courses on these dates, some may want to start earlier or later, and others might want to move faster or slower (FitzGerald et al., 2018), it remains interesting why most providers of education are still focussed on one-size-fits all solutions. Obviously, economic efficiency arguments are provided, like economies of scale, and logistical and administrative processes need to be adjusted to accommodate multiple variations of a course, but with the support of learning analytics and a student-led analytics approach, distance learning organisations could vary their provision to different groups of learners, with specific learning needs. Finally, student-led analytics, whereby students themselves determine what they want to share and see in terms of their own data (Ferguson et al., 2017; Prinsloo & Slade, 2017), will become an emergent issue that distance learning institutions need to plan for. Again the Beyond Prototypes framework could be useful to help distance learning organisations to visualise the complex and changing relations.

References

Adeniji, B. (2019). *A Bibliometric Study on Learning Analytics*. Long Island University, Retrieved from https://digitalcommons.liu.edu/post_fultext_dis/16/

Arbaugh, J. B. (2014). System, scholar, or students? Which most influences online MBA course effectiveness? *Journal of Computer Assisted Learning, 30*(4), 349–362. DOI: 10.1111/jcal.12048

Aznar, A., Rienties, B., & Hillaire, G. (2016). How children use their emotions to learn. *The Conversation*.

Berg, A. M., Mol, S. T., Kismihók, G., & Sclater, N. (2016). The Role of a Reference Synthetic Data Generator within the Field of Learning Analytics. *Journal of Learning Analytics, 3*(1), 107–128. DOI: 10.18608/jla.2016.31.7

Calvert, C. (2014). Developing a model and applications for probabilities of student success: a case study of predictive analytics. *Open Learning: The Journal of Open, Distance and e-Learning, 29*(2), 160–173. DOI: 10.1080/02680513.2014.931805

Chua, S. M., Tagg, C., Sharples, M., & Rienties, B. (2017). *Discussion Analytics: Identifying Conversations and Social Learners in FutureLearn MOOCs*. Paper presented at the FutureLearn data: what we currently have, what we are learning and how it is demonstrating learning in MOOCs. Workshop at the 7th International Learning Analytics and Knowledge Conference, Vancouver, British Columbia.

Clow, D. (2013). An overview of learning analytics. *Teaching in Higher Education, 18*(6), 683–695. DOI: 10.1080/13562517.2013.827653

Conole, G. (2012). *Designing for Learning in an Open World.* Dordrecht: Springer.

Cross, S., Galley, R., Brasher, A., & Weller, M. (2012). *Final project report of the OULDI-JISC project: challenge and change in curriculum design process, communities, visualisation and practice.* Retrieved from York: http://www.jisc.ac.uk/media/documents/programmes/curriculumdesign/OULDI_Final_Report_instit%20story.pdf

Daley, S. G., Hillaire, G., & Sutherland, L. M. (2016). Beyond performance data: Improving student help seeking by collecting and displaying influential data in an online middle-school science curriculum. *British Journal of Educational Technology, 47*(1), 121–134. DOI: 10.1111/bjet.12221

Dalziel, J. (2016). *Learning design: Conceptualizing a framework for teaching and learning online.* New York: Routledge.

de Quincey, E., Briggs, C., Kyriacou, T., & Waller, R. (2019). *Student Centred Design of a Learning Analytics System.* Paper presented at the Proceedings of the 9th International Conference of Learning Analytics Knowledge, Arizona.

Ferguson, R. (2012). Learning analytics: drivers, developments and challenges. *International Journal of Technology Enhanced Learning, 4*(5), 304–317. DOI: 10.1504/ijtel.2012.051816

Ferguson, R., Barzilai, S., Ben-Zvi, D., Chinn, C. A., Herodotou, C., Hod, Y., ... Whitelock, D. (2017). *Innovating Pedagogy 2017: Open University Innovation Report 6.* Milton Keynes: The Open University.

Ferguson, R., Brasher, A., Cooper, A., Hillaire, G., Mittelmeier, J., Rienties, B., ... Vuorikari, R. (2016). *Research evidence of the use of learning analytics; implications for education policy.* Retrieved from Luxembourg: https://ec.europa.eu/jrc/en/publication/eur-scientific-and-technical-research-reports/research-evidence-use-learning-analytics-implications-education-policy

Ferguson, R., & Buckingham Shum, S. (2012). *Social learning analytics: five approaches.* Paper presented at the 2nd International Conference on Learning Analytics and Knowledge, Vancouver, British Columbia, Canada.

Ferguson, R., & Clow, D. (2017). *Where is the evidence? A call to action for learning analytics.* Paper presented at the Proceedings of the 6th Learning Analytics Knowledge Conference, Vancouver.

FitzGerald, E., Kucirkova, N., Jones, A., Cross, S., Ferguson, R., Herodotou, C., ... Scanlon, E. (2018). Dimensions of personalisation in technology-enhanced learning: A framework and implications for design. *British Journal of Educational Technology, 49*(1), 165–181. DOI: 10.1111/bjet.12534

Guri-Rosenblit, S. (2018). E-Teaching in Higher Education: An Essential Prerequisite for E-Learning. *Journal New Approaches in Educational Research, 7*(2), 93–97. DOI: 10.7821/naer.2018.7.298

Hernández-Leo, D., Asensio-Pérez, J. I., Derntl, M., Pozzi, F., Chacón, J., Prieto, L. P., & Persico, D. (2018). An Integrated Environment for Learning Design. *Frontiers in ICT, 5*(9). DOI: 10.3389/fict.2018.00009

Herodotou, C., Rienties, B., Boroowa, A., Zdrahal, Z., Hlosta, M., & Naydenova, G. (2017). *Implementing predictive learning analytics on a large scale: the teacher's perspective.* Paper presented at the Proceedings of the Seventh International Learning Analytics & Knowledge Conference, Vancouver, British Columbia, Canada.

Herodotou, C., Rienties, B., Verdin, B., & Boroowa, A. (2019). Predictive Learning Analytics 'At Scale': Guidelines to Successful Implementation in Higher Education. *Journal of Learning Analytics, 6*(1), 85–95.

Hidalgo, R. (2018). *Analytics for Action: using data analytics to support students in improving their learning outcomes.* Retrieved from Maastricht:

Hillaire, G., Fenton-O'Creevey, M., Mittelmeier, J., Rienties, B., Tempelaar, D. T., & Zdrahal, Z. (Submitted). A student-sourced sentiment analysis to improve detection of (mixed) emotion in online discourse. *IEEE Transactions on Affective Computing.*

Hlosta, M., Herrmannova, D., Zdrahal, Z., & Wolff, A. (2015). OU Analyse: analysing at-risk students at The Open University. *Learning Analytics Review*, 1–16.

Holmes, W., Bialik, M., & Fadel, C. (2019). *Artificial Intelligence In Education: Promises and Implications for Teaching and Learning.* Boston, MA: Center for Curriculum Redesign.

Jivet, I., Scheffel, M., Specht, M., & Drachsler, H. (2018). *License to evaluate: Preparing learning analytics dashboards for educational practice.* Paper presented at the Proceedings of the 8th International Conference on Learning Analytics & Knowledge (LAK'18), Sydney, Australia.

Jones, A., & Issroff, K. (2005). Learning technologies: Affective and social issues in computer-supported collaborative learning. *Computers & Education, 44*(4), 395–408. DOI: https://doi.org/10.1016/j.compedu.2004.04.004

Jones, A., Scanlon, E., Tosunoglu, C., Ross, S., Butcher, P., Murphy, P., & Greenberg, J. (1996). Evaluating CAL at The Open University: 15 years on. *Computers & Education, 26*(1), 5–15. DOI: https://doi.org/10.1016/0360-1315(95)00064-X

Koedinger, K., Booth, J. L., & Klahr, D. (2013). Instructional complexity and the science to constrain It. *Science, 342*(6161), 935–937. DOI: 10.1126/science.1238056

Law, P. (2015). Digital Badging at The Open University: recognition for informal learning. *Open Learning: The Journal of Open, Distance and e-Learning, 30*(3), 221–234.

Lawless, K. A., & Pellegrino, J. W. (2007). Professional Development in Integrating Technology Into Teaching and Learning: Knowns, Unknowns, and Ways to Pursue Better Questions and Answers. *Review of Educational Research, 77*(4), 575–614. DOI: 10.3102/0034654307309921

Li, N., Marsh, V., Rienties, B., & Whitelock, D. (2017). Online learning experiences of new versus continuing learners: a large scale replication study. *Assessment & Evaluation in Higher Education, 42*(4), 657–672. DOI: 10.1080/02602938.2016.1176989

Lockyer, L., & Dawson, S. (2012). *Where learning analytics meets learning design.* Paper presented at the Proceedings of the 2nd International Conference on Learning Analytics and Knowledge, Vancouver, British Columbia, Canada.

Luckin, R., Holmes, W., Griffiths, M., & Forcier, L. B. (2016). Intelligence Unleashed: An argument for AI in Education. In. London: Pearson Education.

Mangaroska, K., & Giannakos, M. N. (2018). Learning analytics for learning design: A systematic literature review of analytics-driven design to enhance learning. *IEEE Transactions on Learning Technologies.* DOI: 10.1109/TLT.2018.2868673

Nguyen, Q., Huptych, M., & Rienties, B. (2018a). *Linking students' timing of engagement to learning design and academic performance.* Paper presented at the Proceedings of the 8th International Conference on Learning Analytics & Knowledge (LAK'18), Sydney, Australia.

Nguyen, Q., Huptych, M., & Rienties, B. (2018b). Using Temporal Analytics to Detect Inconsistencies Between Learning Design and Students' Behaviours. *Journal of Learning Analytics, 5*(3), 120–135. DOI: 10.18608/jla.2018.53.8

Nguyen, Q., Rienties, B., Toetenel, L., Ferguson, F., & Whitelock, D. (2017). Examining the designs of computer-based assessment and its impact on student engagement, satisfaction, and pass rates. *Computers in Human Behavior, 76*(November 2017), 703–714. DOI: 10.1016/j.chb.2017.03.028

Olney, T., Rienties, B., & Toetenel, L. (2018). Gathering, visualising and interpreting learning design analytics to inform classroom practice and curriculum design: a student-centred approach from The Open University. In J. M. Lodge, J. C. Horvath, & L. Corrin (Eds.), *From Data and Analytics to the Classroom: Translating Learning Analytics for Teachers.* London: Routledge.

Prinsloo, P., & Slade, S. (2017). *An elephant in the learning analytics room: the obligation to act.* Paper presented at the Proceedings of the Seventh International Learning Analytics & Knowledge Conference, Vancouver, British Columbia, Canada.

Rets, I. (2018). *Using eye-tracking to research the effects of linguistic text simplification on the reading behaviour of English language learners.* Paper presented at the EuroCALL 2018, Jyväskylä, Finland.

Richardson, J. T. E. (2015). The under-attainment of ethnic minority students in UK higher education: what we know and what we don't know. *Journal of Further and Higher Education, 39,* 278–291. DOI: 10.1080/0309877X.2013.858680

Rienties, B., Brouwer, N., & Lygo-Baker, S. (2013). The effects of online professional development on higher education teachers' beliefs and intentions towards learning facilitation and technology. *Teaching and Teacher Education, 29*, 122–131. DOI: 10.1016/j.tate.2012.09.002

Rienties, B., & Toetenel, L. (2016). The impact of learning design on student behaviour, satisfaction and performance: a cross-institutional comparison across 151 modules. *Computers in Human Behavior, 60*, 333–341. DOI: 10.1016/j.chb.2016.02.074

Rienties, B., Boroowa, A., Cross, S., Farrington-Flint, L., Herodotou, C., Prescott, L., . . . Woodthorpe, J. (2016a). *Reviewing three case-studies of learning analytics interventions at The Open University UK.* Paper presented at the Proceedings of the Sixth International Conference on Learning Analytics & Knowledge.

Rienties, B., Cross, S., & Zdrahal, Z. (2016b). Implementing a Learning Analytics Intervention and Evaluation Framework: what works? In B. K. Daniel (Ed.), *Big Data and Learning Analytics in Higher Education: Current Theory and Practice* (pp. 147–166). Heidelberg: Springer.

Rienties, B., Nguyen, Q., Holmes, W., & Reedy, K. (2017). A review of ten years of implementation and research in aligning learning design with learning analytics at The Open University UK. *Interaction Design and Architecture(s) Journal, N.33*, 134–154.

Rienties, B., Herodotou, C., Olney, T., Schencks, M., & Boroowa, A. (2018a). Making Sense of Learning Analytics Dashboards: A Technology Acceptance Perspective of 95 Teachers. *The International Review of Research in Open and Distributed Learning, 19*(5). DOI: 10.19173/irrodl.v19i5.3493

Rienties, B., Lewis, T., McFarlane, R., Nguyen, Q., & Toetenel, L. (2018b). Analytics in online and offline language learning environments: the role of learning design to understand student online engagement. *Journal of Computer-Assisted Language Learning, 31*(3), 273–293. DOI: 10.1080/09588221.2017.1401548

Rienties, B., Olney, T., Nichols, M., & Herodotou, C. (2019). Effective usage of Learning Analytics: What do practitioners want and where should distance learning institutions be going?. *Open Learning.*

Rizvi, S., Rienties, B., & Rogaten, J. (2018). *Investigation of Temporal Dynamics in MOOC Learning Trajectories: A Geocultural Perspective.* Paper presented at the AIED 2018: Artificial Intelligence in Education, London.

Rogaten, J., Rienties, B., Sharpe, R., Cross, S., Whitelock, D., Lygo-Baker, S., & Littlejohn, A. (2019). Reviewing affective, behavioural, and cognitive learning gains in higher education. *Assessment & Evaluation in Higher Education, 44*(3), 321–337. DOI: 10.1080/02602938.2018.1504277

Scanlon, E., Sharples, M., Fenton-O'Creevy, M., Fleck, J., Cooban, C., Ferguson, R., . . . Waterhouse, P. (2013). Beyond prototypes: Enabling innovation in technology-enhanced learning. In. Milton Keynes: Open University.

Schwendimann, B. A., Rodríguez-Triana, M. J., Vozniuk, A., Prieto, L. P., Boroujeni, M. S., Holzer, A., . . . Dillenbourg, P. (2017). Perceiving Learning at a Glance: A Systematic Literature Review of Learning Dashboard

Research. *IEEE Transactions on Learning Technologies, 10*(1), 30–41. DOI: 10.1109/TLT.2016.2599522

Tait, A. (2018). Open Universities: the next phase. *Asian Association of Open Universities Journal, 13*(1), 13–23. DOI: 10.1108/AAOUJ-12-2017-0040

Tempelaar, D. T., Niculescu, A., Rienties, B., Giesbers, B., & Gijselaers, W. H. (2012). How achievement emotions impact students' decisions for online learning, and what precedes those emotions. *Internet and Higher Education, 15*(3), 161–169. DOI: 10.1016/j.iheduc.2011.10.003

Tempelaar, D. T., Rienties, B., & Giesbers, B. (2015). In search for the most informative data for feedback generation: Learning Analytics in a data-rich context. *Computers in Human Behavior, 47*, 157–167. DOI: 10.1016/j.chb.2014.05.038

Tempelaar, D. T., Rienties, B., Mittelmeier, J., & Nguyen, Q. (2018a). Student profiling in a dispositional learning analytics application using formative assessment. *Computers in Human Behavior, 78*, 408–420. DOI: 10.1016/j.chb.2017.08.010

Tempelaar, D. T., Rienties, B., & Nguyen, Q. (2018b). A multi-modal study into students' timing and learning regulation: time is ticking. *Interactive Technology and Smart Education, 15*(4), 298–313. DOI: 10.1108/ITSE-02-2018-0015

Toetenel, L., & Rienties, B. (2016a). Analysing 157 Learning Designs using Learning Analytic approaches as a means to evaluate the impact of pedagogical decision-making. *British Journal of Educational Technology, 47*(5), 981–992. DOI: 10.1111/bjet.12423

Toetenel, L., & Rienties, B. (2016b). Learning Design – creative design to visualise learning activities. *Open Learning, 31*(3), 233–244. DOI: 10.1080/02680513.2016.1213626

Ullmann, T., Lay, S., Cross, S., Edwards, C., Gaved, M., Jones, E., . . . Rienties, B. (2018). *Scholarly insight Spring 2018: a Data wrangler perspective.* Retrieved from http://oro.open.ac.uk/56732/1/DW_Scholarly_Insight_Report_Spring_2018_oro.pdf.

van Ameijde, J., Weller, M., & Cross, S. (2018). Designing for Student Retention. *Journal of Perspectives in Applied Academic Practice, 6*(2). DOI: 10.14297/jpaap.v6i2.318

van Leeuwen, A., Janssen, J., Erkens, G., & Brekelmans, M. (2015). Teacher regulation of cognitive activities during student collaboration: Effects of learning analytics. *Computers & Education, 90*, 80–94. DOI: 10.1016/j.compedu.2015.09.006

Wolff, A., Zdrahal, Z., Nikolov, A., & Pantucek, M. (2013). *Improving retention: predicting at-risk students by analysing clicking behaviour in a virtual learning environment.* Paper presented at the Proceedings of the Third International Conference on Learning Analytics and Knowledge, Indianapolis.

CHAPTER 8

STEM Learning: Foundations

Eileen Scanlon, Christothea Herodotou,
Denise Whitelock and Chris Edwards

The first joint project undertaken by the Computers and Learning research group was the evaluation of The Open University Science Faculty's CAL offering in 1979. Since then many CALRG activities such as PhD projects, major external research grants, and institutional contributions, have been directed towards a better understanding of what makes science teaching and learning better. In this chapter we will consider our work on conceptual change in science and on the development of pedagogy and technology on personal inquiry using nQuire, and include work integrating these developments into the Open Science Laboratory. Our work has included evaluation of other innovative pedagogical supports such as the Puck-Land simulation for teaching Physics, Virtual Field Trips and the use of the Virtual Microscope both in the UK and a number of other UK and EU universities. We illustrate how judicious use of technology and pedagogy can promote enthusiastic engagement with science and give opportunities for participation and learning.

Introduction

At The Open University's (OU) inception there were those who doubted that science can be taught at degree level to students accepted on an 'open entry'

How to cite this book chapter:
Scanlon, E., Herodotou, C., Whitelock, D. and Edwards, C. 2019. STEM Learning: Foundations. In: Ferguson, R., Jones, A. and Scanlon, E. (eds). *Educational Visions: Lessons from 40 years of innovation.* Pp. 127–138. London: Ubiquity Press. DOI: https://doi.org/10.5334/bcg.h. License: CC-BY 4.0

basis, i.e. without prior entrance qualifications. The OU developed science degrees from its first inception and the number of students registered with the university to start science degrees in the 1990s had reached ten percent of all the full-time science students in the UK (Pentz, 1978). These initial attempts were watched closely as there was some scepticism from the Higher Education establishment of the time that this could be done.

Since the first attempts at teaching science in the OU fifty years ago, the successful learning experiences designed for Open University science students have demonstrated that so much is possible. The change in perceptions about the feasibility of learning and teaching science at a distance is in part due to the developments in the technologies available to support appropriate activities. The courses were designed to help students learning on their own so that every activity was designed carefully, following pedagogical principles, and tested before it was sent to students. This was important because OU students did not have a lecturer to explain things to them if anything was not clear. However, experiments could be refined and revised for residential schools.

The importance of practical work in the teaching of science has always been an essential component of science teaching and emphasized in the literature (see e.g. Hofstein, 2007; Holstermann et al. 2010.) Practical work was dealt with by the incorporation of a variety of media in courses; including home experiment kits, radio or audiotapes, TV and laboratory classes at day schools as documented in Ross and Scanlon, 1995. Technology enhanced learning techniques and tools became more available and these were appropriate to help with this task too.

Why is science hard to learn? There are particular challenges for teaching and learning science at a distance. The OU's system offered the opportunity to study science to those with no previous qualifications in the subject. These ranged from the lack of prerequisites for study, the hierarchical nature of concepts needed to build science content knowledge, the need to develop mathematical skills, and develop practical work (Ross and Scanlon, 1995).

Technology was deployed very early in the development of a pedagogy of teaching science at a distance at the OU. This included the introduction of technology to the mix of media adopted in the first years of the university. A media mix that was heavily text based included also broadcast TV, audio and from the mid-1970s the use of computers. In the late 1970s an evaluation of early attempts at the use of CAL in the science faculty reviewed remedial CAL tutorials delivered on terminals available (for limited access) at study centres and simulation programmes available at residential or day schools (see Scanlon et al. 1987, Jones et al. 1982. 1987a,1987b). In our first case study we consider the use of simulation and modelling arising from these first years' experiences.

Case Study one: Simulations and modelling

Early experiments with the use of computers in teaching science involved simulations and modelling. In a simulation the process or system is modelled and then made available to the user so that, by playing with the system, they can get some insight into what is being modelled. So, experiments can be simulated that would be impossible to interact with in real life for reasons of access, expense time constraints or other considerations. A number of publications trace this work (e.g. Every and Scanlon, 1983; Ross and Scanlon, 1995, Blake & Scanlon, 1996, 2007).

One issue which emerged from the evaluation of our CAL simulations (Jones, Scanlon, and O'Shea, 1987) was the importance of prior knowledge of the concepts which is often assumed in the design of the simulations. Sustained work on science learning in the past 40 years explored how science conceptions are developed. One example of our work on science concepts was the project, funded by the Economic and Social Research Council on using simulations for the development of conceptual change (the ESRC-funded 'Conceptual Change in Science' project). Our aim was to promote change in learners' understanding of physical phenomena. This work included the design and development of a set of teaching materials for the teaching of a topic on mechanics. These teaching materials included interactive computer simulations of force and motion, along with practical activities and written materials. The method involved making learners aware of the limitations of their current conceptions of force and motion. Then, learners would be helped to develop and use a conceptual framework which conformed to current scientific understanding. This would have to be in line with their experience and be internally consistent. Conceptual change was found to be developed in this sequence of lessons. The children on whom the curriculum was tested displayed more sophisticated reasoning than their counterparts in comparison classes (Hennessy et al. 1995a, 1995b). This work influenced the development of simulations used in distance education settings. One particular finding, that the conceptual change in science software was most effective in situations where practical experimental work was combined with work with simulations, was particularly important, see Twigger et al., 1994. (Another example of the influence of this work on the design of teaching, was the Supported Learning in Physics Project (SLIPP), where we used OU expertise in support of teacher education in schools Whitelegg and Edwards, 2001.)

An extension of the simulation which consists of a mathematical model of some process underlying the system is that of a virtual environment. Laurillard (2001 p 36) points out 'virtual environments use a graphical model to display the visual and positional properties of the system rather than its behaviour'. The examples of virtual field trips and virtual microscope are discussed below.

Another connected strand of work involved a number of PhD theses on modelling physics problem solving, and graphical representations (link to CALRG theses lists in the library). These projects looked in detail at students' current conceptions of different science topics and made use of detailed protocol analysis of users' interactions with computer systems as they solved problems to produce rich pictures (thick descriptions of students talking, writing and interacting with technology) to help us understand what ideas and interactions were causing difficulties with instruction (see also Driver and Scanlon, 1988).

One particular problem that Physics students encounter is that of understanding elastic collisions. A simulation known as PuckLand was developed which allowed students to investigate the interaction between two ice pucks. This early work was written in HyperCard for use with the Apple Macintosh and consisted of a pair of pinball-style flippers on either side of the screen with which subjects could flick pucks (see Figure 8.1).

The amount of force with which the flippers hit the pucks could be varied by raising the height of the flippers as could the mass of the pucks. When the 'go' button was activated the pucks moved towards each other on the screen and were animated with speeds proportional to those set by button presses. After the pucks collided, they moved away from each other with a speed that was calculated with the correct Physics formalisms. In this way, the principle of conservation of momentum and kinetic energy were obeyed as illustrated by the apparent screen velocities of the pucks.

The empirical study undertaken with this simulation involved 16–17 year old Physics students working in pairs and this research was an early foray into computer supported collaborative learning. The initial findings revealed that students develop two families of causal models to explain motion after a collision. These have been identified as the linear causal and the resistance/reciprocal causal model. However, these models broke down when the students were confronted with the animations from the PuckLand simulation.

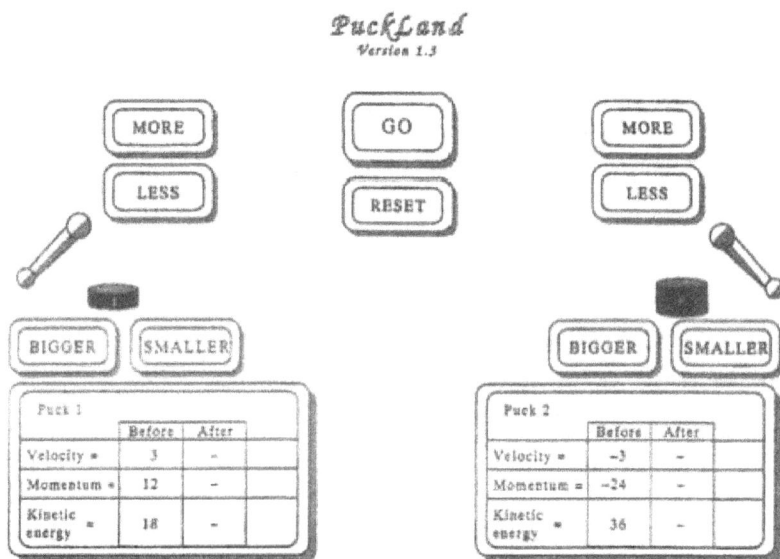

Figure 8.1: Screen dump of the graphic interface to the PuckLand program. Reprinted from *Computers & Education* 20 (1). D. Whitelock, T. Taylor, T. O'Shea, E. Scanlon, R. Sellman, P. Clark, C. O'Malley, Challenging models of elastic collisions with a computer simulation, pp. 1-9, copyright Pergamon Press Ltd (1993), with permission from Elsevier.

The result being that the students were moved to rethink their common-sense ideas about motion which lacked an understanding of conservation of energy.

A second study involved pairing the students with either "similar" or "different" common-sense models of collisions. It is interesting to note this early work suggested that the cooperative construction of shared meaning rather than conflict was more important for successful collaboration (Barbieri & Light, 1993). It is interesting to note that the PuckLand simulation, although routed in Science teaching and learning, was also able to prompt further investigation into computer supported collaborative learning and to provide a further vignette into the practical application of social constructivist theory.

Case study 2: Practical work-home kits, residential schools and multimedia approaches

In an earlier Chapter (4) Coughlan et al. describe an approach to one particular problem of learning science at a distance, that of access to practical experiences. They describe one particular solution in the work researching remote laboratories (see also Scanlon et al., 2004). However, this was only one approach taken to the knotty problem of providing practical experiences for online distance learning of science. Initially the means of making practical experiences available to students was the provision of extensive home experiment kits, residential schools and broadcast TV programmes.

More recently the provision of multimedia meant that students can have vicarious experience of observing experiments. In addition there is the possibility of controlling variables and drawing inferences. An introductory science course offered at The Open University in the 1990s offered students the possibility of interacting with a global warming simulation, taking a virtual desert field trip and conducting Galapagos field trips (see e.g. Taylor et al. 1996; Whitelock, 2001) sometimes with a problem-solving pedagogy applied (see e.g. Ross and Bolton, 1990). Virtual field trips where users explore a three-dimensional environment have been used (see e.g. Whitelock, 2001; Whitelock and Jelfs, 2005).

Furthermore, Whitelock with co-authors Brna and Holland (1996), selected three properties of virtual environments to incorporate into a model that could compare salient properties of virtual systems that would be open to test. These properties included representational fidelity, immediacy of control and presence which could define a finite but still a large space of VE classes. This model was used to understand the factors in virtual environments that promote conceptual learning by comparing two desktop virtual environments which explored field trips to the North Atlantic Ridge by submarine and a walk through an oak wood (Whitelock, 1999). The representational fidelity was rated higher for the oak wood than the North Atlantic Ridge. Immediacy of control was perceived differently in the two VR programs due to the jerky movements experienced in these early desktop VR environments. However, the role of audio was found to be important in more than one way when virtual environments are being built for conceptual learning. this is because they create a sense of presence, engagement and enjoyment but are also important for navigation. The latter is not such a trivial point as first may appear since the cognitive load could be diminished if navigation was easier and students could concentrate on understanding and manipulating concepts within the subject domain. It is interesting to note that virtual reality systems still require navigational and conceptual compasses for conceptual learning as suggested from this 1999 study. Of a similar vintage is our original Virtual Microscope project which simulates the views through a microscope of slides displaying different kinds of materials Whalley et al., 2011. This has particular benefits for students with accessibility issues as described in Chapter 4. For example, it provides access for students with difficulty in reaching laboratories and better access to images for students who are partially sighted.

Case study 3: Personal Inquiry project
A significant advancement in the available technologies to support the development of science understanding had the effect of sparking a new extended investigation into how technologies can enable science learning in contemporary contexts. In the context of a 'Personal Inquiry' (PI) project funded by the ESRC and Engineering & Physical Sciences Research Council (EPSRC), we explored the conditions under which evidence-based inquiry learning can be fostered. The PI project aimed to understand how personal and mobile technologies can be deployed to make the processes of evidence-based scientific inquiry readily accessible to young people (see Anastopoulou et al., 2008, 2012). As Blumenfeld et al. (1991) point out, technology has a potentially useful role to play in structuring the process of inquiry learning with tactical and strategic support.

Making scientific inquiry authentic is a challenge that has been discussed by a number of researchers (e.g. Edelson et al., 1999; Chinn and Malhotra, 2002). A personal inquiry toolkit was developed to scaffold this activity and was tried out in a number of school-based interventions, two in Nottingham schools and two in Milton Keynes. The young people carried out scientific explorations supported by their teachers and also by a personal inquiry toolkit. This toolkit, in its first instantiation, ran on a small portable computer and guided the learners through a process of gathering and assessing evidence, whilst they conducted experiments on topic themes of relevance to the secondary-level UK National Curriculum. Further technology support was provided by data probes connected to the computer. Project partners included schools, technology companies that develop sensing and data-logging equipment, museums, community resource centres and field trip sites. This broad partnership reflected our view that we need to support learning within the classroom and outside it whether on field trips or at home.

At the culmination of this project we developed nQuire, a software application to guide personal inquiry learning. nQuire provides teacher support for authoring, orchestrating and monitoring inquiries as well as student support for carrying out, configuring and reviewing inquiries. nQuire allows inquiries to be scripted and configured in various ways, so that personally relevant, rather than off-the-shelf inquiries, can be created and used by teachers and students. nQuire incorporates an approach to specifying learning flow that provides flexible access to current inquiry activities without precluding access to other activities for review and orientation. Dependencies between activities are automatically handled, ensuring decisions made by the student or teacher are propagated through the inquiry. nQuire can be used to support inquiry activities across individual, group and whole-class levels at different parts of the inquiry. It offers a flexible, web-based approach that can incorporate different devices (smartphone, netbook, PC) and does not rely on constant connectivity (Mullholland et al., 2011). We published a set of studies of orchestration of inquiry within and beyond the classroom (Sharples, 2013; Sharples et al., 2015) and illustrated how the inquiry framework and nQuire toolkit together influenced the performance and effectiveness of inquiry learning (Littleton et al., 2013). This paradigm has been further developed to scaffold online personal inquiry learning within informal settings. For example the nQuire platform has also been used in Higher Education in The Open University's Open Science Lab (see Theme 2) to support informal examples of inquiry learning (Villasclaras Fernandez et al., 2013).

Case Study 4: The iSpot Project
The aim of iSpot (www.ispotnature.org) (see Figure 8.2) is to create a new generation of naturalists by helping students and people of all ages learn how to identify organisms by enhancing natural history identification skills. It was launched in 2009 and developed initially with a five-year, £2 million grant from the Big Lottery Fund for England. This skill (to identify likely IDs for observed flora and fauna) underlies all of biodiversity science. However, this is no longer widely taught in formal curricula in schools or universities. A South African site followed (www.ispot.org.za) and in 2013 a version for Chile was also created (www.ispotnature.org/chile). iSpot has 65,000 registered users who have made more than 550,000 observations of many thousands of species.

In working with the development of iSpot we have contributed to learning but also to scientific discoveries through observations communicated on the platform. The observations included two which had not been recorded in the UK before. A six-year-old girl discovered a moth on her windowsill. The moth, native to Asia, had never before been spotted in the UK. After identification on iSpot, the species was also confirmed by experts and the moth was taken into the Natural History Museum collection. In addition, in South Africa, a doctor submitted a photograph of unknown seeds that were the cause of poisoning in several children presenting at a clinic and these were identified 35 seconds after posting on iSpot (iSpot 2013). Hitherto unknown populations of South African endemic plant species are regularly discovered on iSpot (Silvertown et al., 2015, p. 142).

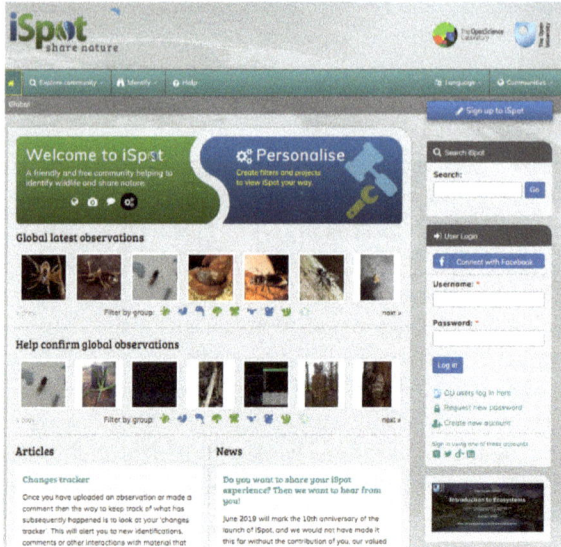

Figure 8.2: The iSpot platform supporting species identification.

iSpot was incorporated into the OU's Open Science Laboratory which allows anyone, anywhere to access practical science education. iSpot also supports Open University / BBC broadcasts, the Open Science Laboratory, and was used in three environmental courses.

We were involved in the design, development and running of the platform and the evaluation of learning on the platform (Scanlon et al., 2014). iSpot provides an online community where novices and experts can work together to identify living organisms and engage in crowdsourcing identification. iSpot allows anyone, anywhere, to upload an image for identification in towns, back gardens, open fields, forests and all sorts of habitats across the country. This contributes to solving the problem of learning about nature. Also, the information gathered by iSpot is used for other data collection for conservation purposes.

The impact of iSpot on learning has been measured in a couple of ways. Learning episodes are short and informal. So, we needed to think about the impact of iSpot and the potential outcomes, including increased awareness and impact on attitudes, as well as engagement and participation. It is complex to examine such learning settings as iSpot. Qualitative analysis does show clear examples of users who start as complete novices, and then come to a good understanding of identification. There is also some quantitative evidence of users learning. For instance, analysis of a sample of 407 users as they progressed through submitting and identifying their first 50 observations within iSpot is strongly suggestive of learning as users showed improvement in their ability to identify other people's observations over the period that they submitted observations:

As users progress from their first to their 50th observation posted on iSpot they have a bigger percentage of correct identifications, that is they are more likely to identify what they have seen for themselves. This change in behaviour probably reflects learning, although other causes of the trend may be possible (Silvertown et al., 2015).

Conclusions

A range of science-related projects have been undertaken over the last 40 years (see also the account in Scanlon 2011) which aims to support learners to learn science from a distance, and without previous academic qualifications, and to build connections between formal and informal learning in order to foster their interest and curiosity in science. Major milestones in the journey of engaging learners with science have been the development of science simulations and modelling and their support of conceptual change (Case Study 1), technology mediated practical work, (Case Study 2), the Personal Inquiry (PI) project that scaffolded the process of scientific inquiry through technology (Case Study 3), and iSpot that leveraged the power of the crowd to support species identification (Case Study 4). This journey aimed to bring science closer to the everyday life of learners and help them understand and appreciate its value by developing bridges between formal and informal education. It also aimed to open up and make science accessible thus enabling potentially anyone to engage with science activities. These technological developments promote enthusiastic engagement with science and give opportunities for participation and learning. For example, the use of simulations allows for hands-on experimental work to take place at any time, in a playful manner and by learning through failure, exploration and experimentation. Simulations lower the barriers to participation and make it easy for people to engage with activities often viewed as determined by scientists. In relation to our Beyond Prototypes themes (see Chapter one) this chapter illustrates the effect of the 'persistent intent' of a succession of teachers and researchers who were determined to meet our initial challenge from many commentators that as far as science learning at a distance goes, '*It can't be done*'.

The above line of work suggests that certain aspects can support the process of engagement with science including an understanding of what people need to know in order to effectively do science, both in formal and informal settings, such as knowledge of basic science-related concepts, and relevant mathematical skills and skills for practical work. Also, an explicit account of hard to grasp concepts should be developed through studies with online learners, in order to identify and improve issues they are struggling with. Such an account could inform the design of more effective science learning experiences that consider the challenges or demands of self-regulated learning, such as the significance of appropriate scaffolding when learners complete tasks on their own.

References

Anastopoulou, S., Sharples, M., Ainsworth, S., Crook, C., O'Malley, C., & Wright, M. (2012). Creating personal meaning through technology-supported science inquiry learning across formal and informal settings. *International Journal of Science Education*, 34(2), 251–273.

Anastopoulou, S., Sharples, M., Wright, M., Martin, H., Ainsworth, S., Benford, S., O'Malley, C. (2008). Learning 21st century science in context with mobile technologies. In J. Traxler, B. Riordan, & C. Dennett (Eds.), Proceedings of the mLearn 2008 conference: The bridge from text to context (pp. 296–303). Wolverhampton, England: University of Wolverhampton.

Barbieri M. and Light, P. (1993). Interaction, gender and performance on a Computer Based Problem Solving Task. *International Journal of Educational Research*.

Blake, C. and Scanlon, E. (2007). Reconsidering simulations in science education at a distance: features of effective use. *Journal of Computer Assisted Learning*, 23(6) pp. 491–502.

Blake, C., Butcher, P., Scanlon, E. and Jones, A. (1996). The Works Metallurgist: an evaluation of a CAL package on phase diagrams. *ALT-J: Research in Learning Technology*, 4(1) pp. 55–57.

Blumenfeld PC, Soloway E, Marx RW, Krajcik JS, Guzdial M, Palincsar A (1991). Motivating project-based learning: sustaining the doing, supporting the learning. Educ Psychol 26(3–4):369–398.

Chinn, C. and Malhotra, B. (2002). Epistemologically Authentic Inquiry in Schools: A Theoretical Framework for Evaluating Inquiry Tasks *Science Education*, Vol 86, No 2.

Driver, R., Scanlon, E. (1988). Conceptual change in science: A research programme, *Journal of Computer Assisted Learning*, Vol. 5, Issue 1.

Edelson, D.C, Gordin, R.D. and Pea, R.D. (1999). Addressing the challenges of inquiry-based learning through technology and curriculum design, *Journal of the Learning Sciences* 8 (3–4), 391–450.

Every, I. and Scanlon, E. (1983). Discovering physics with microcomputers. *Computers and Education*, 8(1) pp. 183–188.

Hennessy, S., Twigger, D., Byard, M., Driver, R., Draper, S., Hartley, J. R., Mohamed, R., O'Malley, C., O'Shea, T., and Scanlon, E. (1995a). Design of a computer-augmented curriculum for mechanics. *International Journal of Science Education*, 17 (1), 75–92.

Hennessy, S., Twigger, D., Byard, M., Driver, R., Draper, S., Hartley, J. R., Mohamed, R., O'Malley, C., O'Shea, T., and Scanlon, E. (1995b). A classroom intervention using a computer-augmented curriculum for mechanics. *International Journal of Science Education*, 17(2) 189–206.

Hofstein, A. and Mamlok-Namman, R. (2007). The laboratory in science education: the state of the art. Chemistry Education Research and Practice 8, 105–107.

Holstermann, N., Grube, D. and Bögeholz, S. (2010). Hands-on activities and their influence on students' interest. Research in Science Education 40, 743–757.

Jones, A., Scanlon, E. and O'Shea, T. eds. (1987a). The Computer Revolution: New Technologies for Distance Teaching. Brighton: Harvester Press.

Jones, A., O'Shea, T. and Scanlon, E. (1987b). Evaluation of Computer Assisted Learning at The Open University. In Jones, A., Scanlon, E. and O'Shea, T. (eds) The Computer Revolution in Education. Harvester Press, ISBN 0-7108-0985-9, pp263–276.

Jones, A., and O'Shea, T. (1982). Barriers to the use of computer assisted British Journal of Educational Technology, Vol 13,No 3.

Laurillard, D. (2001). Rethinking University Teaching, Routledge Press.

Littleton, K., Scanlon, E. and Sharples, M. (2012). Orchestrating Inquiry Routledge Press.

Mulholland, P., Anastopoulou, S., Collins, T., Feisst, M., Gaved, M., Kerawalla, L., Paxton, M., Scanlon, E., Sharples, M. and Wright, M. (2011). nQuire: Technological support for personal inquiry learning. IEEE Transactions on Learning Technologies. First published online, 5th December 2011. 5(2) pp. 157–169 http://doi.ieeecomputersociety.org/10.1109/TLT.2011.32

Pentz, M. (1978). 'It can't be done' Lecture at Royal Institution.

Ross, S. and Scanlon, E. (1995). Technology and Pedagogy. In Open Science; the distance teaching and open learning of science subjects, London: Paul Chapman Publishing.

Ross, S. and Bolton, J. (2002). Physica: a computer environment for Physics problem-solving. Interactive Learning Environments, 10(2) pp. 157–175.

Scanlon, E. (2011). Technology-enhanced science learning at a distance, Open Learning:The Journal of Open and Distance Learning, 24 (2).

Scanlon, E. How novices solve physics problems. pp176–186 In Jones, A., Scanlon, E. and O'Shea, T. (eds) The Computer Revolution in Education. Harvester Press, 1987.ISBN 0-7108-0985-9

Scanlon, E., Woods, W., & Clow, D. (2014). Informal Participation in Science in the UK: Identification, Location and Mobility with iSpot. Educational Technology & Society, 17 (2), 58–71.

Scanlon, E., Jones, A. and O'Shea, T. (1982). Evaluating CAL at The Open University, In The Computer Revolution in Education, Lewes, UK: Harvester Press.

Scanlon, E., Sharples, M., Fenton-O'Creevy, M., Fleck, J., Cooban, C., Ferguson, R., Cross, S. and Waterhouse, P. (2013). Beyond prototypes: Enabling innovation in technology-enhanced learning. Open University, Milton Keynes.

Scanlon, E., Colwell, C., Cooper, M., and Di Paolo, T. (2004). Remote experiments, re-versioning and re-thinking science learning. Computers & Education, 43(1–2) pp. 153–163.

Scanlon, E. (2011). Technology enhanced learning in science: interactions, affordances and design-based research. Journal of Interactive Media in Education, 24 (2).

Sharples, M. (2013). Shared orchestration within and beyond the classroom. *Computers and Education*, 69 pp. 504–506.

Sharples, M., Scanlon, E., Ainsworth, S., Anastopoulou, S., Collins, T., Crook, C., Jones, A., Kerawalla, L., Littleton, K., Mulholland, P. and O'Malley, C. (2015). Personal inquiry: orchestrating science investigations within and beyond the classroom. *Journal of the Learning Sciences*, 24(2) pp. 308–341.

Silvertown, J., Harvey, M., Greenwood, R., Dodd, M., Rosewell, J., Rebelo, T., Ansine, J. and McConway, K. (2015). Crowdsourcing the identification of organisms: a case-study of iSpot. *ZooKeys*, 480 pp. 125–146.

Taylor, J., Scanlon, E. and Hodgson, B. (1996). Multimedia and Science Education, *Education Research and Perspectives*, 23 (2), 48–58.

Twigger, D., Byard, M., Driver, R., Draper, S., Hartley, J. R., Hennessy, S., Mohamed, R., O'Malley, C., O'Shea, T., and Scanlon, E. (1994). The conceptions of force and motion of students aged between 10 and 15 years: an interview study designed to guide instruction. *International Journal of Science Education*, 16 (2), 215–229.

Villasclaras Fernandez, E., Sharples, M., Kelley, S. and Scanlon, E. (2013). Supporting citizen inquiry: an investigation of Moon rock. In: *Scaling up Learning for Sustained Impact, Lecture Notes in Computer Science*, Springer, pp. 383–395.

Whalley, P., Kelley, S. and Tindle, A. (2011). The role of the Virtual Microscope in distance learning. *Open Learning: The Journal of Open and Distance Learning*, 26(2) pp. 127–134.

Whitelegg, E. and Edwards, C. (2001). Beyond the laboratory: learning physics in real-life contexts. In: Behrendt, Helga; Dahncke, Helmut; Duit, Reinders; Graber, Wolfgang; Komorek, Michael; Kross, Angela and Reiska, Priit eds. *Research in science education: past, present and future*. Dordrect, Netherlands: Kluwer Academic Publishers, pp. 337–342

Whitelock, D., Taylor, J., O'Shea, T., Scanlon, E., Clark, P. and O'Malley, C. (1993). 'Challenging Models of Elastic Collisions with a Computer Simulation.' *Journal of Computers in Education*. Vol 20, No. 1 pp 1–9. Pergamon Press.

Whitelock, D.M., Brna., P. and Holland, S. (1996). What is the value of virtual reality for conceptual learning? Towards a theoretical framework. In: P. Brna, A. Paiva and J.A. Self (eds) *Proceedings of the European Conference on Artificial Intelligence in Education*, Lisbon, 127–132.

Whitelock, D. (1999). Investigating the role of task structure and interface support in two virtual learning environments. *International Journal of Continuing Engineering Education and Life-Long Learning*, 9(3/4) pp. 291–301.

Whitelock, D. (2001). *Going Live to the Galapagos Islands and an Oak Wood: S103 Student Responses to some Biological Multimedia Programs* IET internal report Program on Learner Use of Media report No 138.

Whitelock, D. and Jelfs, A. (2005). 'Would you rather collect data in the rain or attend a virtual field trip?': Findings from a series of virtual science field studies. *International Journal of Continuing Engineering Education and Life-Long Learning*, 15(1–2), pp. 121–131.

CHAPTER 9

STEM Learning: Futures

Christothea Herodotou, Eileen Scanlon and Denise Whitelock

Following on from the account of some CALRG research related to STEM learning in the previous chapter we discuss here several examples of attempts to explore the technology and pedagogy of learning science. In one thread we look at informal learning and linking journeys between formal and informal learning and how we have built on previous work on developing inquiry learning. In the second we look at a design to support collaborative working at a distance building on our previous work on learning from simulations. The case studies in this chapter illustrate the persistent intent of supporting science learners and a shared vision of the range of support under development for this end.

Introduction

Recent direction of this research has emphasized informal learning, journeys between formal and informal learning and collaborative working. The development of the nQuire-it project initiated a series of projects in the field of Citizen Science. It resulted in the development of the nQuire-it platform and the Sense-it app supporting the design and implementation of personally meaningful

How to cite this book chapter:
Herodotou, C., Scanlon, E. and Whitelock, D. 2019. STEM Learning: Futures. In: Ferguson, R., Jones, A. and Scanlon, E. (eds). *Educational Visions: Lessons from 40 years of innovation.* Pp. 139–150. London: Ubiquity Press. DOI: https://doi. org/10.5334/bcg.i. License: CC-BY 4.0

investigations outside the classroom, by citizens of all ages. Through the BBC's 'Tomorrow's World nQuire', this has developed further into a dynamic and social toolkit hosting multiple types of Citizen Science projects such as image, audio and text-based projects as well as survey-type projects with personalized feedback. In the LEARN CitSci project, our international Citizen Science collaboration with six natural history museums and universities in the US and UK is aiming to improve the design of existing Citizen Science projects led by museums and make science learning more enjoyable and accessible to young people.

Case study 1: Citizen Inquiry

The story of Citizen Inquiry is a strong example of how an innovative pedagogy reinforced and guided the development of relevant technology. Pedagogy may often be overlooked in technology-enhanced learning (TEL) and this is due to the emphasis often placed upon technological elements rather the learning engagement, processes, and outcomes. In the case of Citizen Inquiry, advancements in technology enabled testing and evaluation of this pedagogy and supported progress towards a learning vision. Citizen Inquiry is an innovative approach to inquiry learning, proposed by OU Emeritus Professor Mike Sharples. It is located at the intersection between 'Citizen Science' and 'inquiry-based learning' and refers to mass participation of the public in joining and initiating inquiry-led scientific investigations. Specifically, "*it fuses the creative knowledge building of inquiry learning with the mass collaborative participation exemplified by Citizen Science, changing the consumer relationship that most people have with research to one of active engagement*" (Sharples et al., 2013, p 36). The 'citizen inquiry' paradigm shifts the emphasis of scientific inquiry from scientists to the general public, by having non-professionals (of any age and level of experience) determine their own research agenda and devise their own science investigations underpinned by a model of scientific inquiry. Citizen inquiry aims to leverage the pedagogical potential of inquiry-based learning – a productive approach to the development of learners' knowledge of the world and the enhancement of higher-order thinking skills – through opening up massive participation in inquiry-based activities.

It becomes evident that Citizen Inquiry emerged from a reconfiguration of existing ideas and social practices, that is the increasing interest and growth of Citizen Science and its consequences for how science is conducted (Bonney et al., 2009) and Inquiry Learning as a problem-solving approach to learning that requires guidance and 'scaffolding'(Quintana et al., 2004). This is an example of 'bricolage' (Scanlon et al., 2013) where the central idea or the vision of TEL innovation resulted from examining available materials, approaches and ideas, and experimentation, rather than the configuration of a vision that is precedes the development of relevant material. A new research project may emerge from either inventing and testing a new idea, or through the process of bricolage, that is bringing together and reconfiguring what is already known.

The first step towards examining or testing the idea of Citizen Inquiry was to attract funding. In 2013, one-year funding from Nominet Trust enabled the recruitment of a software designer and an educational developer to design tools that could scaffold or facilitate learning through Citizen Inquiry. Advancements in technology such as synchronous and asynchronous communication, and the instant data upload from mobile phones to the web could enable communication and mass participation of citizens in inquiry-led learning activities, and thus instantiate the idea of Citizen Inquiry. In partnership with teachers and students from the Sheffield University Technical College (UTC), we designed in a participatory manner the nQuire-it platform and a mobile data collection application, Sense-it (available on Google play). The tools were developed through a design-based research approach, where prototypes of the tools were evaluated by young people, improved and retested (Herodotou, Aristeidou, Sharples, Scanlon, 2018, Herodotou et al., 2014). The delivery of functional versions of the tools was very timely as it coincided with the research activities of a PhD student who was examining inquiry learning in online settings. In practice, this allowed for additional research to take place that could not be supported by the project funding, in two main areas: evaluation of the usability and general functionality of the tools and capturing early evidence of learning impact. It also extended the scope of tools to adult participants through a study with amateur meteorologists and weather watchers and provided recommendations as to how to sustain participation in citizen inquiry learning communities (Aristeidou, Scanlon, Sharples, 2014).

Despite the overall success of the project in developing and evaluating tools to support the process of Citizen Inquiry and a collection of papers published (Herodotou et al., 2017), a period of uncertainty followed the project completion. Additional sources of funding were needed to sustain and monitor the tools, provide support to current and prospective users, develop and enhance the functionality of the tools and disseminate project outputs, and enable uptake of the innovation. During this critical period of no additional financial resources, the OU agreed to provide minimum technical support for maintaining the tools. Also, the research team made systematic attempts to attract additional funding. These efforts were directed both to external funders and the university; in the case of the latter, the intention was to integrate the tools and the new learning approach to the design of new or existing courses. What motivated these efforts was the fact that all involved researchers shared the same vision around the potential of Citizen Inquiry to make learning engaging and interactive while they were also willing to dedicate time to identify new sources of funding. In practice, we scheduled monthly or fortnightly meetings where we discussed our progress towards attracting funding and set actions to be completed before the next meeting. In this way, our efforts were systematic and persistent over time.

Persistent intent (Scanlon et al., 2013) plays a significant role in pursuing and mainstreaming innovation in TEL. The sharing of a clear and common vision amongst a research team can also help steer and plan future activities aiming at extending the project lifecycle. In the case of Citizen Inquiry, persistent intent resulted in a partnership with the BBC's 'Tomorrow's World' science programming (http://www.bbc.co.uk/tomorrowsworld), the aim of which was to extend existing tools and support large-scale public investigations in both the natural and social sciences (e.g., psychology). For example, tools should enable citizens to create and run online studies to explore attitudes and personality. This project, running for a year, involved certain technical developments including new ways to enter responses, secure handling of personal data, and ways for participants to overview results. Overall, this funding enabled the re-implementation of tools to run large studies linked to BBC TV or radio programmes. By the end of the project funding, a new version of the now called nQuire platform had been developed (nQuire.org.uk) (see Figure 9.1).

The platform was launched in 2018 with an investigation proposed by the BBC about the incoming General Data Protection Regulation: 'GDPR – My

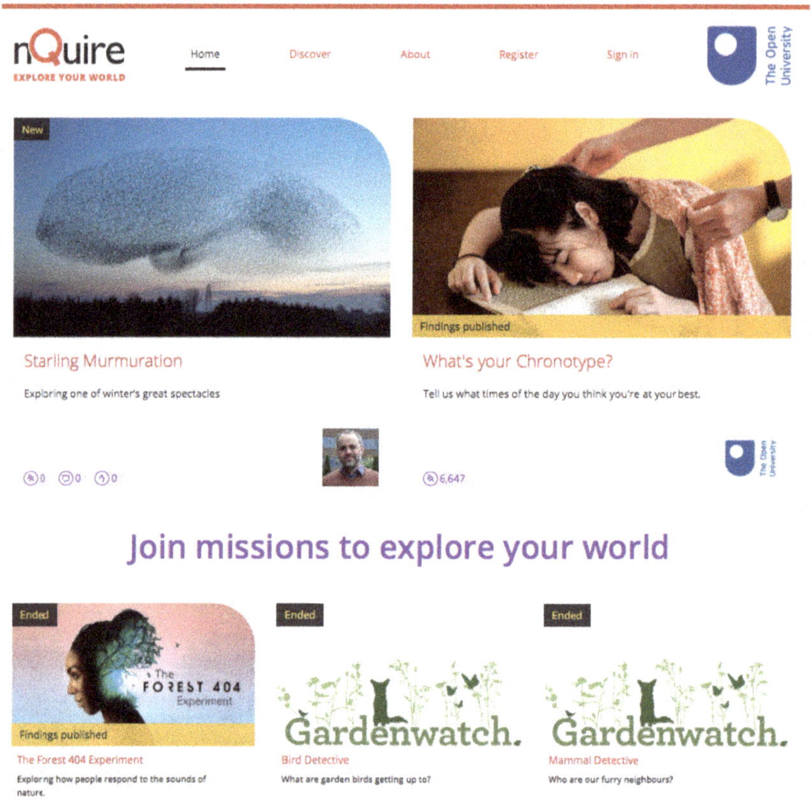

Figure 9.1: The nQuire platform supporting citizen inquiry.

Life, My Data, MyTomorrow'. Advertised on the BBC Tomorrow's World website and systematically shared in social media, the expectation was that a significant number of users would visit the platform and complete the mission, thus raising the profile of the platform as a tool for joining or initiating investigations. A significant aspect of every piece of research is to achieve impact, in the case of Citizen Inquiry this means populating the platform with investigations set by both citizens and scientists, supporting Citizens' Inquiry learning through joining or setting up investigations, and integrating the tools in teaching practices. This first mission did not meet expectations, as only a few people participated. A reflective activity within the team identified that the process of accessing the platform, in particular the requirement to register before joining an investigation, most likely explained the low response rate. Given the remaining funding available, respective changes were made to the platform.

The end of the project with the BBC resulted in a second critical point of uncertainty. Although this partnership had significant outputs, the challenge of achieving impact by having a large number of citizens systematically engaged with the tools had not yet been met. In line with 'persistent intent', the research team shared responsibilities and directed dedicated effort towards two directions: (a) identifying external organisations such as the BBC and schools that would be interested in using the platform and setting up investigations, and (b) identifying courses at the OU that could integrate the platform into their design to support teaching and learning. In this respect, networking was shown to be a critical factor influencing the future of the innovation. Through existing contacts and ongoing communication, the research team identified relevant stakeholders to whom they presented the vision and the tools. This was a fruitful activity as it resulted in a number of outcomes. First, the Chronotype mission was launched and shared with undergraduate students across the university, generating 4,700 responses. Second, leveraging internal funds, a researcher was recruited to identify ways of integrating the platform within Open University courses. Third, the platform was integrated into the design of a new course about technology-enhanced learning, that was managed by colleagues in the same department. This is the first application of the approach and the tools to formal education. Fourth, the partnership with the BBC resulted in the design of additional investigations such as Gardenwatch (See Figure 9.2)- a partnership between the BBC and the British Trust for Ornithology (BTO) surveying gardens across the UK – that engaged thousands of people with the platform and the process of Citizen Inquiry. Finally, relevant applications are under preparation or have been submitted, aiming to attract further funding.

In parallel, the dissemination activities of the research team over time, including presenting at local and international conferences and other universities, attracted the interest of schools. For example, a primary school in China reported high levels of student engagement when students (11–12 years old) were using the platform and the Sense-it application. Students recorded sounds and lights in a shopping mall and conducted interviews with people who live

Figure 9.2: The Gardenwatch mission supported by the BBC and BTO.

around the mall to identify whether living next to the mall affects daily life. In the classroom, students discussed data and wrote a proposal for improving the environment around the shopping mall.

Another example of how supporting distance learning students with their understanding of Science has led to the development of new technologies especially within the realms of Computer Supported Collaborative Learning is our work on shared simulations. Building on the work on learning from simulations in the conceptual change in science projects (see Chapter 8, and shared simulations (see e.g. the SharedArk project, Scanlon et al. 1993) our challenge has been to support learners at a distance working together on complex tasks.

Case study 2: real time working together on simulations

This second case study provides an interesting narrative around the need to reduce the isolation of students working remotely with a positive experience of lerning science together through working in pairs in real time on a computer simulation. This research came to fruition in 2006 by linking together, two software developments, which were built at the OU, known as BuddyFinder and SIMLINK. BuddySpace was the original application that was of interest for this particular Science learning innovation and it was developed as an Instant Messaging environment for community building see Vogiazoglou et al (2005). BuddySpace provided enhanced capabilities for users to manage and visualise the presence of colleagues and friends in collaborative working, gaming, messaging, and other contexts. Of particular interest to our Science project was the role of graphical metaphors for presence, including maps,the BuddySpace team were also studying at this time the semantics of presence, in order to move beyond simple flags such as 'online' and 'busy' to include rich contextual and spatio-temporal information more appropriate to the user's focus of activity.

Buddy Finder was then developed, by the Knowledge Media Institute, to enable users to perform two different functions. First of all it allowed each user to input keywords describing their individual interests and/or skills. Secondly it allowed a user to search the user-defined keyword space to find another user or users that match a specified keyword. The idea being that students would describe themselves, for example, as knowledgeable about or interested in climate change so that other students wishing to discuss this topic would be able to contact them via BuddySpace. Figure 9.3 shows the original BuddySpace messaging Interface while Figure 9.4 illustrates the BuddyFinder interface where students could see from the hotspots on the map, which students were actively online and also search to see if any were interested in working with them on the Global Warming topic see Figure 9.5 below

SIMLINK was the second programme which was built to allow students to work together at a distance with the Global Warming simulation see Figure 9.5. The variables that could be changed in this simulation were those of; cloud cover, amount of ice and snow, albeado, aerosol content, water content, carbon dioxide content and the solar constant. See Figure 9.5 below. Students were linked together remotely using SIMLINK which was in essence a Java based downloadable plugin which formed part of the BuddySpace family of communication tools. It allowed users at a distance to work on a joint simulation together. The users could view the same screen. This meant that when one student made a change to the simulation the other saw this change. In effect the pair working together were viewing identical representations on their monitors, as they would

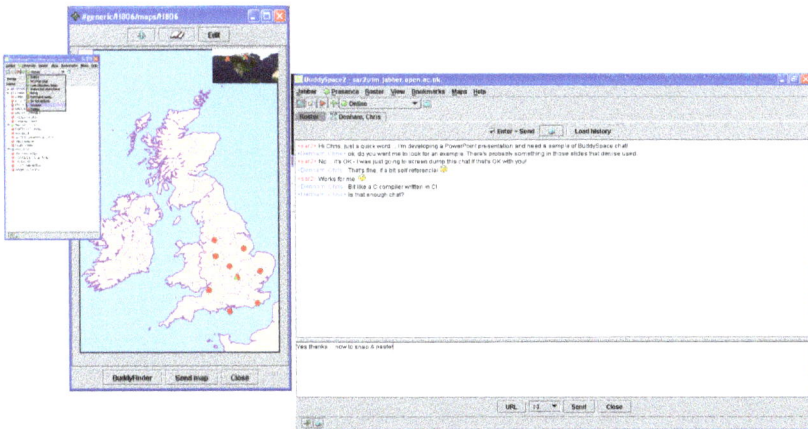

Figure 9.3: BuddySpace messaging Interface.

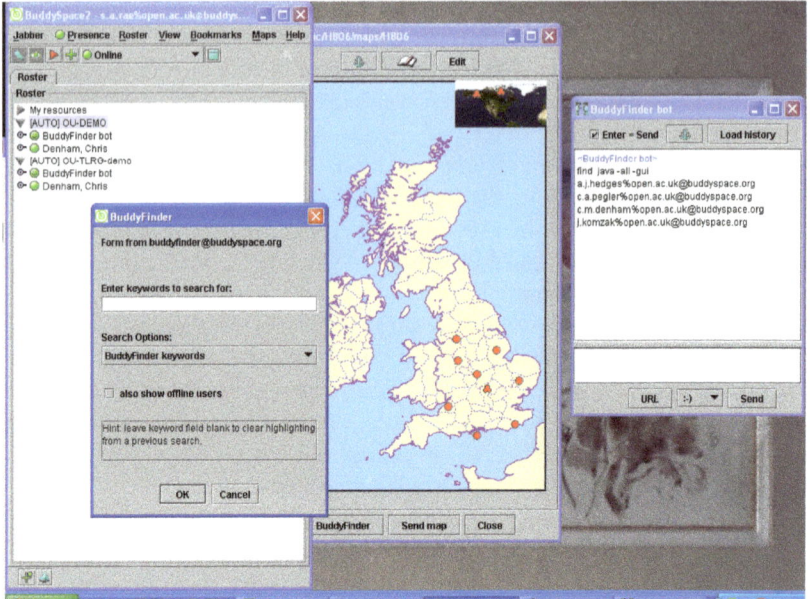

Figure 9.4: BuddyFinder interface.

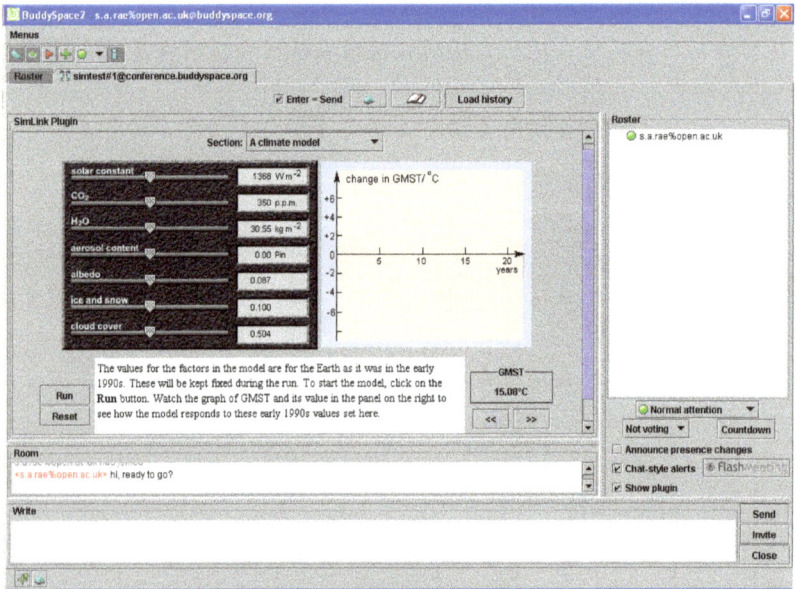

Figure 9.5: SIMLINK with Global Warming.

as if they were working side by side. This was achieved by sending mouse click changes only from one partners application to the other. This avoided bandwith problems and time delays that 'raw' screen sharing would have entailed.

Fourteen volunteers were able to work together in separate rooms using the BuddySpace and SIMLIMK software to solve problems about Global warming together in a session which lasted up to 45 minutes. They quickly became engaged in the topic and cognitive change scores i.e. the difference between pre and post scores showed an increase. This trial illustrated how the system could be used for formative assessment purposes see (Whitelock 2008). The discourse revealed participants were encouraging each other to keep to the task and were happy to explore an unfamilaiar terrain together. The participants agreed that this combination of communication tools to present complex problem solving tasks would be a beneficial asset to OU students. The potential of BuddySpace was then recommended by the Open Content Initiative, to become integrated into Moodle.

The main pedagogical driver for this research was to provide a screen sharing application that would assist with the development of complex problem solving formative assessments for students studying remotely. In this way a 'Predict, Look and Explain' modus operandi for collaborative work around a simulation that has well documented pedagogical benefits could be provided for students studying alone and remotely. One of the major findings of this project is the creativity of staff, both academic and technical, to create formative e-assessments. The development process is time consuming and costly and fewer students benefit from these electronic formative assessments when they are an optional extra in the course. It was recommended that electronic formative assessment become a compulsory element of the course teams teaching learning materials. Learners have been shown to welcome the instant feedback afforded by electronic assessment, which can also be used by tutors to diagnose student misconceptions of a given topic. Designing formative assessments around known misconceptions was a recommended outcome from this work.

Conclusions

The story of Citizen Inquiry combined insights from the Personal Inquiry (PI) project (described further in Chapter 8) and Citizen Science to develop a set of enabling Citizen Science technologies. It suggests new ways of capitalizing on the strength of Citizen Science for the benefits of each citizen and their communities. It is an interactive way of engaging learners with science and a way of making use of the pedagogical benefits of inquiry-based learning at a large scale. Overall, this journey aimed to bring science closer to the everyday life of learners and help them understand and appreciate its value by developing bridges between formal and informal education. It showcases how a successful secondary education project on structuring scientific investigations with the support of technology can be expanded to foster participation in research activities in informal settings, with the support of technology and through communication with others. Similarly, our recent collaboration with three natural history museums and two other universities (funded by the National Science Foundation (NSF), Wellcome Trust and Economic Social Research Council (ESRC)) aims to understand what young people currently learn from their participation in Citizen Science programs led by museums, and to redesign these to effectively scaffold informal learning experiences (LEARN Citizen Science, 2017). These activities emphasise the importance of promoting a continuation of learning across settings, supporting self-regulated learning with the help of technology and social interactions, and promoting lifelong learning inspiration.

Our work on collaboration at a distance supported by technology described here, but also in other accounts of our experiments on collaborative problem solving at a distance using shared simulations (see e.g. Scanlon et al. 2005) also demonstrated the commitment to the judicious use of technology to overcome the challenges of learning science at a distance. These two themes are facing the contemporary challenge of assessing learning appropriately and effectively.

Our research engagement with science projects and activities over the years has been shown to be challenging and has required flexibility to accommodate difficulties, a strong shared vision and persistent intent. Our major challenge has been the lack of funding available that threatened the implementation of our vision of "engaging learners enthusiastically with science". Persistent intent and ongoing communication amongst the research team contributed significantly in identifying solutions and pursuing, slowly but steadily our vision. Reflecting on the last 40 years, we could argue that we did manage to engage learners with science through innovative pedagogies such as Citizen Inquiry, learning from simulations and a range of web-based and mobile technologies. What now requires further work is to ensure that learners engage "enthusiastically" with science; that they are satisfied with their participation in science activities and see learning as fun and enjoyable. Going forward, we need to address the challenges of evidencing learning in informal settings, or connecting learning across settings, and ensuring that this learning is enjoyable and engaging. In pursuit of this we should aim to create learning environments that allow for playful exploration and experimentation, promote making and recovery from mistakes, and expand over and above formal education, to professional and lifelong learning (Ferguson et al., 2019).

References

Aristeidou, M., Scanlon, E. and Sharples, M. (2014). Inquiring Rock Hunters. In: Open Learning and Teaching in Educational Communities, Lecture Notes in Computer Science, Springer International Publishing, pp. 546–547.

Bonney, R., Cooper, C. B., Dickinson, J., Kelling, S., Phillips, T., Rosenberg, K. V., & Shirk, J. (2009). Citizen Science: A Developing Tool for Expanding Science Knowledge and Scientific Literacy. *BioScience*, *59*(11), 977–984. http://doi.org/10.1525/bio.2009.59.11.9

Ferguson, R., Coughlan, T., Egelandsdal, K., Gaved, M., Herodotou, C., Hillaire, G., Jones, D., Jowers, I., Kukulska-Hulme, A., McAndrew, P., Misiejuk, K., Ness, I. J., Rienties, B., Scanlon, E., Sharples, M., Wasson, B., Weller, M. and Whitelock, D. (2019). *Innovating Pedagogy 2019: Open University Innovation Report 7*. Milton Keynes: The Open University.

Herodotou, C., Villasclaras-Fernandez, E. and Sharples, M. (2014). The design and evaluation of a sensor-based mobile application for citizen inquiry science investigations. In: Rensing, C., de Freitas, S., Ley, T. and Muñoz-Merino, P. eds. Open Learning and Teaching in Educational Communities: 9th European Conference on Technology Enhanced Learning, EC-TEL 2014, Graz, Austria, September 16–19, 2014, Proceedings. *Lecture Notes in Computer Science*(8719). Springer International Publishing, pp. 434–439.

Herodotou, C., Aristeidou, M., Sharples, M. and Scanlon, E.(2018). Designing Citizen Science tools for learning: lessons learnt from the iterative development of nQuire. *Research and Practice in Technology Enhanced Learning*, 13(4).

Herodotou, C., Sharples, M. and Scanlon, E. (2017). *Citizen Inquiry: Synthesising Science and Inquiry Learning*. Abingdon: Routledge.

LEARN Citizen Science (2017). Available at https://education.ucdavis.edu/learn-citizen-science

Quintana, C., Reiser, B. J., Davis, E. A., Krajcik, J., Fretz, E., Duncan, R. G., et al. (2004). A scaffolding design framework for software to support science inquiry. *Journal of the Learning Sciences*, 13, 337–386.

Scanlon, E., O'Shea, T., Smith, R., O'Malley, C. and Taylor, J. (1993). Running in the rain-can a shared simulation help to decide? *Physics Education*, 28,107–113, March.

Scanlon, E., Blake, C., Joiner, R. and O'Shea, T. (2005).Technologically Mediated Complex Problem Solving on a Statistics Task, *Learning, Media and Technology*, 30 (2).

Scanlon, E., Sharples, M., Fenton-O'Creevy, M., Fleck, J., Cooban, C., Ferguson, R., Cross, S. and Waterhouse, P. (2013). *Beyond prototypes: Enabling innovation in technology-enhanced learning*. Open University, Milton Keynes.

Sharples, M., McAndrew, P., Weller, M., Ferguson, R., FitzGerald, E., Hirst, T., & Gaved, M. (2013). *Innovating Pedagogy 2013*. Open University Innovation Report 2. Milton Keynes: The Open University.

Vogiazoglou,Y, Eisenstadt,M, Dzbor,M and Komzak, J (2005). From Buddyspace to CitiTag:Large-scale Symbolic presence for Community building and spontaneous play. Proceedings of the ACM Symposium on Applied Computing, Sante Fe, New Mexico, March 13–17.

Whitelock, D., Romano, D. M., et al, (2000). Perfect Presence: What does this mean for the design of virtual learning environments? *Education and Information Technologies* 5(4): 277–289.

Whitelock, D. (2006). Electronic Assessment: Marking, Monitoring and Mediating Learning. In McAndrew, P. and Jones, A. (eds) Interactions, Objects and Outcomes in learning. Special Issue of International Journal of Learning Technology. Vol. 2 Nos. 2/3 p. 264–276.

Whitelock, D. (2008). *Accelerating the assessment agenda: thinking outside the black box.* In Scheuermann, F. & Pereira, A.G. (eds.) Towards a Research Agenda on Computer-Based Assessment: Challenges and Needs for European Educational Measurement, published by the European Commission, Joint Research Centre pp 15–21 ISSN. 1018-5593.

CHAPTER 10

Visions for the Future of Educational Technology

Mike Sharples

Educational Technology is in a period of exciting change, with new technologies such as augmented and virtual reality, new techniques to analyse student data, and new pedagogies for learning online at large scale. Universities are entering partnerships with publishers and startup companies to develop teaching and learning online. As the Computer and Learning research group (CALRG) celebrates its 40th anniversary, The Open University (OU) faces challenges and opportunities. The challenges are to find answers to three big questions. How can providers of online courses develop sustainable business models? How can institutions work together to develop courses that attract substantial numbers of fee-paying students and offer transferrable credit? How can course designers offer education that is both engaging and effective? The opportunities include developing new partnerships though the FutureLearn company to offer professional development courses with transferable credit, exploring inquiry learning at scale with the nQuire platform in collaboration with the BBC, and developing mobile technologies that promote broad and deep access to learning. A promising future research agenda is to examine how new educational technology can combine personalized with social learning. A lesson from 40 years of CALRG is that that successful computer-assisted learning involves not a series of exciting prototypes and quick fixes, but a sustained programme of research into the science of learning and the design of effective interventions.

How to cite this book chapter:
Sharples, M. 2019. Visions for the Future of Educational Technology. In: Ferguson, R., Jones, A. and Scanlon, E. (eds). *Educational Visions: Lessons from 40 years of innovation.* Pp. 151–166. London: Ubiquity Press. DOI: https://doi.org/10.5334/bcg.j. License: CC-BY 4.0

Introduction

The introductory chapter to this book shows an extract from a speech by Lord Crowther, the first Chancellor of The Open University, where he refers to the revolution in communications enabled by computers. Since that speech in 1969, the world has undergone a further technology revolution brought by mobile communications devices: smartphones, tablet computers and wearable communicators.

Equally important is the revolution in education. In 1969, university students listened to lectures, wrote course notes, attended seminars, and sat in exam halls. Many still do. Yet people of all ages and nationalities now learn online. They look up Wikipedia to understand Bitcoin, watch a YouTube video to find out how to bleed a radiator, go to a blog to find a recipe for lasagne, and browse TripAdvisor to plan a holiday. Also, since 2012, Massive Open Online Courses (MOOCs) have allowed anyone with a fast internet connection to study a course in, for example, Mathematics, Machine Learning, or Mindfulness.

The MOOC phenomenon

Many academics at The Open University (OU) were initially blasé about the MOOC phenomenon. Since 1999, we have had our own Open2.net site[1], rebranded in 2006 as OpenLearn[2]. It provides hundreds of hours of free educational content, in collaboration with the BBC. However, in late 2012 the OU made a decision to form the FutureLearn company and build a new platform[3] to offer free online courses from leading universities worldwide. This generated challenges and opportunities.

Project Kyloe

The main challenge was to build a consortium of universities willing to develop free courses, for people from all nationalities with little or no experience of online learning. The opportunity was to develop a new platform that would engage people in sustained, effective, self-managed learning.

In early December 2012, a small group of educational technology experts at the OU were asked to comment on a set of features for Project Kyloe[4], the code name for what was to become FutureLearn. Should the platform have recommendation features, email alerts, ebooks or pdfs, presenters or guest tutors?

---

1   https://www.open.edu/openlearn/about-openlearn/frequently-asked-questions/looking-open2net
2   https://www.open.edu/openlearn/
3   www.futurelearn.com
4   Kyloe is a type of Scottish Highland cattle: Kyloe, cattle, moo, MOOC.

Asking experts to propose a list of features is exactly the wrong way to design a new platform for learning. The right way is to start from the pedagogy. What types of teaching, learning and assessment should be supported? How will people from differing cultures, languages and educational backgrounds be helped to engage and learn? Fortunately, at the end of December 2012, the then Vice Chancellor, Martin Bean, convened a meeting to develop a vision for the new MOOC platform and establish a small team to work with the newly-formed FutureLearn company on pedagogy-informed design of the platform.

Designing FutureLearn

Members of CALRG were prominent in that team, with Sharples as Academic Lead. Together with the software developers, they based design of FutureLearn on a pedagogy of learning as conversation[5]. Conversation is a fundamental process of learning. We converse with colleagues and teachers to share knowledge and coordinate actions. We converse with ourselves to reflect on experience. Conversation can also improve with scale: the more people that take part, the richer and more diverse is the discussion. In FutureLearn, each piece of teaching is linked with a conversation amongst the learners. Conversation for learning has been the guiding principle for designing new features such as peer assessment and online study groups.

In May 2015, 270,00 people started the FutureLearn course 'Understanding IELTS' from the British Council. The biggest-ever online MOOC course, it attracted learners from 190 countries notably in the Middle East and Eastern Europe. For many, it was their first experience of online learning. 25% accessed the courses on mobile devices. The first video in that course (asking participants how they feel about taking exams) attracted 65,000 comments. By the time the course had ended, over 35% of the participants had contributed to the online discussions and many more had learned from viewing the peer contributions alongside educator-designed content. This and subsequent courses have shown how well-conceived social learning can be a basis for open education at scale.

FutureLearn Academic Network

Perhaps the greatest opportunity afforded by FutureLearn has been for academics and educational technologists from 120 institutions to explore new ways to teach online. The FutureLearn Academic Network (FLAN) was set up

---

5   Conversation Theory was developed by Gordon Pask and extended by Diana Laurillard, both of whom worked with The Open University. Laurillard was a former Pro-Vice-Chancellor (Technology Development). Pask obtained the first Open University DSc.

in 2013 to connect academics and research students based in FutureLearn partner institutions. FLAN is coordinated by Eileen Scanlon and Rebecca Ferguson from CALRG. Through quarterly meetings, comparative research studies, joint research bids and collaborative publications, the network has examined successful ways to teach, learn and assess online. Two reports, authored by members of CALRG, surveyed 66 publications on MOOCs from The Open University (Ferguson, Coughlan & Herodotou, 2016) and then 109 publications by FutureLearn partners (Ferguson, Coughlan, Herodotou & Scanlon, 2017). The two reports identify priority areas for universities investing in MOOCs, including: develop a strategic approach to learning at scale, identify and share learning designs, support discussion more effectively and widen access.

The pedagogy of learning through conversation at scale has also posed new questions for educators. What makes a good question to prompt discussion? What should be the role of educators in facilitating conversation – should they ask open questions, offer hints, answer queries, encourage peer discussion, lubricate social interactions? Can learners be trained and supported to act as peer facilitators? How should courses be designed to engage and retain students?

A journey from MOOCs to micro-credentials

FutureLearn, in common with other MOOC platforms, is now on a long-term journey away from a focus on free courses for leisure learners, towards accredited programmes for professional development and lifelong learning. Figure 1 shows the trends, from 2000 to 2020, of open and distance education. In the early 2000s, some universities including The Open University made educational resources such as course notes and recordings of lectures free to browse online.

In the first experiments with MOOCs, from 2008 onwards, learners constructed free online resources into personalized courses and discussed their learning with other participants. In 2012, the major MOOC platforms of Coursera and EdX were established, followed in 2013 by FutureLearn. The courses that run on these platforms, along with others including OpenLearn, have generated rich data on student learning. The fields of social learning analytics, predictive analytics and analytics for learning have sprung up to inform new methods of teaching and learning at scale.

A combination of business imperatives (MOOC companies have belatedly realised that it's hard to sustain a business based on free courses), entrepreneurship, and greater understanding of the needs and profiles of adult learners, have resulted in clusters of courses, dubbed 'nano-degrees'. Each of these nano-degrees provides a credential certified by the providing institution. Combine these clusters, sometimes from multiple providers, and you have a hybrid degree course. Merge them with campus teaching and you get blended courses that can be taken on campus, online, or in combination.

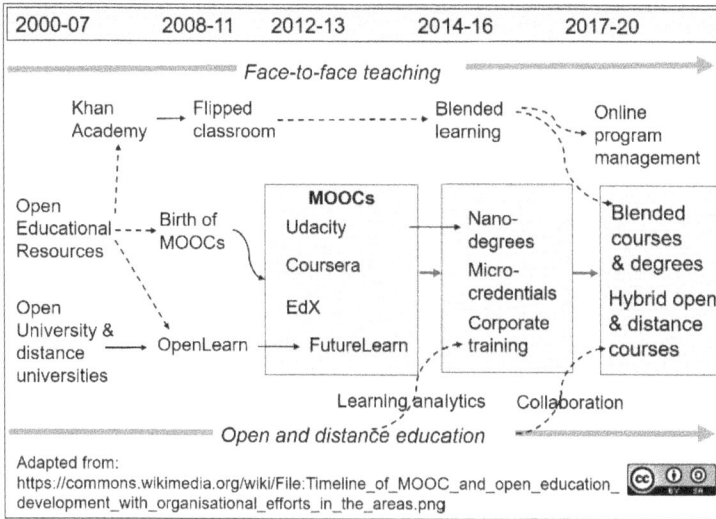

Figure 10.1: Trends for open and distance education from 2000 to 2020.

This complex net of partnerships, providers and pedagogies is still under development, not least at The Open University. A postgraduate degree in Online and Distance Education has been developed by faculty associated with CALRG and now runs on the FutureLearn platform. This degree is both a way to apprentice students into e-learning and a means to research the delivery of accredited courses on a MOOC platform.

The adult learning dilemma

Such courses expose a central dilemma of adult learning: what students like most is generally not what is best for them. In 2016, Rienties and Toetenel, from CALRG, published two papers that analysed student satisfaction, retention and performance for over 150 degree modules offered by the OU (Rienties & Toetenel, 2016; Toetenel & Rienties, 2016). To develop an OU undergraduate module, the course team follow a process of learning design that involves predicting the percentage of different types of student learning: assimilating delivered content, finding information, communicating with other students, producing assignments, experiencing, interacting, and taking assessments.

When the module runs, the university gets data on student satisfaction, retention and exam performance. Thus, for each OU module, we can investigate what type of course design produces what outcomes. In brief, students prefer modules with plenty of delivered content (videos, texts) and some interaction. But the modules best at retaining students are those with communicative and collaborative learning. And student exam performance is *worst* on those modules that are heavy on delivered content.

The future of distance education rests on finding answers to three big questions. How can providers of online courses develop sustainable business models? How can institutions work together to develop courses that attract substantial numbers of fee-paying students and offer transferrable credit? How can course designers overcome the adult learning dilemma to offer education that is both engaging and effective? For The Open University, as one of the largest distance learning universities in Europe, addressing these questions is central to its strategy and future direction.

Inquiry learning at scale

FutureLearn has shown that a platform based on a pedagogy of learning as conversation can be both engaging and effective at massive scale. What other methods of teaching and learning can run at scale? Since 2007, CALRG has designed a series of technologies, collectively named nQuire, to investigate inquiry learning, initially in classrooms then from 2013 for self-directed learning online. The approach of pedagogy-led design is the same as for FutureLearn: start from theory and practice of inquiry learning; let this inform design of a demonstrator system that is tested with learners; apply findings from the system in use to inform both design of the next version and to refine the pedagogy.

Personally meaningful inquiry

nQuire has gone through three main phases, each offering insights into inquiry learning with technology. The first was to explore 'personally meaningful inquiry'. School students investigated topics that had personal significance, such as 'Are animals in cities affected by pollution?' and 'How noisy is my classroom?'. Each student had a computer-based toolkit to guide an entire inquiry process that connected structured learning in the classroom with discovery and data collection at home or outdoors. A visual map of the inquiry process, enacted on a portable computer, was successful in guiding students. However, this schools' version of nQuire placed demands on the teacher to orchestrate the process, particularly for the classroom activity that integrated data collected by all the students into a satisfying conclusion.

Citizen inquiry

The second phase, described in Chapter 9, was to explore how inquiry learning could be managed online, without the guidance of a classroom teacher. The structured inquiry process from the first phase proved too complex and tedious for self-managed inquiries, so we have explored how to implement a new pedagogy of 'citizen inquiry' (Herodotou, Sharples & Scanlon, 2017). This fuses the mass participation of citizen science with the question-led investigation of inquiry learning. In effect, it flips the roles of citizen science. Instead of a scientist designing an investigation to which members of the public contribute, in citizen inquiry any person or group can design an inquiry and then recruit other people, including scientists, to help with carrying it out. The key is to keep each inquiry clear and focused, with an initiating 'big question', a structured activity to investigate it, data that can be collected by members of the public on mobile devices, a way to publish results on the platform, and a conversation between participants to provoke interest and guide the unfolding investigation.

The nQuire-it platform was open to anyone to develop a new inquiry, called a 'mission'. An authoring tool on nQuire-it assisted in designing the mission. Once the mission had been built, it was published on the site for anyone to contribute. Each contribution was visible and, as with FutureLearn, each mission and contribution had a linked discussion. Over the five years that the platform ran, some 150 inquiry missions were developed, ranging from an investigation of noise levels in school classrooms to observations of the impact of flooding on homes and roads in Vietnam's Mekong Delta (Figure 10.2).

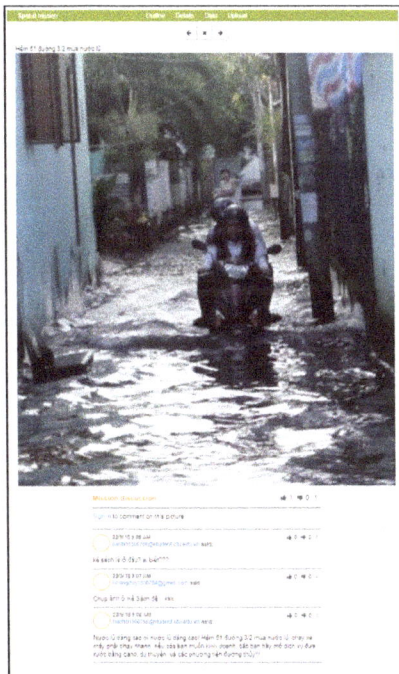

Figure 10.2: A contribution to an nQuire-it mission to log and discuss flooding in Vietnam.

Although nQuire-it demonstrated that people worldwide could design and run investigations, most missions were short-lived with few contributions. A study by Aristeidou with amateur meteorologists (Aristeidou, Scanlon & Sharples, 2017) found that extrinsic factors, such as a well-designed site and thought-provoking questions, attracted and activated participants, but intrinsic factors such as personal interest in the topic and support from the community crucially determined whether the community of inquiry developed and sustained.

Inquiry learning at scale

The new nQuire platform[6] is a collaboration with the BBC. The aim is to demonstrate scale and sustainability in learning by inquiry. Promotion through BBC broadcast media provides the initial recruitment (a mission on nQuire to survey UK gardens has attracted 230,381 responses), but to be successful nQuire must address three challenges: engage participants in valid and meaningful scientific inquiry; provide reward for taking part; enable individuals, groups and organisations to design and run missions on the platform. Some methods we are exploring to meet these challenges include: framing each mission within a scientific process that includes informed consent and ethical scrutiny; offering intrinsic rewards through personalized feedback; giving powerful yet easy-to-use tools to author new investigations; and providing a guided process to design, preview, pilot and launch a mission.

The nQuire project offers an object lesson in developing education technology beyond prototypes (Scanlon, et al., 2013). The persistence has lasted over twelve years and four major versions of the platform. Each iteration of pedagogy and technology has produced a site for bricolage through playful experiment. For example, the Noise Map mission on nQuire-it started as a demonstration of how a mobile phone could capture sound data to the platform, then was taken up by a teacher in Argentina who used it with students to explore environmental noise, then it spread to schools in Hong Kong, Taiwan, China and New Zealand where they compared noise levels in classrooms, labs and school cafes:

"Our MindLab Manurewa recorded a sound level of 44 to 68dB. While this seemed somewhat reasonable, I think this was a little loud for groupwork indoors. At a high of 68dB we struggled to hear each other or follow the conversation." ejenkins@ormiston.school.nz

Each iteration of the nQuire project has produced evidence of the value to learners of engaging in inquiry learning, both to investigate personally-meaningful

---

6 www.nquire.org.uk

issues and to understand how to be a scientist. It has also raised issues – such as teacher orchestration, self-managed inquiry, and inquiry at scale – that have been examined by successive iterations. However, if this suggests a smooth path of design-based research, it certainly does not feel that way to the research team. Each version of the project has involved debate about the value and direction of the research and a continual struggle to get funding.

Inquiry, like conversation, is a fundamental process of learning. Through inquiry learning students learn to pose thoughtful questions, make sense of information, and learn about the world around them. They develop the skills and attitudes needed to be self-directed, lifelong learners (National Library of New Zealand, n.d.). Citizen inquiry learning that is online, open and scalable offers new opportunities for people to learn by investigating themselves and their environment.

Mobile and accessible learning

Personal investigations require mobile technologies to record and share data. Members of CALRG have been active since the early 2000s in development of mobile technologies for learning. Sharples held the first international conference on mobile and contextual learning, to become the mLearn conference series, and both Sharples and Kukulska-Hulme have served as Presidents of the International Association for Mobile Learning[7].

Learning and context

The large European MOBILearn project, which ran from 2002–2004, developed an architecture for mobile learning. As with FutureLearn and nQuire, the focus was not on the technology alone, but the combination of pedagogy and technology. One important legacy of MOBILearn is a theory of mobile learning as a contextualised practice (Sharples, Taylor & Vavoula, 2016).

As learners, we are always immersed in a context. For traditional education, this is the classroom, managed by a teacher and mediated by familiar tools such as blackboards and textbooks. When education is taken beyond the classroom, the context becomes more fluid and unpredictable. As well as being *in* a context, as learners we also *create* context out of our available resources of location, technology and social setting. For example, a family standing before an exhibit in a museum is creating a context for learning out of the exhibit and its labelling, the route through the museum to reach that exhibit, existing knowledge

---

7 https://iamlearn.org/

brought by each family member, mobile devices including handheld museum guides and mobile phones, and the conversation amongst the family members.

Since people have a diversity of needs and cultures, own a range of technologies, and move through varying locations and social engagements, it follows that researching mobile learning is complex and challenging. To design mobile technologies involves either adapting them to rapidly changing contexts or providing a generic aid to learning that will offer useful learning despite context (Sharples, 2015). To evaluate the effectiveness of mobile learning requires new methods for understanding how knowledge is created within and across contexts.

Mobile support for migrants

Of all the contexts for mobile learning, perhaps the most difficult to research and design involve support for migrants. Immigrants to a country bring their own knowledge, language, technologies, expectations and concerns to a new setting. Just providing migrants with a mobile visitor guide in their own language in by no means sufficient. They have needs to gain work, find friends, understand cultural norms and expectations, and learn how to survive and prosper in the new environment. CALRG, led by Agnes Kukulska-Hulme, has had a central role in the European MASELTOV project to support immigrants in cities through mobile technologies. Its aim has been to understand the changing contexts of the immigrants as they go about their daily lives and how combinations of mobile technology and peer support can give help when needed (Kukulska-Hulme, et al., 2015).

Accessible learning

Viewing learning as a mobile and contextualised activity prompts us to rethink accessibility. As Chapter 4 discusses, allowing people with a broad variety of abilities and disabilities to enter online learning is necessary but not sufficient. We must also support them to stay and learn. Each person has a different context for learning – with unique needs, barriers, resources, culture, and social network. This context frames how that person understands what it means to learn, what will be gained from engaging in education, and how the learning activity will progress. The implication is that we must look for new ways to support the resourcefulness of students from their contexts, not just provide our resources.

As an example, members of CALRG have been exploring the value of predictive analytics. Computational techniques can analyse the online interactions of students on a course and predict, with high accuracy, which students are at risk of failing. What then? One use of such methods is to alert teachers to poorly-performing students. Another is to let the students themselves know what they could do to get back on track – such as join a discussion forum or read a supplementary text. However, this is analytics seen from the perspective of the course provider. To the student, being given yet more resources is unlikely to help if they are already overloaded, or if they view learning as a process of trying to digest everything they are given. Understanding students' context, history and culture may contribute more to effective learning than diagnosing failure – but that is hard to program into software. A better approach may be to offer analytics that empower teachers to understand not just which students are at risk, but the contextual factors involved (Herodotou, et al., 2019).

Merging personal and social learning: a research agenda

It is an exciting time for educational technology. There's a plethora of new tools for learning: virtual and augmented reality, chatbots, predictive analytics, personalized learning systems. The Bill and Melinda Gates Foundation has teamed up with the Zuckerberg Initiative (founded by Facebook CEO, Mark Zuckerberg) to promote and invest in personalized technology for classroom instruction (New Profit, 2017).

However, technology alone will not transform education. An analysis of 40 years of research into the impact of educational technology on educational performance shows only a small to moderate effect size of 0.33 (Tamin, et al., 2011). The successes in computer-assisted learning come from understanding how to use technology effectively in the classroom and online. Future research must explore good combinations of technology and pedagogy. For example, a RAND study of personalized learning in schools showed that it could be effective, but only if students learn in groups, the classroom is re-designed to accommodate the new way of learning, and the students are given opportunities to discuss their performance with the teacher (Pane, Steiner, Baird & Hamilton, 2015).

A promising research agenda for educational technology is to examine how personalized and social learning can fit together. Personalized learning offers content and activity that is matched to the needs, abilities and context of each learner. It can drive mastery learning where the student continues with a topic until it is well understood, and cognitive tutoring that diagnoses each student's knowledge and gives remedial help to correct misconceptions.

Social learning is a great success of educational innovation (Johnson & Johnson, 2009). When students cooperate in small groups of between four and eight people, this results in greater creativity and better outcomes than working alone. Over the past 40 years, hundreds of studies in labs, classrooms and online, have uncovered conditions for successful cooperative learning. For groups to work well, they need to have shared goals, each person should know how and when to contribute, and everyone should make an appropriate contribution. They should share rewards such as group marks in a fair way, and members of a group should all have opportunities to reflect on progress and to discuss contributions. For many students, learning in groups is not a natural process, and they need to learn how to cooperate by arguing constructively and resolving conflicts. The key phrase is *positive interdependence* – everyone sees the benefits of learning together and works to achieve the group's goals. Social learning platforms such as FutureLearn are starting to show how positive interdependence can enhance learning online at large scale.

How can personalized and social learning be made to work together, so that they compliment rather than conflict? It means designing learning environments that encourage students to examine their personal learning goals and work to achieve mastery of a subject, not alone but alongside others with similar aims and contexts. Successful learning environments of the future will be based on a deep understanding of the science of learning, support students to set and meet their goals, offer a combination of personalized tuition and social learning, harness predictive analytics to assist teachers and students, and provide a delightful experience.

Ethical EdTech

Yet even an environment for successful learning is not enough, if it fails to reach the standards expected of ethical research and development. Too many educational technology studies in the past have treated students as if they were subjects in a laboratory experiment. That is no longer acceptable. The new direction is not to claim that the outcomes of an educational intervention justify the means, nor to rely on an ethical review board to police educational research, but for the researchers themselves to engage actively in a process of ethical research design (Head, 2018).

The first consideration is whether it is ethical for any piece of educational research to take place at all. Researchers should engage in questioning the assumptions of their research from the outset. Part of developing as an educational researcher is learning how to work with participants, to be sensitive to their needs and contexts, and to address and resolve ethical dilemmas. "Becoming an ethical educational researcher, then, is a matter of pedagogy." (Head, 2018, p.11). The CALRG is contributing to that pedagogy of ethics for fields that include mobile learning (Lalley, et al., 2012) and AI and education (Holmes, Iniesto, Sharples & Scanlon, 2019).

It is not possible here to summarise the rich ongoing discussions about ethics for educational research. Instead this chapter ends with some provocative guidelines framed as a mnemonic: MISSION.

Multiple media, devices, partners
Independent verification

Secure environment
Support for learners
Inquiry process
Open access
aNalytics for learning

Educational technology requires understanding the *multiple media* and devices that people use in their everyday lives and designing new ways to augment their learning across contexts. It also involves multiple partners as design informants, including learners, teachers and policy makers.

As design of an educational technology progresses, there is increasing need to bring in *independent verification* of the educational need, the user experience, the validity of the learning and its ethical soundness. For CALRG projects, this has included expert testing of early prototypes, recruiting teachers as experts in educational effectiveness and curriculum relevance, and commissioning independent reviews of data security.

A *secure environment* for learning covers not only ensuring security of data produced by learners, but also providing safe and enjoyable places to learn online. For example, the FutureLearn and nQuire sites provide ways for users to report inappropriate comments, checked by moderators.

Support for learners starts from their first engagement with the educational technology. For our projects, we put great effort into designing the 'first five minutes experience' so learners know how to take part, what to expect, and what to do first. On nQuire, users can view content without registering for the platform, so they know what to expect before providing personal data. Support for learners can extend to recruiting expert and peer facilitators and embedding effective pedagogies into the learning experience, such as formative testing with immediate feedback.

An *inquiry process* is central to active learning. It involves learners setting personal goals and asking questions to themselves that require investigation and reflection. The teacher becomes a partner in the learning process, guiding students to create knowledge. Good teachers and researchers inquire into their own practices and share knowledge of what works.

For ethical education, *open access* should be the norm, not only to enter education but to profit from the full richness of the experience. That means designing for cultural, physical and mental diversity and providing ways for like-minded students to share their knowledge and experience. It also means giving students access to the process and results of their unfolding study, through techniques such as dynamic knowledge maps, skill charts and open learner models (Bull & Kay, 2010).

Learning online creates a rich seam of data that can be mined to show progress and performance. An ethical approach to educational technology harnesses that data to provide *analytics for learning*. This could take the form of predictive analytics to guide students in what to do next based on their performance, or it could assist teachers and course designers to understand which topics students find difficult and how to improve the course quality and access.

CALRG at 40

As the Beyond Prototypes framework indicates (Scanlon, et al., 2013), technology enhanced learning is a complex system of technologies and practices, developed and embedded over many years. We are fortunate to be part of a research group that has prospered for 40 years and is still thriving. Some themes that influenced the formation of CALRG, such as designing and testing open and accessible educational technologies, are as important now as then. Some themes have come to prominence more recently, such as developing learning environments that are scalable and sustainable. And some themes set an agenda for future research and development, including analytics for learning and how to combine personalized with social learning online. Over the years, PhD students have made a major contribution to CALRG, opening new areas of research and bringing their personal and cultural perspectives. So too have the system developers and programmers – they have built the technologies and platforms, sometimes through many versions, that support the learning and test the theories.

We now know for certain that successful computer-assisted learning involves not a series of exciting prototypes and quick fixes, but a sustained programme of research into the science of learning and the design of effective interventions. Continued support for research and development in education technology is essential for the next generation of students to benefit from the current advances in educational technology and pedagogy.

References

Aristeidou, M., Scanlon, E., and Sharples, M. (2017). Profiles of engagement in online communities of citizen science participation. *Computers in Human Behavior*, 74 pp. 246–256.

Bull S., & Kay J. (2010). Open Learner Models. In: Nkambou R., Bourdeau J., Mizoguchi R. (eds) *Advances in Intelligent Tutoring Systems*. Studies in Computational Intelligence, vol 308. Springer, Berlin, Heidelberg.

Ferguson, R., Coughlan, T., & Herodotou, C. (2016). *MOOCS: What The Open University research tells us*. Institute of Educational Technology, The Open University, Milton Keynes.

Ferguson, R., Coughlan, T., Herodotou, C., & Scanlon, E. (2017). *MOOCs: What the research of FutureLearn's UK partners tells us*. Institute of Educational Technology, The Open University, Milton Keynes.

Head, G. (2018). Ethics in educational research: Review boards, ethical issues and researcher development. European Educational Research Journal. Published online at https://doi.org/10.1177%2F1474904118796315.

Herodotou, C., Sharples, M., & Scanlon, E. (Eds.)(2017). *Citizen Inquiry: Synthesizing Science and Inquiry Learning*. Routledge.

Herodotou, C., Hlosta, M., Boroowa, A., Rienties, B., Zdrahal, Z., & Mangafa, C. (2019). Empowering online teachers through predictive learning analytics. *British Journal of Educational Technology*, 50(6), 3064–3079.

Holmes, W., Iniesto, F., Sharples, M., & Scanlon, E. (2019). ETHICS in AIED: Who Cares? An EC-TEL workshop. In: *EC-TEL 2019 Fourteenth European Conference on Technology Enhanced Learning*, 16–19 Sep 2019, Delft, Netherlands.

Johnson, D.W., & Johnson, R.T. (2009). An educational psychology success story: social interdependence theory and cooperative learning. *Educational Researcher*, 38(5), 365–379.

Kukulska-Hulme, A., Gaved, M., Paletta, L., Scanlon, E., Jones, A., & Brasher, A. (2015). Mobile Incidental Learning to Support the Inclusion of Recent Immigrants. *Ubiquitous Learning: An International Journal*, 7(2), 9–21.

Lally, V., Sharples, M., Bertram, N., Masters, S., Norton, B., Tracy, F. (2012). Researching the Ethical Dimensions of Mobile, Ubiquitous,and Immersive Technology Enhanced Learning (MUITEL) in Informal Settings: a thematic review and dialogue. *Interactive Learning Environments*, 20 (3), 217–238.

National Library of New Zealand (n.d.). *Understanding inquiry learning*. Retrieved from https://natlib.govt.nz/schools/school-libraries/library-services-for-teaching-and-learning/supporting-inquiry-learning/understanding-inquiry-learning

New Profit (2017, April 13). *New Profit launches personalized learning initiative*. Retrieved from http://blog.newprofit.org/amplify/new-profit-launches-personalized-learning-initiative

Pane, J. F., Steiner, E. D., Baird, M. D., & Hamilton, L. S. (2015). *Continued Progress: Promising Evidence on Personalized Learning*. RAND Corporation.

Rienties, B. & Toetenel, L. (2016). "The impact of learning design on student behaviour, satisfaction and performance: A cross-institutional comparison across 151 modules. *Computers in Human Behavior*, 60, 333–341.

Scanlon, E., Sharples, M., Fenton-O'Creevy, M., Fleck, J., Cooban, C., Ferguson, R., . . . Waterhouse, P. (2013). *Beyond Prototypes: Enabling Innovation in Technology-Enhanced Learning*. Retrieved from http://beyondprototypes.com/

Sharples, M. (2015). Seamless Learning Despite Context. In L-H. Wong, M. Milrad & M. Specht (eds.) *Seamless Learning in the Age of Mobile Connectivity*. Springer, Singapore, pp. 41–55.

Sharples, M., Taylor, J., & Vavoula, G. (2016). A Theory of Learning for the Mobile Age. In C. Haythornthwaite, R. Andrews, J. Fransman &

E.M. Meyers (eds.) The SAGE handbook of e-learning research, 2nd edition. SAGE, pp. 63–81.

Tamim, R. M., Bernard, R. M., Borokhovski, E., Abrami, P. C., & Schmid, R. F. (2011). What forty years of research says about the impact of technology on learning: A second-order meta-analysis and validation study. *Review of Educational Research*, 81(1), 4–28.

Toetenel, L. & Rienties, B. (2016). Analysing 157 learning designs using learning analytic approaches as a means to evaluate the impact of pedagogical decision-making. *British Journal of Educational Technology*, 47(5), 981–992.

Acknowledgements

Over the CAL research group's 40 years, it has been influenced, shaped and supported by all its members. There are so many that we cannot mention them all, but we are grateful for the support of every one of them. Individual researchers have influenced our work and the field more generally. Our apologies for omissions, but we would particularly like to acknowledge the following people.

- Professor Sir Tim O'Shea, who first came up with the idea of the CALRG and it being a cross-university group.
- The Directors of the Institute of Educational Technology: Professors David Hawkridge, Clive Lawless, Mary Thorpe, Peter Knight, Josie Taylor, Patrick McAndrew and our current Director, Denise Whitelock.
- The contributions made by our research students over the years to the group and to the fun we've had. Many have remained engaged with the group, including: Professor Cathy Lewin, Professor Jenny Preece, Dr Katy Jordan, Dr Koula Charitonos, Dr Maria Aristeidou, Dr Pat Fung, Professor Rick Holliman and Professor Rupert Wegerif.
- Group convenors Adrian Kirkwood, Dr Canan Blake, Dr Doug Clow (who also blogged our talks tirelessly), Dr Kim Issroff, Dr Liz Fitzgerald, Dr Mark Gaved, Professor Max Bramer and Dr Wayne Holmes.
- Our student organisers: Dr Francisco Iniesto, Irina Rets, Jake Hilliard, Dr Janesh Sanzgiri, Dr Jenna Mittelmeier, Lesley Boyd, Dr Tina Papathoma and Dr Vicky Murphy.
- Our research fellows: Professor Claire O'Malley, Dr Erica Morris, Dr Canan Blake, Dr Laurence Alpay, Professor Marian Petre, Dr Mark Treglown and Dr Yibing Li.
- Diana Laurillard, who joined the group early on and is now Professor of Learning with Digital Technologies at the London Knowledge Lab, UCL.

Diana first talked about her influential Conversational Framework, which owed its origins to the work of Gordon Pask, at an early CALRG conference. This approach, which continues to influence our work, formed the basis of her highly influential book 'Rethinking University Teaching' (Routledge 2002).

- Dr James Aczel, Professor Karen Littleton and Professor Neil Mercer for contributions over the years.
- Professor Tom Vincent who, in the early days, developed a research programme on accessibility and using technology to support disabled students; work that was taken up by our first research student, Dr Alistair Edwards and that continues today.
- The Institute's support staff, who have provided so much support for our technical reports, run our conferences, and enabled us to celebrate our anniversaries: Di Mason, Hansa Solanki, Kylie Matthews, Maria Di Gennaro, Michelle Peralta, Natalie Eggleston and Vicky Cole.
- We would also like to thank Stylianos Hatzipanagos (University of West London) and Richard Joiner (University of Bath) for taking time to peer review chapters of the book prior to publication. Their comments provided valuable insights into how to improve on our draft texts.

www.ingramcontent.com/pod-product-compliance
Lightning Source LLC
Chambersburg PA
CBHW051211090426
42740CB00022B/3460